AF652263

Human Rights and Child Labour in Indian Industries

Human Rights and Child Labour in Indian Industries

ANU SAKSENA

SHIPRA

All rights reserved. No part of this work may be reproduced, stored in a retrieval system or transmitted in any form or by any means, electronic, mechanical, photocopying, recording or otherwise without the prior written permission of the copyright owner and the publishers.

(Published in 1999, 2001)

ISBN: 978-81-7541-590-4

2011 Edition

Human Rights and Child Labour in Indian Industries

© Anu Saksena

Published by:
SHIPRA PUBLICATIONS
H.O.: LG 18-19, Pankaj Central Market, I.P. Ext.,
Patparganj, Delhi 110092, Ph. 22235152, 22236152
Br. Off.: 4617/18, Ansari Road, Daryaganj,
New Delhi 110002; Ph. 65946453, 9810522367
Email: info@shiprapublications.com
Website: www.info@shiprapublications.com

PREFACE

I sincerely thank Dr. B . N. Mehrish, Department of Civics and Politics, University of Bombay for his inspiring guidance and critical suggestions at every stage of this work. In the course of this work, I also had discussions with Mrs. Shashi Jain, Joint Secretary, Ministry of Labour, Govt. of India, Prof. K.P.Saksena, Jawaharlal Nehru University, Mr. Jerry Pinto, co-ordinator UNICEF, and Mr. Mahavir Jain, co-ordinator Child Labour Cell, National Labour Institute, all of whom helped me greatly in understanding the problems of child labour. I am also grateful to Mr. Balakrishnan, Director, Ministry of Labour, Govt . of India and Ms. Meena Gupta, project co-ordinator, CLASP, ILO, for providing me with the relavant information.

I am deeply indebted to my husband, Rishabh, for the constant encouragement and support, which made this work possible. I am also grateful to my father-in law Mr. K.D.Saksena and my father Mr. S.K.Bhatia, for their guidance and support.

Anu Saksena

CONTENTS

List of Tables

Chapter 2

Chapter 3

I
Introduction

All human beings possess certain intrinsic rights solely by reason of being human. Human rights need to be protected and respected by all because they allow one to develop fully and without them one cannot live as a human being. Thus human rights are for all and need to be respected by all. However, there are certain groups which require special protection. Children constitute one such group because they are extremely vulnerable to exploitation. They depend on adults for survival and are one of the weakest sections of society.

It is therefore imperative that children are given a fair and equitable deal in society to enable them to realise their full potential. The rights of the child are recognized in the Universal Declaration of Human Rights adopted in 1948. For the care of children, the United Nations International Children's Emergency Fund was established by the United Nations General Assembly in 1946. UNICEF was initially established to care for children of war-torn Europe. Its mandate was later extended to provide services for the survival and development of children. In 1959, the UN General Assembly adopted the Declaration of the Rights of the Child which states that "mankind owes to tne child the best it has to give...". The UN Convention on the Rights of the Child (1989) lays down the framework of basic norms for an incremental human rights regime which would be committed to protect and promote the rights of the child.

Children are subjected to various forms of exploitation, abuse and inhuman treatment. One such form of exploitation is child labour. Sending children to work may seem rational in poverty-stricken societies but it is at the cost of their physical, intellectual and emotional development. Despite being universally condemned by the international community, children continue to be a sizeable section of the workforce. The Rights of the Child are marginalised, particularly in developing countries. Child labour is largely concentrated in Asian, African and Latin American countries. In India, millions of children are at work rather than being at school. The increasing incidence of child labour is a critical problem faced by the country. India has the largest child labour force in the world. Despite efforts made by the government to deal with the problem of child labour, it continues unabated.

The problem of child labour is a complex and multi-dimensional one. The phenomenon of child labour is dependent on several variables. Assessing the problem becomes difficult because of multiplicity of definitions of child labour. There is lack of systematic information on the causes of child labour and its magnitude. This study addresses the following questions:

- What are the forms of child employment in general and in India in particular.

- What are the factors responsible for the prevalence of child labour. A statistical analysis of the causes of child labour in India has been attempted.

- What is the magnitude of the problem of child labour in India.

- What are the consequences and repurcussions of sending children to work

- What steps have been taken by the Government of India since independence to tackle the problem.

- To what extent are international norms and standards observed in India.

- How far the existing legislation, policies and programmes adopted to deal with the problem of child labour have been successful.

Owing to the nature of the subject matter, both quantitative and qualitative methods are used to analyse the pattern, distribution and magnitude of child labour. Qualitative assessment of the probable causes of child labour is substantiated by statistical analyses of data. Various sets of data, each using incidence of child labour as the dependent variable, are subjected to statistical regression to find out the correlation with the probable causal factors.

This study attempts to analyse and discuss child labour as a human rights issue. A large section of literature available on child labour deals with child labour in various industries. An attempt has been made in this study to apply statistical methods to establish the significance of the correlation of various causal factors with the actual incidence of child labour. A detailed and comprehensive review of governmental action—legal as well as developmental—to ameliorate the problem of child labour has also been undertaken in this study.

The first introductory chapter deals with the importance and objectives of the study. The second chapter discusses the causes, forms and magnitude of child labour in general. It traces the emerging importance of children's rights within the framework of promotion of human rights and international action against child labour. The third chapter deals with the problem of child labour in India. It analyses the causes of child labour in India. It also discusses the types of child labour and consequences of child labour in India.

The fourth chapter discusses the prevalence of child labour in various Indian industries where children are employed in large numbers and are exposed to exploitative and hazardous conditions. The four industries featured in this chapter are match industry of Sivakasi, glass industry of Firozabad, carpet industry of Mirzapur-Bhadoi and brassware industry of Moradabad. The fifth chapter reviews the constitutional, statutory and developmental measures adopted by the Indian Government to deal with the problem of child labour. It examines the assistance offered by international organisations like the International Labour Organisation and the UNICEF to the Indian Government. This chapter also examines India's response to the international efforts to ban child labour. In the last chapter concluding observations are made.

II
Child Labour and Human Rights

Children in every society have always participated in economic activities. Children assist their families at home, in farms, in shops, etc. All work is not bad for children. Some activities make a positive contribution to their development, prepare them for their future tasks and help pass traditional skills from one generation to another. It inculcates a sense of responsibility in children and helps them to take pride in their work.

The term child labour, however, denotes something quite different Child labour implies that children are being exploited or overworked or deprived of their rights to health, education or just to childhood.[1] Child labour implies jobs that are imposed upon the child, that are occasioned by imperative need, that are carried out under conditions of exploitation, that call for greater physical and mental resources than the exploited child possesses—because they are monotonous, strenuous, hazardous or unduly prolonged, because they are a source of worry and because they inevitably imply a lack of schooling, relaxation and general well-being. Jobs of this sort are found in both self-employed, wage-earning and even in family enterprises—albeit usually in a less extreme form. The children who are engaged in such jobs grow up prematurely and sadly, instead of leading a carefree existence during what should be the happiest days of their lives.[2] Child labour, therefore, is the work which involves some degree of exploitation—physical, mental, and social—and therefore impairs the development of children.

Before arriving at a comprehensive definition of child labour, the term 'child' also needs to be clarified. Childhood may be defined in terms of age but different societies have different age thresholds for demarcating childhood and adulthood. In some societies, age may not be a sufficient basis for defining 'childhood'. The fulfilment of certain social rites and traditional obligations may well be important requirements in defining 'adult' and 'child' status. In still others, the integration of children into socio-economic life may begin so early and the transition from childhood to adulthood may be smooth and gradual, making it virtually impossible to identify clearly the different life phases. Thus the concept of 'child' may mean different things in different societies and at different times.[3] In the context of child labour, a working definition of 'child' may be a person below the internationally agreed age limit of 15 years. However, different countries have different basic minimum age of employment. This point will be discussed later.

The term child labour covers children under the age of 15 years, working to support themselves or their families, at the cost of their physical, social and mental development. The International Labour Organisation has given some characteristics of child labour.

1. Working too young, often at the age of 6 or 7.
2. Working long hours, in some cases 12 to 16 hours a day.
3. Working under strain—physical, social or psychological, in mines or sweat shops for example.
4. Working on the streets in unhealthy and dangerous conditions.
5. For very little pay, as little as $3 for a 60-hour week.
6. Work with little stimulation that does not facilitate the child's social and psychological development as in dull and repetitive tasks.
7. In some situations children are made to take too much responsibility. Children often have charge of siblings only a year or two younger than themselves.
8. Work subject to intimidation which inhibits self-confidence and self-esteem, as with slave labour and sexual exploitation.

There are no reliable statistics on the number of child workers because a large number of children work in family enterprises or are employed in the informal sector or work illegally. In 1979, the ILO had estimated the number of working children to be around 50 million. This figure is considered to be a serious underestimate. The United

Nations estimates that as many as 200 million children are at work in the world's fields and factories. According to a recent ILO report, some 250 million children between the ages of 5 and 15 are working in developing countries. Around 60 percent of them—or nearly 153 million are found in Asia, 32 percent or 80 million are in Africa and 7 percent or 17.5 million live in Latin America.

At least one child out of every four in the developing world is toiling under conditions resembling slavery, according to the 1997 UNICEF report on the state of the world's children. An estimated 250 million children aged 5-14 years are engaged in hazardous work, prostitution, bonded labour.

Causes of Child Labour

Child labour is a combination of number of factors: poverty, illiteracy, traditional beliefs and attitudes and employers' preference for hiring children.

The driving force behind every case of child labour is generally poverty but the basic cause is an interplay of some of the above factors. A child goes out to work in order to contribute to the family income. Broadly speaking, child labour persists in inverse relation to the degree of economic advancement of a society or country. The exploitation of children is one of the consequences of complex situations of insufficient progress.[4] ILO observed that 98 percent of the economically active children are found in developing countries. The Special Rapporteur of the United Nations Sub-Commission on Prevention of Discrimination and Protection of Minorities also observed that poverty and exploitation of child labour go hand-in-hand. It is the poorest populations, at the lowest levels of human existence, who are forced to work the most prematurely, he noted.[5]

Children may be forced to work due to poverty but child labour in turn accentuates poverty. Children are engaged in jobs that can be done by adults too, thus depriving adults of jobs. Employers prefer to hire children because they can extract the same work from children at lower wages, in the process bringing down the overall wages for such jobs. Thus child labour increases adult unemployment and reduces their income and thus forces adults to send their children to work to supplement the family income. The poor are thus caught in a vicious circle. Rather than improving the household income, child labour helps to reduce it.

In a large number of developing countries, migration from rural areas has also intensified the problem of child labour. In most developing countries, developmental efforts have neglected the agrarian sectors, resulting in growing pauperisation of small farmers, increasing landlessness and rural differentiation. This has led to search for wage employment in commercial farms, as well as to rapid migration away from rural areas. Children from poor families are forced into the labour market to work either individually or as part of contracted family labour. Given the need to meet subsistence requirements on the one hand and growing pauperisation resulting from land alienation on the other, the pressure on rural households to find alternative sources of survival by all means, whether under family control or under contract to prospective employers and labour recruiters, becomes almost insurmountable. When a rural family migrates to the town, the adults are straightaway faced with a new and unknown environmental and labour situation. As a result of the instability and insecurity that this causes, the children are often sent to work so that the family may survive.

Child labour is not merely a consequence of poverty. There is also a correlation between literacy rate and the magnitude of child labour. Countries having low literacy and school attendance rates generally have the most acute child labour problems. It has been often stated that education can bring the dramatic exploitation of child labour to an end. The example of the developed countries confirms this conclusively. The historical record reveals an astonishing correlation between the progress of education in Europe and decrease in the volume of child labour and the transformation of its very nature. A glance at the educational statistics shows that it is almost always the same countries that admit to being the most behind in school enrolment and teacher-student ratio, that have the greatest problems as regards the exploitation of child labour.

Figure 1 shows that the highest rates of school enrolment coincide with the lowest numbers of school-age children per teacher and are found in the most developed countries: the United States of America, the United Kingdom and New Zealand, which are countries in which child labour is least apparent. Countries such as Somalia and Chad are characterized by a poor staffing ratio, a low percentage of children enroled in school and the exploitation of child labour. Figure 2 also provides a systematic confirmation of this fact, a fact that is presented globally, and for all countries.[6]

Figure I : Percentage of School-age Population (5-19) Enrolled in School and Number of School-age Children per Teacher, Selected Countries, 1975

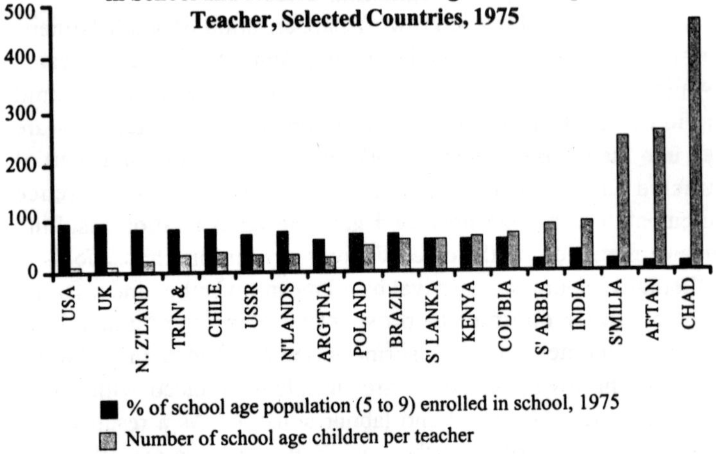

Source: M. C. McHale & J. McHale, Children in the World (Washington D. C. Population Reference Bureau, 1979) in A. Bouhdiba, Exploitation of Child Labour : Final Report of the Special Rapporteur of the U. N. Sub Commission on Prevention of Discrimination & Protection of Minorities (Geneva : U. N., 1983), p. 26

It is said that governments in developing countries lack the financial resources for universal compulsory primary education and parents often find schools irrelevant to meet their needs. Professor Myron Weiner puts forth the argument that many countries successfully made primary school education compulsory and universal when per capita incomes were low, poverty was widespread and parents would have employed their children had they been permitted to do so. Japan introduced compulsory education in 1872, North and South Korea, Taiwan and the People's Republic of China made education compulsory shortly after the Second World War. All these countries introduced compulsory education when per capita incomes were low. By 1910, Japan was able to ensure that 98 percent of the 6 to 13 age group attended school. In 1943, Taiwan made 6 years of primary school education compulsory. Both North and South Korea launched massive campaigns in the 1950s to get all their primary school age children into school. The People's Republic of China is another

Figure II : Percentage of Children Aged 6 to 11 & 12 to 17 Enrolled in School in Developed & Developing Countries

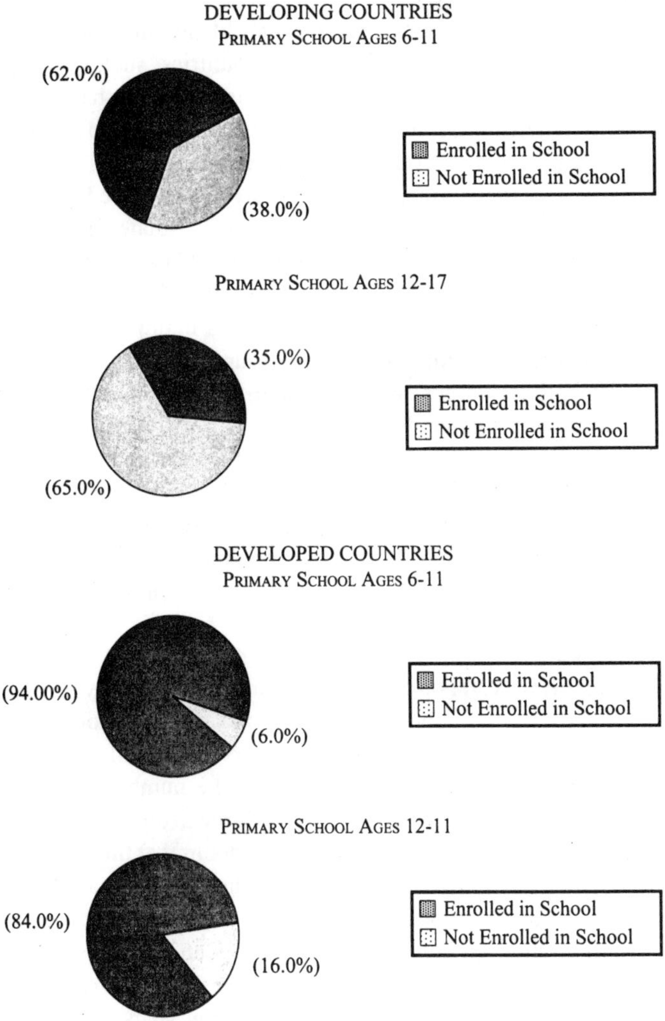

Source: M. C. McHale and J.McHale, Children in the World (Washington D. C. Population Reference Bureau, 1979) in A. Bouhdiba, Exploitation of Child Labour : Final Report of the Special Rapporteur of the U. N. Sub-Commission on Prevention of Discrimination & Protection of Minorities (Geneva : U.N., 1983), p. 9.

dramatic case. In 1949, only one fourth of the children in China were in primary school, by 1982 the figure was 93 percent, with 70 percent completing sixth grade. The story is similar for most of the countries of Southeast Asia.

However, the relationship between child labour and illiteracy may not be one of cause and effect. Some countries, such as Mexico, Colombia and Thailand, not to mention Spain and Italy, have largely succeeded in eradicating illiteracy but remain confronted by the child labour problem, which is sometimes very acute.[7]

In Thailand, for example, four years of primary education is compulsory for all children. According to one estimate, literacy rate in Thailand is 87.7 percent. According to the 1984 census, Thailand has a population of 50 million, with a little over 20 million people under the age of 15. Thai government sources claim there are only 1.07 million working children in the age group 11-14 years. However, according to other sources, in 1984 there were about 10.7 million working children in Thailand. While rural poverty is the driving force behind child labour in Thailand, the role of vested interests cannot be underestimated. There is a tremendous demand for children as workers in factories, restaurants and private houses and as prostitutes in brothels. There is a need to increase compulsory education from four to six years and forcefully implement the compulsory school system.[8]

Sri Lanka is another example of a country that massively expanded its primary school enrollments in the 1950s. By 1981, 90 percent of the primary school-age children were in school and 70 percent of all children completed five years of schooling. Labour force statistics indicated a sharp decrease in the number of children in the age group of 10-14 in the labour force from 1946-63 as a result of school enrolment.[9] While there is no doubt that the Sri Lankan example is a success story, particularly in the South Asian context, the situation is not so optimistic. According to the 1980 census, there are 3.8 million children between the ages of 5 and 14 in Sri Lanka, but only 2.7 million are attending school, the other 1.1 million are working. However, children do at least get a few years of schooling and manage to work at the same time. Their entry into the labour force takes place at a later age.[10]

Thus the importance of compulsory schooling in the struggle against child labour cannot be undermined. However, the educational system adopted by countries concerned must be meaningful and realistic and must adapt itself to the real needs of society.

The role of vested interests in perpetuating child labour also needs to be highlighted. Employers often claim that there are types of work for which children are particularly suited. However, most work done by children can also be done by adults. The real reason behind employers preference in hiring children is the desire to maximise profits. Children can be made to work for long hours for low wages. Employers find it easier to deal with children because they do not organise themselves in trade unions, can be easily intimidated and are not capable of defending themselves and insisting on their rightful due.

The notion of child labour is also rooted in the traditions and attitudes of the regions where it is practised, as a remnant of the past, a form of resistance to change. For example, it is widely believed in many developing countries that the more the children in a family, the more the hands to help increase the family income. Again, in the developing countries the idea that a child who is no longer a baby should be maintained without working is uncommon. The idea stems not so much from poverty as from traditional beliefs.[11] In many societies, child labour is not considered a problem and is regarded as part of a child's normal socialisation even if exploitative work conditions are present. On the other hand, the attitudes and beliefs of policy makers in several developing countries regarding the respective roles of upper and lower classes have perpetuated the problem. It is often argued that the children of the poor should be prepared for their future roles from an early age.

Child labour persists in some countries because of lack of political will to deal with the problem and because child labour laws cannot be adequately enforced because of shortage of qualified labour inspectors.

Thus children work because of poverty, lack of compulsory education, rapid rural-urban migration and because of prevailing social, cultural and political attitudes.

Forms of Child Employment

Elias Mendelievich suggested that as far as employment status of working children is concerned, the following are the main types:

a) Children who work on their account;
b) Wage earners paid time or piece rates;
c) Apprentices;

d) Children who assist an adult worker who in turn works for an employer;
e) Children who work with their family without any direct remuneration.

The Special Rapporteur of the Sub-Commission on Prevention of Discrimination and Protection of Minorities has arrived at a comprehensive list of types of child labour. These are as under:[12]

I. Work carried out within the family

A. Without a middleman
   1. Family farming
   2. Family craftwork
B. With a middleman
   1. Craft piecework

II. Work outside the family

A. Without a middleman
   1. Tasks carried out by the child on his own account
B. With a middleman
   1. Tasks carried out for third parties
   2. Seasonal workers in agriculture
   3. Apprentices
   4. Sweat-shop system

III. Three Specific Cases

1. Maid-of-all-work in a situation of virtual bondage
2. Bond Service
3. Child Prostitution

Family farming makes the greatest use of child labour in the context of unpaid family assistants. In this type of labour it is not so much the child who is exploited by the general social system as the whole family. The economic, social and cultural situation of the family obviously has repercussions on the child but he at least remains integrated in a social context that is in principle protective. Children are also engaged in family craftwork. The intricate rules governing the market for the crafts produced also makes possible exploitation and abuses. As in the case of family farming, there is no question of wage and the situation remains one of joint production at the group level. This type of activity, in which the exploitation of child labour is no less real because it is indirect, to be found in most parts of the world. Craft piecework is a more highly evolved form than the previous type. It meets the same needs, is carried out in the same places, and employs the same manufacturing techniques. However, a middleman or a capitalist is involved who picks up the products from the families to market them, having first secured a more or less extensive and more or less excessive sales monopoly. The family no longer has direct access to the market. To be in a better position to exert pressure he gives a small advance on the wage. The threat of exploitation is clearly greater and affects the child along with the family. Since payment is made on the basis of amount and quality of work, to earn more money the family calls upon its children and becomes the more or less willing and conscious accomplice of the middleman. The Satwargaon brickworks in India is the classic example: it employs 600 to 700 children with their families.

Children also carry out small tasks on their own account. However, two subtypes, differing radically, according to the level of development of the country, must be distinguished in this type of work. In developing countries, the child usually works in order to live, and in order to survive. In developed countries children usually work in order to satisfy secondary or even superfluous needs. Small tasks called out by the child for third parties are different in that they produce a relationship of dependence which can very easily become one of exploitation, For example, children who sort through rubbish for old rags and wastepaper have to share the better part of the money obtained with someone else. Moreover, the dividing line between small tasks, dubious practices and even near-delinquency is truly a fine one.

The seasonal labour of children in agriculture is more organised and also more prevalent. Seasonal labour is in general remunerative and is carried out under widely varying conditions. However, to the extent that it is work that is very difficult to control and in which middlemen are fairly numerous, the loopholes for abuse are quite large.

Children also work as apprentices. Learning how to work is a part of any sound and balanced education. Apprenticeship enables the child to try his hand at a task at a fairly early age and then to improve in skill until all operations have been mastered. But very frequently apprenticeship is simply subterfuge for evading legislation on minimum age. The exploitation of child labour is perpetuated through apprenticeship. More often than not, supposed apprentices are in fact working rather than learning and not being paid for it. Such a state of affairs may sometimes last for years. There is too much fake apprenticeship, which is merely a facade behind which there is nothing at all, since the activities performed require no qualification, provide no training and at best are carried out for paltry sums. Even the most thankless and hard tasks are sometimes given to children.

The sweat-shop system in much of the Third World, more especially in Asia, is the equivalent of the European workshops at the beginning of the 19th century. A large number of children work in them under terrible conditions. In Bangkok, a police raid discovered 63 children—49 girls and 14 boys—between the ages of 8 and 14, working under atrocious conditions in one of the 10,000 sweat-shops which abound in Thailand and which, being illegal, pay scant attention to the laws governing employment.

Maids-of-all-work in situation of virtual bondage are to be found everywhere. This type of child labour is very widespread. A study conducted in urban areas of Colombia found that 40 percent of all 11 and 12-year-old child workers were domestic servants. It is generally girls who are employed as domestic servants. In Bolivia and Colombia little Indian girls are 'adopted' from the age of 3 by white families to do the household work.

Bonded labour is the ultimate stage of exploitation of child labour. Debt bondage can arise in a number of ways. In agrarian societies land tenure patterns impose on tenants, sharecroppers and similar categories of workers obligations over and above household consumption requirements. In some cases, these obligations, may take the form of providing the landlord a share of the produce. But in others they may involve the provision of labour services, including those of children. The prevalence of such relations is known to lead to a severe and high incidence of debt bondage.

Debt bondage is often also the result of the parents being given a loan to meet some urgent need. The debtor then has to repay by working. Parents may send children to work in the house of the moneylender. In practice the debt does not decrease; it climbs ever upwards—a combination of usurious interest rates and outright fraud. These children may stay for many years, not knowing how long they must work or even the size of the debt they are paying off. While bonded labour is prohibited by law, it is still found, for example, in parts of South and Southeast Asia. According to ILO, there are several million child bonded labourers in South Asia.

All child labourers, wherever they work, sell some of their childhood but none sell as much as those driven to prostitution. It is a problem for rich countries as well as poor. Studies in Europe and America show how runaway children are most likely to sell their bodies. Children in most countries have always been used as prostitutes but the situation in some Asian countries, like Thailand, has been aggravated by the expansion of mass tourism. Both boys and girls are used in the flesh trade. In Sri Lanka, for example, the majority of child prostitutes are boys.

The problem can also be analysed by examining the sectors in which children are employed. Sectors employing child labour vary from one country to another but child labour is most common in agriculture followed by service sector, largely in street trades, and in third place industry.

Most child work is agricultural. Starting with light tasks, such as looking after animals, collecting firewood and fodder and drawing water, they later learn to sow and to reap. In commercial agriculture, on plantations for example, they often work as part of the family team: weeding, spreading fertilizer, tending plants, though they often share in the heavier tasks.

Figure III : The Work of Street Children in Asuncion, 1987

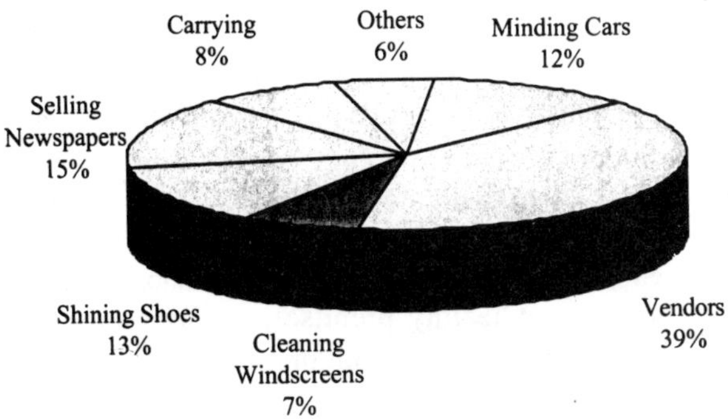

Source: International Labour Organisation, World Labour Report (Geneva: ILO, 1992).

The rapid urbanisation process of recent decades has led to a marked increase in child labour in the cities. Children work in a wide variety of street trades: as shoeshine boys, messengers, sellers of magazines, food, flowers, lottery tickets, etc. These children are often termed as street children because they may be literally living on the streets or at the place of their work. The boys very often work as waiters in roadside cafes and restaurants and as pageboys and the girls as hotel maids or domestic servants. The range of occupations of street child workers in Asuncion, Paraguay, is shown in Figure 3 on page 15.

Children who work in industries are generally employed in the informal sector. While in some industries children perform secondary tasks, they may also directly participate in the main tasks of production.

Working Conditions

Where children work in a family undertaking, generally working conditions may not be too arbitrary. However, these traditional situations are declining in many areas, especially where plantation agriculture is becoming established or where there is massive out-migration, as in southern Africa for example.[13]

When children are employed outside the family, the way they are treated, as well as their conditions of work, are usually determined by the employer. The possibilities of ill-treatment are unlimited. Ill-treatment may include corporal punishment, abuses of all kinds, humiliation and frustration. Children are usually employed in the informal sector, where conditions of work are appalling and welfare facilities are conspicuous by their absence. The tasks in which they are employed are generally monotonous and repetitive in nature and often they are ill-suited to the child's physical and mental capacities.[14]

The working conditions severely tax the child's physical and mental resistance as a result, for example, of suffocating heat in enclosed premises or exposure to rain or sun in open-air work. They may be forced to work in an awkward position in badly lit, badly ventilated, noisy or unhealthy premises, in damp and unhygenic surrounding, in an atmosphere contaminated with dust or gases, crammed together with other workers, in workshops without adequate safety devices, rest areas, medical and toilet facilities, having to carry excessively heavy loads, etc. all in violation of the principles set forth in international instruments to protect their rights.[15]

Children who are more or less self-employed and child street traders generally feel they are freer than other working children. Despite their relative freedom, they too are an exploited lot because they too have to bear the demands of the market. Although many self-employed workers work in their own home, others have to travel varying distances to reach their workplace as many wage-earners do. When carrying out their activities they are hardly ever protected from the vagaries of the weather. They may be harassed by the police or by groups of youths or adults.[16]

Hours of Work

The length of time that children work each day and over the year varies considerably according to their schooling status, their parent's wish to keep them at work more or less continuously, how long the employer needs them and so on. Some children work only during the school holidays, at weekends, early in the morning or late at night. Seasonal work is also often undertaken by children, in agricultural work for tasks such as sowing and harvesting. Since the general conditions of work are generally fixed by the employer alone, all kinds of abuses are encountered: working days of 10, 12 or 14 hours for some times seven days a week, that is to say far beyond what the child can tolerate both physically and mentally.

In some countries, girls work longer hours than boys because boys spend more time at school. It is common knowledge that children in domestic service work long hours since they must be available at virtually any time to carry out their employer's bidding. Two studies carried out in Indonesia and Nepal produced the details shown in Table 1 of the daily hours of work for children of both sexes.[17]

Some wage earning children are permitted to take work breaks at fixed intervals during the working day. Others are not allowed to do so despite the fact that a child needs a break more often than an adult if he is to recharge his physical and mental batteries. The period of daily rest is often not sufficient, especially in agricultural work, industry, some service industries and domestic service. The weekly rest is sometimes granted and paid, sometimes granted but not paid and sometimes not allowed at all, *i.e.*, the working week is a seven-day week. In many undertakings, children do not enjoy annual paid holidays.

Table 1
Indonesia (JAVA) and Nepal: Daily Hours Worked by Children

Country and Age Group	Hours Worked per Day	
	Boys	Girls
INDONESIA (JAVA)		
6-8	3.6	3.5
9-11	3.3	5.4
12-14	4.8	8.7
NEPAL		
6-8	3.7	4.9
9-11	6.5	8.4
12-14	7.5	9.9

Source: M. Nag, R. C. Peet and B. White, "Economic Value of Children in Two Peasant Societies, International Population Conference (Liege, 1978) in Elias Mendelievich, Children at Work (Geneva, 1979), p. 39.

Remuneration

Children who work in the family undertaking usually receive no payment for their work, since the family income is considered to be one indivisible whole. This is equally true when the family carries out work for a third party. The children take part in the work and the family receives the total sum earned.

When the child is a wage earner, he may be paid a salary, a daily wage or piece-rate wage. The wage that a child earns is much lower than those received by an adult for doing the same work. While they work for long hours, their wages are pitifully low. Children in electric light bulb factories in Indonesia, for example, work from 7.00 am to 3.00 pm, six days a week, for US$3 per week. Child coffee pickers in Zimbabwe earn roughly the same for a 10-hour-day, six-day-week. In Nepal, children in carpet factories earn US$1 per day or less. A still more flagrant example of exploitation of child workers is that of supposed apprentices who are infact working than learning and are not being paid for it. Finally, in another types of exploitative relationship, payment is symbolic or non-existent or supplied in kind: food, lodging or 'presents' to the child or to the family.[18] This is often the case for those working in restaurants or in domestic services.

Consequences of Child Labour

Sending children to work may seem a rational approach to poverty but employment of children has profound repercussions. ILO research shows that child labour is almost universally recognized as being undesirable, harmful for the children themselves and harmful for the future of their nations. Mendelievich in his book "Children at Work" has classified repercussions of child labour into three:

Social and Labour Repercussions

When a child joins the workforce at a young age, he is deprived of the opportunity to educate himself and acquiring qualifications which will help him in getting a better job in future. It is therefore very likely that a child who has been at work from an early age will spend his whole life at the bottom of the social ladder.

Thus child labour has become a mode of perpetuating an unjust social system and of ensuring the continued availability of subservient, unskilled, illiterate labourers who do not have the bargaining power to question the system that marginalises them and deprives them of their right to lead a decent life.[19]

Physical Repercussions

Many of the jobs that children do are harmful for their physical development. The physical susceptibility of working children also has a lot to do with the fact that they have very different capacities and needs from adults, and this fact is very rarely taken into account by employers. The manner of their employment, the nature of their work and the conditions under which they are often employed subject them to severe health and safety hazards.

Work in agriculture is also characterised by certain hazards, particularly with the introduction of advanced farming practices, new techniques and chemicals. There is also prolonged exposure to heat, sunlight, dust, wind and insects and the high costs in terms of safety and health associated with work in commercial and plantation agriculture. Children are particularly at risk from endemic and parasitic diseases, diseases of the respiratory tract, dermatosis and fatal accidents.[20]

However, these problems are multiplied several fold in industries. Work may be heavy and intense; it may be highly mechanised and extremely monotonous; it may involve the use of sharp and dangerous objects and toxic substances; it may be carried out in conditions of extreme heat, dust and noise. Child workers in industries are faced with serious risks to their health and physical development. They may be required to undertake tasks for which they are entirely unprepared physically. In a number of industries children are exposed to lead poisoning which may have no noticeable effect on adults. There are claims that children's brains are detrimentally affected due to exposure to lead poisoning. There are documented cases of paralysis caused by the use of toxic glues. There is documentation on the paralytic effects of a number of chemicals on children in Morrocan workshops where children were gluing suitcases and shoes. In these cases the toxic effects were accentuated by poor sanitation and ventilation and the younger the child, the more serious the paralysis.

The risk of occupational diseases or accidents are higher among child workers because their growing bodies are not as strong as adult workers. Several studies show that child workers have greater health problems than adults even if both are placed in the same working environment.

There can be special risks associated with the working environment. For example, young migrant workers in Peruvian gold panning are unaccustomed to the insects, heat and humidity and have no defences against the diseases prevalent in the jungle. In Bogota's quarries and brickyards children undertake dangerous tasks such as unloading hot bricks from kilns and transporting heavy loads. Heavy loads and awkward body positions in particular can affect physical growth, especially the growth of bones, which are still soft in children. When a child is regularly bent under a heavy burden or is forced to stay in an unnatural position for long periods, deformation of the spinal column, pelvis or thorax may be the result. A World Health Organisation report on child workers cites health hazards such as bony lesions and postural deformity attributable to such work as carpet weaving, embroidery and lifting heavy weights.

Children generally work for long hours, which results in excessive fatigue and stunted growth. Poor children are generally malnourished but their work increases their energy requirement and calorie deficit.

Moreover, if they suffer from anaemia, fatigue and inadequate sleep, they become more susceptible to accidents and infectious diseases. Reports on the carpet factories in Pakistan estimated that half of the 50,000 bonded children in the industry never reach the age of 12—victims of malnutrition and disease.

Excessively hot, damp or dusty conditions also create a milieu which favours the transmission of communicable diseases. Many of these diseases, for example tuberculosis or bronchitis, may be very difficult to cure and involve lifelong illnesses. Once again, malnutrition, anaemia, inadequate sleep, etc. lower resistance. Once infected at an early age, and through constant reinfection, it becomes difficult to break the vicious cycle of contact. In many cases workplaces do not meet hygenic standards. There is often no running water or toilet facilities. In these situations gastro intestinal diseases flourish and it is difficult to break the oral-faecial cycle.[21]

The self-employed child who has an accident or contracts a disease of occupational origin obviously benefits from no form of social protection. If the child is a wage-earner he is not usually protected either since in the vast majority of cases he is working illegally. If he is the victim of an occupational accident or disease he and his parents must be prepared for fearful and irreversible consequences. The official statistics reveal a very small proportion of the occupational accidents or diseases that affect children.

Thus many jobs done by children are the cause of physical deformities and illnesses such as deformities of the spine, stunted growth, infections, burns, sores etc. or else they may aggravate defects or maladies. Child labour involves both short-term and long-term health risks. Some of the hazards may not be immediately apparent but may take some years to manifest.

Mental Repercussions

Child labour has mental repercussions also since the age at which he usually starts to work coincides more or less with a period of profound mental change in the child. If to the working child's unfavourable intellectual status an ill-directed mental development is added, there will be undesirable mental consequences and behavioural problems, caused by the child's inadequate comprehension of the adult world and by his imitating, distorting and exaggerating what he wrongly believes to be the essence of that world.[22]

The mental consequences of child labour are not just the result of the work situation but the violent change to which the child is exposed. In many cases children are separated from their families when they migrate to cities and other places in search of employment. Migration, for example in many African areas, may affect 2 out of 3 households. Children are thrust into a new urban slum. An unfamiliar, often oppressive work situation, exacerbates the stresses and leads to socio-cultural disorganisation. There is a breakdown of effective communication, impaired human relations, insecurity, problems of identification, a high prevalence of psycho-neurotic reactions and psychosomatic disorders.[23]

Moreover, since a large number of children work for long hours, their social interactions are limited and this affects their emotional development. Lack of leisure time activities and repression of childhood desires have harmful impact on the harmonious development of a child's personality.

Child Labour in Developed Countries

Until a few centuries ago, children everywhere worked alongside their parents. Only the children of the privileged classes could escape manual work. In 19th-century Europe children were employed in factories, some worked in tenements with their parents who in turn were paid for the output of the household. Industrialisation increased job opportunities for working-class families. Urban working class families dependent on daily wages sought to reduce risk through the employment of their children. Children's work became more dangerous: machines and chemicals endangered their well-being, working conditions were poor, hours long and wages low.[24]

It was not until the 19th century that governments began to regulate the conditions of employment for children and restrict the ages at which children could work. However, much of the early legislation proved to be ineffective, although the passage of the legislation itself was indicative of changing attitudes towards children and work and towards the responsibility of the state as the protector of children against employers and parents.

With the spread of compulsory schooling, the rapid and considerable improvement in levels of living and the enforcement of anti-child labour laws there was a significant decline in child labour.

However, child labour is still prevalant in the developed nations, according to an ILO report. In the poverty pockets of the industrialised countries there may be as many as another 10 million or more working children, many of whom are not in school fulltime and many may not be reached by health services. These children are found particularly amongst illegal migrant families; but also in certain occupations in the entertainment or publicity industries.

Italy has some of the highest number of working children in Western Europe. There have been reports of tens of thousands in Naples region alone, with the leather industry a particular cause for concern. Spain, too, has some significant numbers—some sources suggest more than 100,000—with most of the children working in agriculture, generally on family farms.

There are reports about girls in Portugal who work in the clothing industry or as servants. According to a recent study in Birmingham, Britain, some 43 percent of all children between 10 and 16 years work under abject conditions and 75 percent are illegally employed.[25]

In the United States of America the majority of child workers are employed in agriculture and a high proportion of these are from immigrant families. According to an ILO report, more than 500,000 children in the USA are forced to work on farms in California. Most of these children are Mexican and they lack even the most rudimentary social and health care. In a clothing factory in New York, government inspectors found children working in circumstances considered inhuman even at the beginning of this century. "It was so cold that children would not even notice if they hurt themselves", the government inspectors stated. A study conducted in 1990 by the General Accounting Office showed a 250 percent increase in child labour law violations from 1983 to 1990. In an operation carried out by the US Department of Labour for 3 days in 1990, 11,000 children were found working illegally.[26]

The problem of child labour is also emerging in East European countries which are making a transition to market economy.

Thus child labour may be concentrated in developing countries but is certainly not confined to them. According to the ILO report, the upsurge in the reported cases of child labour in the industrialised world stemmed mainly from the recent economic recession.

Table-2

Number and Percentage of Boys and Girls Aged 10 to 14 in the Labour Force of Selected Countries

Country	Boys		Girls		Total	
	No.'000s	Percentage	No.'000s	Percentage	N0'000s	Percentage
USA	221	2.1	106	1.1	327	1.6
China	5397	12.1	4128	9.6	9525	10.9
Sweden	2	0.6	1	0.3	3	0.4
Italy	70	3.1	44	2.0	114	2.6
Hungary	2	0.6	4	1.3	6	1.0
Egypt	426	18.2	101	4.5	527	11.5
Mozambique	220	41.8	77	14.5	297	28.1
Tanzania	334	35.9	223	23.9	557	29. 9
Brazil	1054	15.8	382	5.8	1436	10.8
Peru	44	4.6	40	4.3	84	4.5
Mexico	390	10.0	91	2.4	481	6.3
India	7620	19.4	7537	20.7	15157	20.0
Indonesia	1425	16.5	1048	12.5	2473	14.5
Thailand	623	23.0	730	27.7	1353	25.4

Source: M.C.Mc Hale and J.Mc Hale, Children in the World (Washington D.C, 1979), in Abdelwahab Boudhiba, *Exploitation of Child Labour: Final Report of the Special Rapporteur of the United Nations Sub-Commission on Prevention of Discrimination and Protection of Minorities* (Geneva: UN, 1983) p. 7.

Child Labour in Developing Countries

Table II shows that though child labour is prevalent in most countries, it is of minimal intensity (less than 3 percent) in the developed countries of Europe and North America. Developing countries of South Asia, Latin America and Africa show a high incidence of child labour, with Tanzania showing a peak of 29.9 percent.

Figure 4 shows the extraordinary extent to which child labour is concentrated in Asian, African and Latin American countries. Both the charts show clearly the disparity between the percentages of children between the ages of 10 and 14 who work in different parts of the world. Asia has the largest child workforce. According to ILO estimates, child workers constitute as much as 7 percent of the population under 15 years of age as high as 11 percent of the overall labour force in some Asian countries.

Figure IV : Number of Children aged under 15 in the Labour Force by World Regions, 1975 and 2000

1975 : TOTAL LABOUR FORCE UNDER 15 = 54.7M

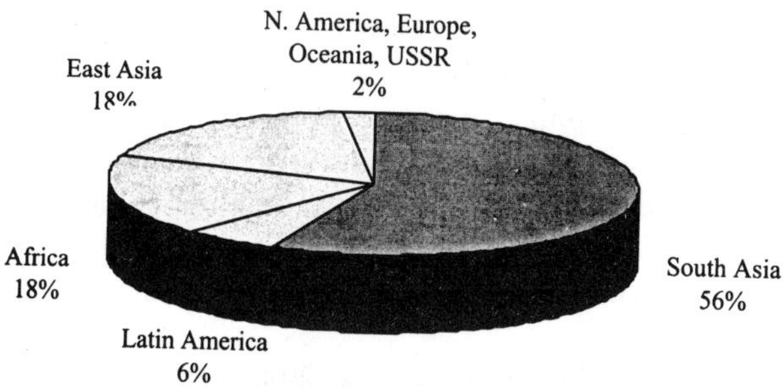

2000 : TOTAL LABOUR FORCE UNDER 15 = 37.3M

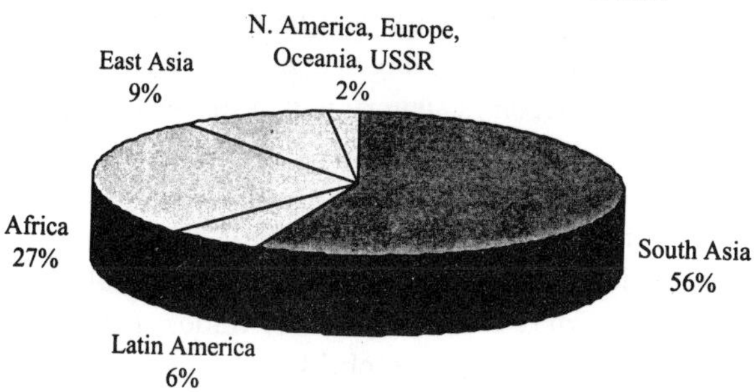

Source: M.C.Mc Hale and J.Mc Hale, Children in the World (Washington D.C, 1979), in Boudhiba, *Exploitation of Child Labour: Final Report of the Special Rapporteur of the United Nations Sub-Commission.*

The Country Report on Human Rights Practices of US Senate Foreign Relations Committee revealed that of a total child population of 9 million in Nepal, 4.8 million children work.[27] Overall Bangladesh has 18 million child workers. It's garment industry alone employs 40,000 children. Pakistan has an estimated 8 million working children. The carpet looms in Pakistan alone employs 500,000 children.[28] The situation in Sri Lanka is different compared to other South Asian countries but is no less worrying. According to the 1980 census, there are 3.8 million children between the ages of 5 and 14 in Sri Lanka, but only 2.7 million are attending school, the other 1.1 million are either working or begging. According to a recent survey, of the 1.9 million Sri Lankan children in the age group of 10-14 years, about 250,000 are in the non-formal labour market. Around 20,000 are engaged in male prostitution and some 10,000 are estimated to be street children.[29]

According to a recent study on child labour in the Philippines, roughly 2.7 million children are working full time and if the number of children working part time is added, the figure could range from 3 million to 8 million, depending on the definition used. Child labour in the Philippines is to be found in every sector of the economy—on the streets as vendors, in small-scale factories, in rural areas, where they work as part of family labour, in cottage industries making baskets, embroidering, sewing, as domestic servants and in the fishing sector.[30] In Thailand, there are 10.7 million working children—88.2 percent in the agriculture sector, 10.2 percent in the industrial sector. A large number of Thai children also work in restaurants, in homes and as prostitutes.

In some African countries, as many as 20 percent of children are reported to be working, and child workers make up as much as 17 percent of the workforce. The work assigned to children in rural areas in Africa may be divided into three categories. The first consists of domestic chores. The second category is that of farm work, which children have to sometimes perform beyond their physical strength. The third category is that of work in the informal sector of the rural economy. This includes crafts and small trades that are essential to village life, especially shopkeeping. In the urban informal sector in Africa, child labour is of 3 types: (1) Street trades, (2) Domestic service, in which 90 percent of the children employed are girls, sometimes as young as 7 or 8 years old. (3) Begging. In this context, the problem of AIDS and its relation to child labour must be mentioned. Adults who suffer from AIDS, without employment or social protection, are entirely dependent on their children for a living. Furthermore, sexual exploitation of children exposes them to infection since they have no means of protection and because sexual exploitation is a part of their working conditions.[31]

In Ethopia, 41.7 percent children aged between 10 and 14 years are employed—49.9 percent of the males are economically active while 32.3 percent female children are working. In some Latin American countries upto 26 percent of children are working. Latin America is the urbanised region of the developing world so children are more likely to be working in cities. Brazil has the greatest number of working children—7 million—according to a government household survey which indicates that around 18 percent of Brazilian children between 10 and 14 are economically active. A similar propotion of Mexican children between 12 and 14 are working. National census data on the labour force exclude children under the age of 12 and there are no public figures on the overall distribution of the economically active population by age. One source puts the number of working children in Colombia at 3 million.

The problem of child labour has assumed serious proportions. Their continued and widespread employment in the workforce is a denial of their basic rights. The repercussions of child labour are confined not only on the children individually but on the society as a whole because the contribution of these children to society in future will suffer on account of the sacrifices made in terms of their health and education.

International Action Against Child Labour

Child labour subjects children to exploitation and forces them to work in conditions dangerous to their physical, social and mental development. The growing magnitude of the problem has made it a cause for international concern. Efforts have been made at the global and national level by various international organisations along with their member nations to expose the problem and to cope with it. The beginning of the industrial revolution brought about the enactment of child labour laws. In the international arena, the first conventions indirectly protecting children began in the late 19th and early 20th century.

Children's right emerged as a sub-category in the development of the rules of war and of the international labour conventions. The idea of grouping children into a distinct category was gradually promoted. Children have been a silent and unrepresented minority, they used to belong to one of those groups in history which Martin Luther King Jr described as "nobodies". Non Governmental Organisations played a very important role in giving shape to the rights of the child. The whole process started at the outset of this century, when some British women in Cambridge made a survey of the charitable societies at that time to determine what protection was provided to children. These pacifist women worked throughout the First World War to alert the general public to the plight of children in war-affected areas. After the war, they founded the "Save the Children" movement, whose lobbying led to the recognition of the rights of the child in the League of Nations.[32] In January 1924, a committee was set up in the league whose scope included the protection of children in general. This was later divided into two sections, one of which was specifically devoted to child welfare. The Geneva Declaration of the Rights of the Child was adopted in 1924. The Geneva Declaration recognizes the principle that childhood is entitled to special care, assistance and safeguards. The Geneva Declaration contains a sentence that has become the motto of all supporters of the children's cause: "mankind owes to the child the best it has to give." Geneva Convention IV and the additional protocols incorporated and expanded many of the principles contained in the Hague Conventions and specifically provided for protection of children. Children were provided general protection by Article 14, 17 and 24 of the Geneva Convention IV and 76, 77, 78 of Protocol I. But with the outbreak of World War II, it lost its significance. The Declaration of Geneva formed the basis of the 10-point 'Declaration of the Rights of the Child', which was unanimously adopted by the UN General Assembly on 20th November, 1959.

The General Assembly of the UN adopted on 10th December, 1948, a Universal Declaration of Human Rights. Portions of the Universal Declaration of Human Rights apply specifically to minors. It contains 30 articles, 21 of which spell out civil and political rights, and 6 articles deal with economic and cultural rights.

The UN adopted a Convention on the Abolition of Slavery, the Slave Trade and Institutions and Practices similar to Slavery in 1956. This convention prohibits the exploitation of child labour in cases where children are delivered to another person for that purpose. Article 1 of the Convention states that "Each of the practicable and necessary measures to bring about progressively and as soon as possible the complete abolition and abandonment of ... any institution or practice whereby a child or young person under the age of 18 years is delivered by either or both of his natural parents or by his guardian to another person, whether for reward or not, with a view to the exploitation of the child or young person or his labour."[33]

The General Assembly adopted the International Covenant on Human Rights in December, 1966. The covenant consists of 3 seperate instruments: the International Covenant on Economic, Social and Cultural Rights; the International Covenant on Civil and Political Rights; and the Optional Protocol to the International Covenant on Civil and Political Rights.

The International Covenant on Economic, Social and Cultural Rights imposes a general prohibition on the employment of children under a certain age and the employment of children in work constituting a threat to their health or morals. More specifically, Article 10, paragraph 3, provides that "... children and young persons should be protected from economic and social exploitation. Their employment in work harmful to their morals or health or dangerous to life or likely to hamper their normal development should be punishable by law. States should also set age limits below which the paid employment of child labour should be prohibited and punishable by law."[34]

Though the Universal Declaration of Human Rights, 1948, implicitly included the freedom and rights of children, it was believed that this was not enough. It was felt that the special needs of children justified a seperate document because children are particularly vulnerable to arbitrary deprivation of their human rights. This led to the adoption of the Declaration of the Rights of the Child in 1959.

The 1959 declaration enunciates general principles for the care and protection of children. It is mainly concerned with economic, social and cultural rights. It must be noted that it was in the preamble of 1959 declaration that the problem of implementation of children's rights was first mentioned. The preamble to the declaration states that the child because of his physical and mental immaturity needs special safeguards and care. "Mankind", it says, "owes the child the best it has to give."[35]

The Declaration of the Rights of the Child also prohibits the employment of children under a certain age and the employment of children in work which endanger their development. Principle 9 states: "The child shall be protected against all forms of neglect, cruelty, and exploitation. He shall not be the subject of traffic in any form. The child shall not be admitted to employment before an appropriate minimum age; he shall in no case be caused or permitted to engage in any occupation or employment which would prejudice his health or education or interfere with his physical, mental or moral development."[36]

The Government of Poland submitted a draft Convention on the rights of the child to the General Assembly in 1978. In 1979, it submitted an amended version of the draft to the Commission on Human Rights. The General Assembly requested the Commission to give the highest priority to the question of completing the draft convention, "bearing in mind the children's rights are basic human rights and call for continuous improvement of the situation of children all over the world as well as their development and education in conditions of peace."[36] As a result, the General Assembly decided to set up a working group within the Human Rights Commission, which from 1979, the International Year of the Child, met regularly to complete the Convention. On November 20, 1989, the General Assembly at its 44th session adopted the Convention. It came into force on September 2, 1990, following ratification by the stipulated minimum of 20 member states.

The Convention recognizes the exceptional vulnerability of children and proclaims that childhood is entitled to special care and assistance. It is guided by the principle of "first call for children"— a principle that the essential needs of children should be given highest priority in the allocation of resources at all times. It obligates the state to respect and ensure that children get a fair and equitable deal in society.[38]

The Convention's provisions can be categorised under the headings of civil and political rights, social rights and cultural rights. Article 3 states that "in all actions concerning children ... the best interests of the child shall be a primary consideration." It implies that whenever a child's right is in the process of being affected, the focus must be on the child's welfare and not on the parents' or guardians' will. The extraordinary importance of Article 3 lies in the fact that for the first time it grants children the right to their best interests. Article 27 makes it obligatory for the state to recognize the right of every child to have a standard of living which may ensure requisite physical, mental, spiritual, moral and social development of each child. Article 28 of the convention imposes a liability on the state to recognize the right of the child to education and for that purpose it is expected on the part of each state to make primary education compulsory and it should be available to all children free of cost. The state is also expected to take measures to encourage regular attendance at school and the reduction of dropout rates. Under Article 32 obligation has been imposed on each member state to recognize the right of each child for being protected from economic exploitation and from doing work of hazardous nature which may prove to be harmful to the health of the child or retard the physical, mental, spiritual, moral or social development of the child. Article 35 requires state parties to take all appropriate measures to prevent the abduction, the sale of or traffic in children for any purpose or in any form. As of 1995, 181 countries had ratified the convention.

ILO and Child Labour

The ILO has concerned itself with the question of child labour since its foundation in 1919. The abolition of child labour has been one of its basic aims since its establishment. At the same time, it has pursued a systematic policy of protection of working children from undesirable conditions of work. The ILO's traditional approach to child labour has been to lay down international labour standards through ILO conventions and recommendations. There are thus two main categories of ILO instruments concerning child labour:

1. Instruments prohibiting child labour
2. Protection of child labour

Instruments Prohibiting Child Labour

The first instrument which set a minimum age for admission to employment was the Minimum Age (Industry) Convention (No. 5), adopted by the ILO General Conference at its first session in 1919. This convention fixed the minimum age for admission of children to industrial employment at 14 years.

At subsequent sessions the ILO adopted various other conventions and recommendations fixing minimum age standards for admission to employment in different sectors of economic activity:
Minimum Age (Sea) Convention, 1920 (No. 7);
Minimum Age (Agriculture) Convention, 1921 (No. 10);
Minimum Age (Trimmers and Stokers) Convention, 1921 (No. 15);
Minimum Age (Non-Industrial Employment) Convention, 1932 (No. 33);

Minimum Age (Non-Industrial Employment) Recommendation, 1932 (No. 41);
Minimum Age (Sea) Convention (Revised), 1936 (No. 58);
Minimum Age (Industry) Convention (Revised), 1937 (No. 59);
Minimum Age (Non-Industrial Employment) Convention (Revised), 1937 (No. 60);
Minimum Age (Coal Mines) Recommendation, 1953 (No. 96);
Minimum Age (Fishermen) Recommendation, 1953 (No. 112);
Minimum Age (Underground Work) Convention, 1965 (No. 123)

In 1973, the ILO decided that the time had come, as stated in the preamble to the convention, to establish a general institution on the subject, which would gradually replace the existing ones applicable to limited economic sectors, with a view to achieving the total abolition of child labour.

Convention No. 138 provides that "each member should pursue a national policy to ensure the effective abolition of child labour and to raise progressively the minimum age for admission to employment or work to a level consistent with fullest physical and mental development of young persons." This age should not be less than 15 years.

However, the above Convention provides the possibility of lowering these age limits in certain circumstances. Article 2 lays down that a country "whose economy and educational facilities are insufficiently developed may, after consultation with either the organisation of employers and workers concerned, where such exist, initially specify a minimum age of 14 years". Moreover, a member state whose economy and administrative facilities are insufficiently developed may initially limit the scope of application of the Convention and may extend the scope at a later date. However, the provisions of the Convention must be applicable as a minimum to the following: mining and quarrying; manufacturing; construction; electricity; gas and water; sanitary services; transport, storage and communications; and plantations and other agricultural undertakings mainly producing for commercial purposes, but excluding family and small-scale holdings producing for local consumption and not regularly employing hired workers.

Article 7 lays down that "states which have ratified the convention may permit the employment of children 13 to 15 years of age (12 to 14 for states which have adopted 14 years as a general minimum age), and of older children who have not completed their compulsory schooling, in 'light work' which is not likely to be harmful to their health or development " and not such as to prejudice their attendance at school or their participation in vocational orientation or training programmes."

As regards work which is likely to jeopardise the health, safety or morals of young persons, the convention lays down that the minimum age for admission to any type of employment or work of this kind shall not be less than 18 years. However, Article 3 provides that a country may authorise employment in dangerous work as from the age of 16 years on the condition that health, safety and morals of the young persons concerned are fully protected and that the young persons have received adequate instruction or vocational training in the relevant branch of activity.

In addition, the International Labour Conference adopted the Minimum Age Recommendation, 1973 (No. 146) to supplement the Minimum Age Convention, 1973. This recommendation invites states to give high priority to planning for and meeting the needs of children and youth in national development policies and programmes and to extend inter-related measures necessary to provide the best possible conditions of physical and mental growth for children and young persons. It recommends that members take as their objective the progressive raising to 16 years of the minimum age for employment or work specified in pursuance of the Minimum Age Convention. In countries where the minimum age for employment is still below 15 years, urgent steps should be taken to raise that level. In countries where the minimum age for admission to types of employment or work which are likely to jeopardise the health, safety or morals of young persons is still below 18 years, steps should be taken to raise it to that level.

With a view to facilitating the goals set forth in the convention, the recommendation advocates the adoption of measures designed to achieve full employment of adults; the progressive extension of other economic and social measures to alleviate poverty so as to make recourse to child labour unnecessary; the adoption and extension of adequate facilities for educational and vocational guidance and training; the adoption of special measures for children who do not have families or do not live with them, as well as for migrant children; and the introduction of compulsory full-time attendance at school or participation in vocational training courses at least upto the age specified for employment in Convention No. 138

As of 1993, 40 governments had ratified the Minimum Age Convention No. 138. Convention No. 138 and Recommendation No. 146 are reproduced in Annexures II and III of the book. In practice, most governments have set 14 or more as a basic minimum age (Table 3), with variations: for light work the minimums are generally about 12 and for hazardous work between 16 and 18.

TABLE 3

Basic minimum age for employment in various countries

12 Years	Bangladesh, Belize, Costa Rica, Equador, Egypt, Figi, Haiti, Jamaica, Morocco, Nigeria, Qatar, St Lucia, Sierra Leone, Singapore, Solomon Islands, Sudan, Syria, Thailand, Trinidad and Tobago, United Republic of Tanzania, Uganda, Yemen.
13 years	Cyprus, Jordan, Lebanon, Myanmar, Saudi Arabia, Swaziland, Tunisia, United Kingdom
14 years	Angola, Argentina, Bahamas, Bahrain, Belgium, Benin, Bolivia, Brazil, Burkina Faso, Cameroon, Cape Verde, Central African Republic, Chad, Columbia, Cote d'Ivoire, Djibouti, Dominican Republic, EI Salvador, Equatorial Guinea, Ethiopia, Gautemala, Guinea-Bissau, Guyana, Honduras, Indonesia, Italy, Kuwait, Liberia, Madagascar, Malaysia, Mali, Malawi, Mauritania, Mexico, Namibia, Nepal, Nicaragua, Niger, Pakistan, Panama, Papua New Guinea, Peru, Portugal, Rwanda, Sao Tome and Principe, Senegal, Suriname, Sri Lanka, Togo, Veneguela, Zamibia.
15 years	Afghanistan, Albania, Austria, Barbados, Botswana, Chile, Comoros, Cuba, Denmark, Dominica, Finland, Ghana, Greece, Hungary, Iceland, India, Islamic Republic of Iran, Iraq, Ireland, Israel, Japan, Lao Peoples Democratic Republic, Lasotho, Libyan Arab Jamahiria, Luxembourg, Malta, Mauritius, Mozambique, Netherlands, New Zealand, Norway, Paraguay, Philippines, Poland, Seychelles, Somalia, Switzerland, Turkey, United Arab Emirates, Uruguay, Yugoslavia.
16 years	Algeria, Antigua and Barbuda, Bulgaria, Burundi, China, Congo, Czechoslovakia, France, Gabon, Guinea, Kenya, Mongolia, Romania, Spain, Sweden, United States, Zaire.

SOURCE: International Labour Organisation, World Labour Report (Geneva: ILO, 1992), p. 18.
Note: This table is intended to give a general picture. In many countries the basic minimum varies according to the sector of production.

Protection of Child Labour

While maintaining the long-term aim of achieving the prohibition of child labour, the ILO has also pursued a policy of fixing standards with the objective of protecting child labour against exploitation. This has led, since 1919, to the adoption of a number of conventions and recommendations prohibiting the employment of children and/or young persons in certain types of work, and regulating their working conditions. There are several major categories of such instruments:[39]

I. Instruments prohibiting night work by children and young persons:

- Night Work of Young Persons Industry Convention, 1919 (No. 6);
- Night Work of Children and Young Persons (Agriculture) Recommendation, 1921 (No. 14);
- Night Work of Children and Young Persons (Non-Industrial Occupations) Convention, 1946 (No. 79);
- Night Work of Young Persons (Non-Industrial Occupations) Recommendation, 1946 (No. 80);
- Night Work of Young Persons (Industry) Convention (Revised), 1948 (No. 90);
- Wages, Hours of Work and Manning (Sea) Convention, 1958 (No. 109).
- *II. Instruments prohibiting the employment of children and young persons in certain categories of hazardous work:*
- Leading Poisoning (Women and Children) Recommendation, 1919 (No. 4);
- White Lead (Painting) Convention, 1921 (No. 13);
- Radiation Protection Convention, 1960 (No. 15);
- Conditions of Employment of Young Persons (Underground Work)

- Recommendation, 1965 (No. 125);
- Maximum Weight Convention, 1967 (No. 127);
- Benzene Convention, 1971 (No. 136).
- *III. Instruments making provisions for stricter standards for young workers with regard to hours of work, weekly rest, paid holidays and apprenticeship:*
- Utilization of Spare Time Recommendation, 1924 (No. 21);
- Holidays with Pay Recommendation, 1936 (No. 47);
- Apprenticeship Recommendation, 1939 (No. 60);
- Holidays with Pay (Agriculture) Recommendation, 1952 (No. 93);
- Holidays with Pay Recommendation, 1954 (No. 98);
- Weekly Rest (Commerce and Offices) Recommendation, 1957 (No. 103);
- Reduction of Hours of Work Recommendation, 1962 (No. 116)

Legislation alone is not enough to deal with the problem of child labour. There is a wide gap between the legal instruments and the actual state of affairs, as is borne out by ILO case studies. Child labour seems to be effectively abolished in the formal sector, characterised by large enterprises using highly mechanised or capital-intensive techniques. Even here, it is not clear whether this is due to a strict enforcement of child labour legislation or to the fact that child workers are of little use and uneconomical in a production system which uses advanced technology and less labour input. In any case, child labour continues to be widespread in the unorganised sector of industry, agriculture and services in much of the developing world, despite national legislation prohibiting it. There are many factors responsible for the poor enforcement of existing legislation. The availability and quality of education along with the poverty of the families of school age children act as a brake on the effectiveness of legislation. The inadequacy and low standards of education results in a very high school dropout rate and undermines the parents expectations concerning the benefits of schooling. Moreover, governments lack effective enforcement machinery to monitor regulations and standards governing child labour. Such machinery is seriously deficient in most developing countries. The inspectorate system is generally understaffed and thus unable to cope with child labour. In the Philippines, for example, there are less than 200 labour inspectors nationwide for almost 40,000 employers. Many countries have a bureau or a unit for child labour but generally these bureaux do not have an enforcement mechanism of their own.[40]

Hong Kong is striking example of what can be achieved through rigorous enforcement of legislation, effective campaigns and spread of education. In Hong Kong, inspections are regularly and persistently carried out by the Women and Young Persons Division of the Labour Department. In 1986, for example, 250, 167 inspections were carried out in 19, 274 establishments. Such a strict approach evidently works. In 1986 only 123 cases were discovered and most of these were technical offences rather than serious exploitation.[41] Other than rigorous inspections, each year special campaigns are launched for detecting child employment. Above all, the Hong Kong government has been able to check child labour because of spread of education. In 1971, the government introduced free primary education. This was followed in 1978 by a phased programme of secondary education and in 1980 schooling became compulsory for all children under 15. Finally, the introduction of social security contributions in respect of young workers has reduced employers' reliance on child labour.

Since child labour is closely linked with poverty, lack of development and inadequate schooling in the countries in which it is prevalant, child labour legislation must be accompanied by a wide range of measures concerning employment and income generation programmes, and by a reform and expansion of education facilities. Keeping these realities in mind, the ILO has not confined its activity to the establishment of standards and monitoring of the application of conventions. In recent years, the ILO has supplemented its standard-setting work with research, information dissemination and technical assistance.

ILO extends technical cooperation to member states to enable them to bring national laws and practice closer to the model set out in international labour standards. The ILO technical cooperation activities focusses attention on eliminating forced labour or bonded labour and child labour in industries and occupations which are detrimental to the safety, health or morals of children. It recognised that employment of children in certain dangerous types of occupations, such as work which involves exposure to toxic substances, use of pesticides or insecticides in agriculture and recycling of household waste in dumping sites, may not be prohibited by national legislation, but should be eliminated. ILO technical cooperation programmes also support NGOs which are active in this field.

The ILO recognises the fact that though it has been playing a leading role in the struggle against child labour, some of the action required to attack the underlying causes of child labour—poverty, insufficient economic growth and deficiencies in the education system —is within the competence of other international organisations like the International Monetary Fund (IMF), the World Bank, the General Agreement on Tariff and Trade (GATT) and the United Nations International Children Emergency Fund (UNICEF). Thus the ILO proclaims that diversity of mandates for action in the struggle against child labour should therefore be reflected in strengthened cooperation between the ILO and these other organisations and, most importantly, by close collaboration with the UNICEF.

Another way the ILO addresses the problem of child labour is through programmes and projects at the national and local community level. The ILO has committed itself to a major effort to halt child labour. In 1990, the German government offered to support the ILO in launching a major global offensive against child labour. The International Programme on the Elimination of Child Labour (IPEC) came into being with a view to giving a new impetus to the ILO's operational activities in this field.

A financial agreement was signed between the Government of Germany and the ILO in December 1991 to the amount of DM 50,000,000 for a period of 5 years. The programme is global in its scope and provides technical advisory services to all ILO member states on request. Six countries—Brazil, India, Indonesia, Kenya, Thailand and Turkey—sought ILO assistance and were selected as priority countries. In the next phase 6 additional countries chosen for the action plan are Bangladesh, Cameroon, Egypt, Pakistan, the Philippines and the United Republic of Tanzania. Besides Germany, other countries have also shown interest in supporting IPEC. In September 1992, Belgium became the second donor.

The operational structure of IPEC is based on ILO rules and procedures and on Memoranda of Understanding between the ILO and participating countries. The MOU finalises the agreement on the development and execution of national IPEC activities. It establishes the areas, principles and modalities of cooperation between the ILO and the government. IPEC seeks collaboration with other UN agencies, particularly the UNICEF, the United Nations Educational,

Scientific and Cultural Organisation (UNESCO), and the World Health Organisation and also with international NGOs to avoid duplication of effort and to maximise the impact of all available resources against the problem.

IPEC focusses on the worst abuses of child labour: hazardous work, forced labour, the employment of working children who are less than 12 or 13 years old, girls and street children.

Organisations directly involved in initiating and implementing the action programmes include governmental institutions, policy makers and political leaders, in particular the ministries of labour, education, health and welfare and information and statistics. Partner organisations include NGOs, including voluntary agencies, workers and employers' groups, religious organisations and the media.

The immediate objectives of the programme are as under:[42]

- to have enhanced the capability of ILO constituents and NGOs to design, implement and evaluate policies and programmes aimed at the elimination of child labour and the protection of working children;
- to have determined the comparitive strengths and weaknesses of various types of intervention at the local and national levels for replication and adoption; and
- to have established mechanisms at both the national and international level capable of generating and supporting public awareness and social mobilisation campaigns to combat child labour.

In order to promote action against bounded child labour, the ILO, within the ambit of IPEC, organised the Asian Regional Seminar on Children in Bondage in Islamabad in November 1992. It was held in collaboration with the United Nations Centre for Human Rights and the Government of Pakistan. Judges, lawyers, labour officials, representatives of employers' and workers' participated in the seminar. The seminar culminated in the formulation and adoption of 'A Programme of Action Against Child Bondage'.

UNICEF, UNESCO and Child Labour

Elimination of child labour is also a key component of UNICEF's policy. UNICEF is the only UN agency devoted exclusively to the needs of children. Founded in 1946, initially to care for the children of war-torn Europe, its mandate was gradually expanded. UNICEF supports government efforts in providing services essential to the survival and development of children, such as clean water, safe sanitation, immunisation and other health measures. It also seeks to provide to children skills essential for leading a healthy and productive life and thus education is a major priority of the UNICEF.

UNICEF collaborates with governments, international agencies, NGOs, trade unions and legal experts to promote the elimination of child labour and integration of children released from labour into the educational system. It has been a major funding agency for improving the lot of children in general and child labour in particular. UNICEF has sanctioned $0.5 million for child labour programmes for the five year period commencing from 1991.

The United Nations Educational, Scientific and Cultural Organisation (UNESCO) is another of the UN's specialised agencies. UNESCO has special responsibility for everything involving prevention of the various forms of discrimination and promotion of the educational and cultural rights.

UNESCO has also been making efforts to combat with the problem of child labour. Set up in 1946, UNESCO aims at promoting cooperation among nations through education, science and culture and thereby contribute to peace and security and enhance universal respect for justice, fundamental freedoms and human rights, including rights of the child. It has tried to attack the problem of child labour through the spread of education.

Thus the efforts of these international organisations are in the right direction and indeed commendable. However, the goal of complete abolition of child labour is still a distant one. In order to be effective, it is essential that international organisations arrive at programmes and campaigns suited to national conditions. Moreover, there is a need for greater coordination of efforts of international organisations in the struggle against child labour. International organisations also need to develop their campaigns within the framework of a partnership with concerned governments and NGOs if their efforts are to have a lasting impact on the status of the working children of the world.

References

1. International Labour Organisation, *World Labour Report* (Geneva: ILO, 1992) p. 14.
2. Elias Mendelievich, "Children at Work" (Geneva: ILO, 1979) p.3.
3. International Labour Organisation, *Child Labour: A Briefing Manual* (Geneva: ILO, 1986) p. 11.
4. Elias Mendelievich, "Children at Work"*op.cit.*p.4.
5. Abdelwahab Boudhiba, *Exploitation of Child Labour: Final Report of the Special Rapporteur of the United Nations Sub-Commission on Prevention of Discrimination and Protection of Minorities* (Geneva: UN, 1983) p. 11.
6. Abelwahab Bouhdiba, *op. cit.*, p. 25.
7. Abdelwahab Bouhdiba, *op. cit.*, p. 6.
8. Nerra Burra, "Issues Emerging from the Experience of some Developing Countries of Asia", *Child and Education,* Digest 28, (Paris : UNESCO-UNICEF, 1989) pp. 45-52.
9. Myron Weiner, *The Child and the State in India. Child Labour and Education Policy in Comparative Perspective* (Oxford: Oxford University Press, 1991) p. 174.
10. Neera Burra, *op. cit,* pp. 41-42
11. Elias Mendelievich, "Child Labour", *International Labour Review,* Vol. 118, No. 5, September October 1979, p. 560.
12. Abdelwahab Bouhdiba, *op. cit.*, p: 18.
13. David C. Pitt, "Child Labour and Health," in Usha. S. Naidu and Kamini Kapadia (eds.), *Child Labour and Health: Problems and Prospects* (Bombay: Tata Institute of Social Sciences, 1985) p. 12.
14. Elias Mendelievich, Children at Work, *op. cit.,* p. 36.
15. Elias Mendelievich, International Labour Review, *op. cit.*, p. 562.
16. *Ibid.*
18 Abdelwahab Bouhdiba, *op. cit.*, p. 16.
17. Elias Mendelievich, Children at Work, *op. cit.*, pp. 38-39.
20. Elias Mendelievich, Children at Work, *op. cit.*, p. 41.
21. David C. Pitt. *op.cit.* p.17.
22. Elias Mendelievich, Children at Work, *op. cit.*, p.41.
23. David C. Pitt. *op.cit.* pp.18-19.
19. Walter Fernandez, Neera Burra and T. S. Anand, "Child Labour in India", (New Delhi, 1986) pp. 2-3.
24. Myron Weiner, The Child and the State in India: Child Labour and Education Policy in Comparative Perspective, *op. cit.*, pp. 109-110.
25. "Child Labour in West too: ILO", *National Herald,* May 30, 1993.
26. International Labour Organisation, World Labour Report, *op. cit.*, p. 14.
27. Explosion of Child Exploitation in South Asia", *SAARC Link,* No. 2, 1993, p. 1.
28. Teddy Arellano, "Child Labour in South Asia", *Asian Labour Update.* Issue 14, January-March, 1994.
29. SAARC Link, *op. cit.*, p. 1.
30. Neera Burra, *op. cit.*, pp. 35-36.
31. "Child Labour in Africa," *International Labour Review* Vol. 132, No. 2, 1993, pp. 382-84.
32. Robert Ricci, "The Rights of the Child," in Abdulrahim. P. Vijaypur (ed.), *Essays on International Relations* (New Delhi: South Asian Publishers, 1991) pp. 192-93.

33. Abdelwahab Bouhdiba, *op. cit.*, p. 30
34. *Human Rights: A Compilation of International Instruments* (New York: UNO, 1983) p. 129.
35 *Ibid.*
36. *Ibid.*
37. *The United Nations and Human Rights* (New York: UNO, 1984) pp. 18-19.
38. UNICEF, *The Right to be a Child* (New Delhi: UNICEF, 1994) p. 1.
39. Abdelwahab Bouhdiba, *op. cit.*, p. 30.
40. Asseta Bequelc and Jo Boyden."Working Children: Current Trends and Policy Response",*International Labour Review* Vol. 127 No 2, 1988, p.163.
41. International Labour Organisation, *World Labour Report, op cit* . p. 164.
42. International Labour Organisation, *IPEC Programme Document* (Geneva: ILO, 1993) p.12.

III
Child Labour in India

Children in India constitute a formidable section of the work force. A large number of children spend their growing years toiling in order to survive. They lead a life of misery, deprivation and exploitation. India has the dubious distinction of possessing the largest child labour force in the world.

As has already been mentioned, there is no consensus on a valid definition of child labour in the national or international context. The term 'Child Labour' is variously defined, depending on the meaning attached to the term 'child' and 'labour'. The term 'child' is generally defined in terms of chronological age and the term 'labour' is defined in terms of nature and magnitude of production capacity.

The term 'child' has been differently defined in India. The Child Labour (Prohibition and Regulation) Act, 1986, states that "Child is a person who has not completed his fourteenth year of age". According to the Baroda-based organisation, Operations Research Group, "A working child is one who was enumerated during the survey as a child falling within the five to fifteen age bracket and who is at remunerative work, may be paid or unpaid, and busy in any hour of the day within or outside the family...."[1]

There are also varying definitions of the term 'work' or 'labour'. This has resulted in varying estimates on child labour in India. The term 'work' may be defined as either employment for wages or full-time work, whether or not for wages or even part-time work, with or without wages.

As per the 1971 census, there were 10.74 million working children in India. In the 1981 census, the number of working children was estimated at 13.6 million. This figure rose to 17.58 million

Table 1
Projections of Child Labour in India: 1971 to 2000 A.D.
(in Millions)

Year	Child Labour (5 to 14 years of age)
1971	10.74
1981	13.64
1983	17.36
1985	17.58
1990	18.17
2000	20.15

Source: Child Labour in India (New Delhi: Ministry of Labour, Government of India, 1994)

according to the estimates of the 43rd round of the National Sample Survey conducted in 1987-88. The census data of 1991 on child labour has not yet been released. The projection of child labour estimates indicate 18.17 million in 1990 and 20.15 million in the year 2000 (Table 1). However, the Operations Research Group estimates that 44 million children in the 5-15 age group are in the labour force. The Chamber of Commerce and Industry (CCI) estimates that child labour in the organised, unorganised and the household sector in India is over 100 million. These variations in data arise because of the problems related to defining child labour. The census figures are substantially lower than the figures cited by other organisations because the census categorises child by its participation in the wage labour force while most children work outside the wage sector. The estimates of the Operations Research Group are much higher because they include children who do not receive wages but work full-time.

Table 2 shows the extent of increase in the incidence of child labour in respect of changes in total population, child population and total labour force over the period 1961-81. Total population increased by 24.9 percent in 1971 and 51.6 percent in 1981 with 1961 as the base year. Child population increased by 27.9 percent in 1971 and 46.1 percent in 1981, with 1961 as the base year. Child labour decreased by 25.7 percent in 1971 and 22.8 percent in 1981 with 1961 as the base year. During the period 1961-81, child labour was 5.66 percent of the total child labour force. However, it should be noted that figures in Table 2 do not include children engaged in

Table 2
Index of Population, Labour Force, Child Population and Child Labour

(Base 1961=100)

Year	Population	Labour Force	Child Population	Child Labour
1961	100.00	100.00	100.00	100.00
1971	124.90	95.66	127.90	74.30
1981	151.60	117.94	146.10	77.20

Source: Census of India Reports of 1961, 1971 & 1981

marginal occupations such as shining shoes, cleaning vehicles, invisible domestic activities and illegal occupations.[2]

Table 3 reveals that there is a wide disparity in the prevalence of child labour amongst states. In Andhra Pradesh 8.5 percent of the children work for wages, in Meghalaya 6.9 percent children work, in Karnataka 6.58 percent of children work, in Madhya Pradesh 6.38 percent of children work, while in Kerala only 0.76 percent of children are working.

Table 5 shows that girls account for 33.57 percent of child labour in the country. In Manipur, Nagaland, Sikkim, Himachal Pradesh, Mizoram and Goa, girl workers outnumber boy workers. Table 6 shows that Andhra Pradesh has the largest number of girl child labour followed by Maharashtra, Madhya Pradesh, Karnataka and Tamil Nadu. Table 5 also shows that child labour is primarily concentrated in rural areas. Out of the total child work force in India, 91.14 percent were working in rural areas and 8.86 percent in urban areas in 1981.

The problem of child labour cannot be easily quantified. Its extent as an evil practice also needs to be understood by qualitative analysis, *viz.*, the stress and dangers working children are exposed to and the opportunities they are deprived of. In order to gain greater insights into the problem, attention has to be focussed on the basic causes of child labour.

Table 4 shows state-wise distribution of child labour in 1971 and 1981. Andhra Pradesh has the largest number of working children at 1.95 million in 1981, followed by Madhya Pradesh (1.7 million), Maharashtra (1.56 million), Uttar Pradesh (1.43 million), Karnataka (1.13 million), Bihar (1.1 million) and Gujarat (0.61 million). Over 90 percent of the child labour population in the country is to be found in 11 states .

Table 3

State wise Distribution of Child Workers

S. No.	State	% age of child workers to total: Population	Workers	Children
1.	Andhra Pradesh	3.28	7.75	8.50
2.	Bihar	1.28	4.31	3.07
3.	Gujarat	1.36	4.31	3.07
4.	Himachal Pradesh	1.41	4.11	3.56
5.	Haryana	1.10	3.89	2.64
6.	Jammu & Kashmir	1.82	6.00	4.44
7.	Karnataka	2.60	7.08	6.58
8.	Kerala	0.27	1.00	0.76
9.	Madhya Pradesh	0.63	6.85	6.38
10.	Maharashtra	2.01	5.20	5.25
11.	Manipur	1.25	3.11	3.19
12.	Meghalaya	2.93	6.75	6.91
13.	Nagaland	1.89	3.98	5.14
14.	Orissa	1.95	5.97	4.93
15.	Punjab	1.07	3.64	2.90
16.	Rajasthan	1.72	5.65	4.06
17.	Sikkim	2.50	5.37	6.32
18.	Tamil Nadu	1.80	4.58	5.14
19.	Tripura	0.96	3.45	2.45
20.	Uttar Pradesh	1.14	3.90	2.74
21.	West Bengal	0.96	3.39	2.47
22.	A&N Islands	0.45	1.35	1.13
23.	Arunachal Pradesh	2.37	4.78	6.02
24.	Chandigarh	0.43	1.24	1.29
25.	Dadra & Nagar Haveli	2.52	6.17	5.93
26.	Delhi	0.40	1.25	1.12
27.	Goa, Daman & Diu	0.63	2.05	1.78
28.	Lakshadweep	0.08	0.39	0.19
29.	Mizoram	0.92	2.20	2.32
30.	Pondicherry	0.53	1.83	1.44
	India	**1.68**	**5.03**	**4.26**

Source: Census of India, 1981.

Table 4
Statewise Distribution of Child Labour(0-14) Age Group

S. No.	State/UT	Workers in the (0-14 age group)	
		1971 census	1981 census
1.	Andhra Pradesh	1,627,492	1,951,312
2.	Assam	239,349*	*
3.	Bihar	1,059,359	1,101,764
4.	Gujarat	518,061	616,913
5.	Haryana	137,826	194,189
6.	Himachal Pradesh	71,384	99,624
7.	Jammu & Kashmir	70,489	258,437
8.	Karnataka	808,719	1,131,530
9.	Kerala	111,801	92,854
10.	Madhya Pradesh	1,112,319	1,698,597
11.	Maharashtra	988,357	1,557,756
12.	Manipur	16,380	20,217
13.	Meghalaya	30,440	44,916
14.	Nagaland	13,726	16,235
15.	Orissa	492,477	702,293
16.	Punjab	232,774	216,939
17.	Rajasthan	587,389	819,605
18.	Sikkim	15,661	8,561
19.	Tamil Nadu	713,305	975,055
20.	Tripura	17,490	24,204
21.	Uttar Pradesh	1,326,726	1,434,675
22.	West Bengal	511,443	605,263
23.	A&N Islands	572	1,309
24.	Arunachal Pradesh	17,925	17,950
25.	Chandigarh	1,086	1,986
26.	Dadra & Nagar Haveli	3,102	3,615
27.	Delhi	17,120	25,717
28.	Goa, Daman & Diu	7,391	9,378
29.	Lakshwadeep	97	56
30.	Mizoram	***	6,314
31.	Pondicherry	3,725	3,606
TOTAL		10,753,985	13,640,870

Source: Census of India, 1971 & 1981.

* Includes figures of Mizo district also which then formed a part of Assam **1981 Census could not be conducted in Assam due to disturbed conditions prevailing at that time. ***Census figures of 1971 in respect of Mizoram included under Assam

Table 5
Percentage Distribution of Child Workers by Sex Rural and Urban Areas

S. No.	State/UT	Male		Female		Total
		Rural	Urban	Rural	Urban	
1.	Andhra Pradesh	52.79	5.26	39.60	2.35	100.00
2.	Bihar	71.34	4.19	23.63	0.84	100.00
3.	Gujarat	61.20	8.34	28.81	1.65	100.00
4.	Himachal Pradesh	40.26	1.17	58.04	0.53	100.00
5.	Haryana	74.02	6.83	18.44	0.71	100.00
6.	Jammu & Kashmir	68.05	10.74	27.85	2.53	100.00
7.	Karnataka	54.87	8.36	33.11	3.66	100.00
8.	Kerala	42.77	8.60	40.80	7.83	100.00
9.	Madhya Pradesh	56.70	3.10	38.88	1.32	100.00
10.	Maharashtra	48.83	5.62	43.28	2.27	100.00
11.	Manipur	38.22	3.62	53.34	4.82	100.00
12.	Meghalaya	56.84	1.68	39.89	1.59	100.00
13.	Nagaland	41.68	2.51	54.20	1.61	100.00
14.	Orissa	71.49	3.76	23.37	1.38	100.00
15.	Punjab	83.36	12.18	3.68	0.78	100.00
16.	Rajasthan	62.13	5.52	31.13	1.22	100.00
17.	Sikkim	38.25	4.31	54.89	2.55	100.00
18.	Tamil Nadu	45.98	10.71	37.32	5.99	100.00
19.	Tripura	69.09	2.17	25.70	3.04	100.00
20.	Uttar Pradesh	75.67	8.82	14.72	0.79	100.00
21.	West Bengal	73.50	8.30	14.51	3.66	100.00
22.	A & N Islands	66.19	19.39	11.70	2.72	100.00
23.	Arunachal Pradesh	42.88	1.19	55.36	0.57	100.00
24.	Chandigarh	6.64	74.36	1.23	17.77	100.00
25.	Dadra & Nagar Haveli	50.93	2.38	44.27	2.42	100.00
26.	Delhi	5.87	80.12	2.63	11.38	100.00
27.	Goa, Daman & Diu	34.06	12.49	36.82	16.33	1000.00
28.	Lakshwadeep	25.81	25.81	35.48	12.90	100.00
29.	Mizoram	42.26	2.40	53.33	2.01	100.00
	TOTAL	**59.83**	**6.60**	**31.31**	**2.26**	**100.00**

Source: Census of India, 1981, Series-I, Part III A, General Economic Tables, Table B-3

Causes of Child Labour in India

There are several causes responsible for the growing incidence of child labour. These causes are all intrinsically related to one another. However, the main cause responsible for the prevalence and perpetuation of child labour is poverty. Nearly half of India's population lives below the poverty line. A child is forced into employment because of the need to supplement the meagre family income. Even the smallest contribution made by the child is welcome in the poor family in which he generally lives. In some families due to the death or disability of the bread-winner the child is forced to work.

A report prepared by the Anti-Slavery Society, which has consultative status with the UNESCO, cited poverty as the main force that drives children to work.[3] According to estimates, almost half the families with working children are below the poverty line.

A report compiled by the labour, social welfare and education ministries in collaboration with UNICEF reveals that almost 40 percent of households have one-third to half the family income supplemented through children's contribution and around 31 percent have 21-30 percent share. A pilot study conducted by the Madras School of Social Work in Madras, Madurai and Coimbatore found that 60 percent of child workers were found at work to supplement their family income, 23 percent were forced to take up employment on account of the death of their father and 17 percent of them began working on the insistence of their parents. Another study conducted in the unorganised sector by the Centre for Social Research in 1984 found that most child workers were under compulsion to work due to poverty.[4]

Migration from rural areas to urban areas also encourages child employment. With growing commercialisation and mechanisation of agriculture a large number of farm workers become redundant and are forced to migrate to cities. The search for work is the main reason for migration. Placed in an unfamiliar environment and severe deprivation, children of migrant families are forced to join the work force. A study conducted by the National Labour Institute with the assistance of UNICEF on the working children of Delhi shows that migrants comprise more than two-thirds of working children.

Table 6
Statewise Distribution of Child Labour in India, 1981

(in millions)

S.No	States/UT	Rural			Urban			Grand Total
		Male	Female	Total	Male	Female	Total	
1	2	3	4	5	5	7	8	9
1.	Andhra Pradesh	0.9700	0.8300	1.8000	0.0920	0.0450	0.1500	1.9500
2,	Assam	—	—	—	—	—	—	
3.	Bihar	0.6900	0.3400	1.0300	0.0360	0.0085	0.0440	1.0700
4.	Gujarat	0.3100	0.2500	0.5600	0.0400	0.0095	0.0500	0.6100
5.	Jammu & Kashmir	0.1200	0.1300	0.2500	0.0120	0.0051	0.0170	0.2700
6.	Kerala	0.0400	0.0380	0.0780	0.0069	0.0062	0.0131	0.0920
7.	Madhya Pradesh	0.8700	0. 7600	0.1600	0.0450	0.0220	0.0670	0.1700
8.	Tamil Nadu	0.4300	0.4000	0.8300	0.0950	0.0560	0.1510	0.9800
9.	Maharashtra	0.6900	0.7600	1.4500	0.0750	0.0340	0.1100	1.5600
10.	Karnataka	0.5600	0.4500	0.0100	0.0840	0.0390	0.1240	1.1300
11.	Orissa	0.4200	0.2600	0.6800	0.0200	0.0090	0.0290	0.7100
12.	Punjab	—	—	—	—	—	—	—
13.	Rajasthan	0.4200	0.3500	0.7700	0.0310	0.0100	0.0410	0.8100
14.	Uttar Pradesh	1.0000	0.3000	1.3000	0.1100	0.0100	0.1250	0.1420
15.	West Bengal	0.4100	0.1100	0.5200	0.0470	0.2700	0.0740	0.5900
16.	Himachal Pradesh	0.0390	0.0580	0.0970	0.0008	0.000440	0.0012	0.0980
17.	A&N Islands	—	—	0.0011	—	—	—	—
18.	Delhi	—	—	—	—	—		
19.	Lakswadeep	—	—	0.000025	—	—	0.000021	0.000040
20.	Manipur	—	—	0.0180	—	—	0.0020	0.0200

1	2	3	4	5	6	7	8	9
21.	Tripura	—	—	0.240	—	—	0.0010	0.0250
22.	D&N Haveli	—	—	—	—	—	—	—
23.	Goa, Daman & Diu	—	—	0.0071	—	—	0.0022	0.0093
24.	Pondicherry	0.0011	0.000880	0.001980	0.0016	0.000360	0.0020	0.003980
25.	Chandigarh	—	—	—	—	—	—	—
26.	Nagaland	—	—	0.0150	—	—	0.006	0.0156
27.	Sikkim	—	—	0.0079	—	—	0.000540	0.008440
28.	Haryana	—	—	—	—	—	—	—
29.	Arunachal Pradesh	—	—	0.0180	—	—	0.0003	0.0183
	All India	**7.3400**	**5.2100**	**12.5500**	**0.7600**	**0.2900**	**1.05000**	**13.5900**

Source: Compiled from Census of India, 1981

Children also seek employment because the adult wage earners of their families are unemployed or underemployed. Poverty and unemployment may be the twin ills that perpetuate child labour but employment of children in turn accentuates poverty and unemployment. While children in India work in large numbers, adults are faced with the problem of unemployment or underemployment. The existence of child labour forces many adults out of work. It also considerably lowers down the rate of wages in the society. Child labour is as much a cause as consequence of adult unemployment and underemployment. It both supplements and decreases family income.

A study carried out on child labour in the lock industry of Aligarh by the Aligarh Muslim University substantiates the above argument. While child labour is widely used in this industry, many adults are unemployed or under-employed. The average number of days when employment is possible in this industry works out to be 264 days. Workers consider themselves to be fully engaged when they could find work for 180 days a year. A lock worker feels lucky if he gets work for 4 days in a week. Thus, even those adults who are termed permanently employed are unemployed for more than 3 months and others are unemployed for periods ranging between 6 to 9 months.

"The entrance of children into the labour market reduces the volume of employment for the adults and lowers the bargaining power of adults workers. Some experts argue that if all the children were eliminated from the labour force in India, employment opportunities for at least 15 million adult unemployed workers would be increased."[5]

The paradox of a high incidence of child labour and adult unemployment in India lies in the fact that children can be paid less. They are a source of cheap labour and can be easily exploited. Employers find it more advantageous to employ children because children cost less, they can be easily laid off when business is slack and they can be easily disciplined. Child workers constitute a mute, docile and uncomplaining work force. Thus employers have a vested interest in maintaining child labour.

Inadequate educational facilities and lack of compulsory education for all children below the age of 14 years is also an important cause for the high incidence of child labour in India. Child labour is closely related to the school drop-out rates. Wherever drop-out rates are high at the primary and middle levels, incidence of child labour is also high. This is manifested in the 10 states with a high child labour population. In India, at the primary school level there is a 47 percent drop which increases to 64 percent at the middle school level. The net result is that half of India's children between 6 and 14 are not in schools. It can be assumed that a sizeable number of these dropout children find employment of some kind. Cumulative dropouts are the highest in Bihar (80.53 percent) and Andhra Pradesh (74.81 percent), which also have a high incidence of child labour. The lowest dropout occurs in Kerala (15.92 percent), which has the lowest incidence of child labour (Table 7).

Since independence the Government of India has advocated ending child labour and establishing compulsory and universal primary education for all children up to the age of 14. However, the goal of universal primary education is far from becoming a reality. In 1981, only 41.4 percent of India's population above the age of five are literate (53.05% males and 28.5% females), with the highest literacy rate among urban males (74%) and the lowest among rural females (20.7%). In 1981, 56.6 percent of the 10-14-age group, 55.4 percent of the 20-24 age-group and 45.1 percent of the 25-34 age-group were literate.

Professor Myron Weiner in his book 'The Child and the State in India' puts forth the view that child labour is not simply a feature of low income developing countries that cannot be eliminated until national incomes grow, but is in fact sustained by government policies on primary education. He says that since education is not compulsory in India, children readily drop out of school to enter the labour force. Weiner says that it is incorrect to assume that primary education cannot be universalised because of low national income. "Among contemporary developing countries there is no clear relationship between literacy and per capita income. India has an adult (over 15)literacy rate of 40.8 percent, while in China it is 72.6 percent; Burma, 78.5 percent; Indonesia, 74.1 percent; Tanzania, 85 percent; Sri Lanka, 86.1 percent; and the Philippines, 88.7 percent. And while literacy for India as a whole is low, the state of Kerala, with a per capita income no different than that of the rest of the country, has a literacy rate of 85 percent".

"A number of Asian countries experienced spectacular primary-school attendance rates prior to their rapid economic growth. In the short space of 1873 and 1903, the Japanese government increased elementary-school attendance from 28 percent to 94 percent. By 1913, 98 percent of the age group was attending school. South Korea,

Table 7

Percentage Distribution of Children attending School and Drop Out Rates in Primary and Middle School 1985-86

State	Children at tending School Aged 5-9 years						Dropout Rates					
							Primary School			Middle School		
	Male			Female			Male			Female		
	R	U	C	R	U	C	R	U	C	R	U	C
AndhraPradesh	42.33	65.06	47.30	44.59	73.87	51.37	53.47	57.50	55.18	70.89	80.08	74.81
Bihar	30.08	38.69	31.47	14.79	46.97	18.46	63.33	67.06	64.50	78.14	85.90	80.53
Gujarat	42.27	60.25	49.58	33.03	55.49	39.44	40.74	43.05	41.73	65.34	72.96	68.50
Haryana	42.25	64.36	46.50	2.94	59.11	30.08	26.13	31.78	28.28	36.24	52.50	41.93
Karnataka	43.49	61.58	48.41	30.67	56.98	37.74	50.11	65.67	57.66	67.85	78.29	72.69
Kerala	74.36	79.74	35.32	72.22	79.63	75.17	3.18	4.57	3.86	16.17	15.66	15.92
MadhyaPradesh	33.14	59.20	37.89	15.43	51.47	21.99	36.13	45.60	39.55	48.97	67.46	55.29
Maharashtra	52.01	69.09	57.47	38.98	64.78	47.08	39.63	50.47	44.61	59.09	73.35	65.59
Orissa	47.24	61.90	48.89	31.58	53.80	34.01	48.60	51.42	49.77	60.06	69.65	63.94
Punjab	51.26	66.00	55.20	45.38	60.23	48.68	49.78	51.47	50.56	62.26	69.27	65.52
Rajasthan	32.35	55.12	36.76	9.55	42.50	16.03	47.42	53.64	49.02	59.86	71.20	62.66
Tamil Nadu	59.69	72.21	63.75	47.95	68.35	54.58	20.13	25.20	22.48	47.63	58.72	52.73
Uttar Pradesh	30.03	46.77	32.74	13.65	39.35	18.00	42.63	45.89	43.68	50.63	66.70	55.91
West Bengal	35.52	59.28	41.65	27.2	53.75	32.70	58.57	62.61	60.25	70.63	74.46	72.27
ALL INDIA	39.76	61.81	44.47	25.94	55.83	32.32	45.84	50.27	47.61	60.70	70.04	64.42

Source: Child Labour in India, Reference note prepared by the Ministry of Labour, Govt. of India, 1993.

with only a third of its children in primary schools in 1941, universalised primary education by the early 1970s. Its literacy rate increased from 55 percent in 1944 to 90 percent. In China, primary-school education expanded rapidly after 1949. In 1979, China enrolled close to 147 million children in 920,000 formal schools, an enrolment ratio of 93 percent, compared with 25 percent in 1949. The literacy rate among the population aged 15 and above is 72.6 percent, an increase of 52 percentage points since 1949".[6]

Weiner says that resource constraints also do not explain the differences in educational performance between India and other countries. India spends 3.6 percent of its gross national product on education—less than Kenya (6.7%), Tanzania (4.3%), or Malaysia (7.8%), but more than Burma (1.6%), China (2.7%), Sri Lanka (3.5%), and Indonesia (2.0%). Compared to these countries, a larger proportion of India's budget is spent on higher education.

According to Weiner, India has made less of an effort to remove children out of the labour force into the school system not for economic or demographic reasons but because of attitudes of politicians, government officials, intellectuals, voluntary agencies and the influential middle class towards child labour and compulsory primary-school education. The desires of low-income parents to send their children to work or to employ them at home and of employers to seek low-wage, pliable, non-unionised labour is of secondary importance because elsewhere in the world a large number of parents and employers have also supported child labour and opposed compulsory education. According to Weiner, the root cause of the problem lies in the Indian view of the social order, notions concerning the respective roles of upper and lower social strata, concerns that 'excessive' and 'inappropriate' education for the poor could disrupt existing social arrangements. "Indians reject compulsory education, arguing that primary schools do not properly train the children of the poor to work, that the children of the poor should work rather than prepare them for white collar occupations".[7]

A point of view frequently propounded by professionals in the field of education and policy makers is that the existing school system is irrelevant to the needs of working children. However, it is incorrect to argue that parents of working children do not send them to school primarily because of the supposed irrelevance of the curricula. Evidence suggests that parents have a deep interest in educating their children for education alone can provide mobility to the socially and economically disadvantaged sections of society. Commonly, difficult economic circumstances prevent the fulfilment of this aspiration; inadequate school infrastructure tilts the balance in favour of work.[8]

However, the above argument does not detract from the shortcomings of the Indian school system, which is not meaningful, realistic or flexible. Moreover, about 90 percent of India's working children live in rural areas and are usually involved with some kind of agricultural or allied activity. During the seasonal operations, such children are unable to attend school even if they wished to and were able to. Noted educationist, the late J.P. Naik, called for a radical transformation of the traditional model of formal education. He made a number of constructive suggestions to orient the school system to the needs of the rural working children. For one, the school calendar should be adjusted as to allow time off for agricultural operations like sowing and harvesting. Another important recommendation he made is to have pre-schools or creches attached to primary schools so that girls could bring their younger siblings there and have them looked after as well as get an education.[9]

Finally, Weiner propounds that "compulsory primary education is the policy instrument by which the state effectively removes children from the labour force. The state thus stands as the ultimate guardian of children, protecting them against both parents and would be employers".[10]

Thus several factors are responsible for the existence and perpetuation of child labour in India. While poverty is the root cause of child labour, we cannot wait for economic benefits to trickle down and ease poverty. The prevalence of child labour and lack of compulsory education cannot be justified on the grounds of poverty. The state needs to take positive action and intervene to end this aberration and bring justice to its working children.

Statistical Analysis of the Causes of Child Labour in India

A statistical analysis of historical data has been carried out to identify the actual correlation between the incidence of child labour and the various causal factors of child labour identified by our analysis above. The correlation is indicated by value of the regression correlation coefficient(r^2)arrived at by statistical regression of data pertaining to the causal factor and child labour at a point in time. The results of the analysis can be summarised as follows:
(for details of regression data, please refer to Annexure I-IX)

a) Poverty as a cause of child labour

Table 8 shows the state-wise distribution of child labour, poor and unemployed persons in rural and urban areas in 1981, and forms the basis of our analysis to see the correlation between the incidence of child labour and poverty.

While child labour shows a moderate correlation with poverty in rural India (r^2 = 0.4874), the correlation with poverty is much stronger in urban India (r^2 = 0.7726). On an overall basis, the correlation coefficient of 0.5673 lends substance to our hypothesis that poverty is one of the main causes of child labour.

b) Unemployment as a cause of child labour

Table 8 also neıps us to study unemployment as a causal factor for child labour. It is seen that though the correlation coefficient is quite low at the rural level (0.1270), it is strong at the urban level (0.66520). The low correlation at the rural level also distorts the overall picture (r^2 = 0.1704). This apparently low correlation is to be viewed keeping in mind that in rural India, underemployment also plays a significant role, especially in an economy dependent on the seasonal nature of the demand for labour resources from the agrarian sector.

c) Illiteracy and Child labour

Table 9 gives data on literacy in rural and urban India. Illiteracy data has been derived from this information, and has been used with the data on incidence of child labour in Table 8 to study the correlation between child labour and illiteracy at the rural, urban and all-India levels. Illiteracy in both rural India (r2= 0.67) and urban India (r2 = 0.78) is found to be strongly correlated with the incidence of child labour. This correlation is also reinforced by the high correlation coefficient (0.70) at the all-India level, strongly supporting our hypothesis that illiteracy is one of the important causes of child labour. Thus the results of the statistical analysis on causes of child labour points to a strong correlation between child labour and poverty and illiteracy.

Table 8

No. of Child Labour, Poor and Unemployed Persons on Daily Status Basis by States in India, 1981

State/UT	Rural			Urban			Total		
	Child Labour	Poor Persons	Un-Emp. Persons	Child Labour	Poor Persons	Un-Emp. Persons	Child Labour	Poor Persons	Un-Emp. Persons
1	2	3	4	5	6	7	8	9	10
Andhra Pradesh	1.8000	18.0200	1.8300	0.1400	4.4600	0.3800	1.9400	22.4800	2.2100
Assam	-	9.4000	0.1000	-	0.7700	0.0400	0.0000	10.1700	0.1400
Bihar	1.0300	36.0000	1.5400	0.0440	4.0200	0.1900	1.0740	40.0200	1.7300
Gujarat	0.5600	10.1500	0.4600	0.0500	3.0800	0.3300	0.6100	13.2300	0.7900
Haryana	-	2.3400	0.1500	-	0.9000	0.6500	0.0000	3.2400	0.8000
Himachal Pradesh	0.0970	1.1100	0.0240	0.0012	0.0500	0.0060	0.0982	1.1600	0.0300
J&K	0.2500	1.5400	0.1800	0.0170	0.5000	0.0260	0.2670	2.0400	0.2060
Karnataka	1.0100	13.1700	0.8900	0.1240	4.7200	0.5200	1.1340	17.8900	1.4100
Kerala	0.0780	9.5100	1.6600	0.0130	2.4500	0.3200	0.0910	11.9600	1.9800
Madhya Pradesh.	1.6300	24.8800	0.3900	0.0670	5.0900	0.2100	1.6970	29.9700	0.6000
Maharashtra	1.4500	22.7800	1.1500	0.1100	6.9500	0.5600	1.5600	29.7300	1.7100
Manipur	0.0018	0.3200	0.0010	0.0020	0.960	0.0006	0.0038	0.4160	0.0016
Meghalaya	-	0.5900	-	-	0.0400	-	0.0000	0.6300	0.0000
Nagaland	0.0150	-	-	0.0006	0.0040	-	0.0156	0.0040	0.0000
Orissa	0.6800	16.0400	0.7900	0.0290	1.3100	0.1300	0.7090	17.3500	0.9200
Punjab	-	1.4400	0.1900	0.0000	1.1500	0.1100	0.0000	2.5900	0.3000
Rajasthan	0.7700	9.1300	0.4700	0.0410	2.4400	0.1400	0.8110	11.5700	0.6100

1	2	3	4	5	6	7	8	9	10
Sikkim	0.0079	-	-	0.0005	-	-	0.0084	0.0000	0.0000
Tamil Nadu	0.8300	18.0700	2.8500	0.1500	7.1700	1.0200	0.9800	25.2400	3.8700
Tripura	0.0240	1.1800	0.0250	0.0010	0.0600	0.0070	0.0250	1.2400	0.0320
Uttar Pradesh.	1.300	45.6900	1.0700	0.1250	9.800	0.4000	1.4250	55.4900	1.4700
West Bengal	0.5200	23.6500	2.1600	0.0740	5.0200	0.67800	0.5940	28.6700	2.8400
A&N Island	0.0011	-	-	0.0003	-	-	0.0014	0.0000	0.0000
Arunachal Pradesh.	0.0180	-	-	0.0003	-	-	0.0183	0.0000	0.0000
Chandigarh	-	-	-	-	-	-	0.0000	0.0000	0.0000
D&N Haveli	-	-	-	-	-	-	0.0000	0.0000	0.0000
Delhi	-	-	0.0150	-	-	0.0280	0.0000	0.0000	0.0430
Goa, Daman	0.0071	-	-	0.0022	-	-	0.0093	0.0000	0.0000
Lakshwadeep	0.0003	-	-	0.0000	-	-	0.0003	0.0000	0.0000
Mizoram	-	-	-	-	-	-	0.0000	0.0000	0.0000
Pondicherry	0.0020	-	-	0.0022	-	-	0.0042	0.0000	0.0000
ALL INDIA	**12.5500**	**267.0400**	**9.2100**	**1.0500**	**61.0000**	**5.2200**	**13.6000**	**328.0400**	**14.4300**

Source: Planning Commission, Sarvek Shana, April, 1986

Table 9
Rural Urban Literacy 1981

State	Given Data				Derived Data		
	Literates Rural	Literacy Rate Rural	Literates Urban	Literacy Rate Urban	Illiterates Rural	Illiterates Urban	Illiterates Total
1	2	3	4	5	6	7	8
ANDHRA PRADESH	9.54	27.90%	6.49	61.00%	24.66	4.15	28.81
ARUNACHAL P.	0.11	·22.80%	0.02	63.80%	0.37	0.01	0.38
ASSAM							
BIHAR	13.77	27.50%	0.46	61.80%	36.31	0.28	36.59
GOA	0.37	61.60%	0.21	74.30%	0.23	0.07	0.30
GUJARAT	8.50	43.60%	6.39	71.00%	11.00	2.61	13.61
HARYANA	3.06	37.30%	1.61	66.80%	5.15	0.80	5..95
HIMACHAL PRADESH.	1.60	48.90%	0.22	77.80%	1.67	0.06	1.73
J & K	1.02		0.57				
KARNATAKA	8.20	37.60%	6.09	66.90%	13.61	3.01	16.62
KERALA	14.29	80.30%	3.63	86.90%	3.51	0.5	4.05
MADHYA P.	8.83	26.30%	5.72	64.60%	24.73	3.13	27.87
MAHARASHTRA	15.56	45.70%	14.06	74.30%	18.49	4.86	23.35
MANIPUR	0.39	45.00%	0.20	62.60%	0.48	0.12	0.60
MEGHALAYA	0.30	34.40%	0.16	75.10%	0.57	0.05	0.62
MIZORAM	0.21	69.20%	0.09	89.50%	0.09	0.01	0.10
NAGALAND	0.25	45.60%	0.08	76.10	0.30	0.02	0.33
ORISSA	7.32	37.80%	1.70	64.80%	12.05	0.93	12.98

1	2	3	4	5	6	7	8
PUNJAB	4.28	41.70%	2.59	65.00%	5.98	1.39	7.37
RAJASTHAN	4.87	22.50%	3.49	58.10%	16.77	2.51	19.28
SIKKIM	0.08	36.90%	0.03	64.90%	0.14	0.02	0.15
TAMIL NADU	12.52	45.00%	10.12	73.30%	15.30	3.69	18.98
TRIPURA	0.70	45.80%	0.17	83.40%	0.83		
SIKKIM	0.08	36.90%	0.03	64.90%	0.14	0.02	0.15
TAMILNADU	12.52	45.00%	10.12	73.30%	15.30%	3.69	18.98
TRIPURA	0.70	45.80%	0.17	83.40%	0.83	0.03	0.86
UTTAR P.	20.98	28.50%	9.13	54.90%	52.62	7.50	60.12
WEST BENGAL	13.29	40.20%	9.05	70.70%	19.77	3.75	23.52
UT'S							
ANDMAN	0.07	58.10%	0.03	76.70%	0.05	0.01	0.06
CHANDIGARH	0.01	53.30%	0.28	76.20%	0.01	0.09	0.10
DADRA & NAGAR HAVELI	0.02	30.30%	0.00	65.70%	0.06	0.00	0.06
DAMAN & DIU	0.02	50.40%	0.02	75.30%	0.02	0.01	0.03
DELHI	0.22	57.80%	3.61	73.00%	0.16	1.34	1.49
LAKSHWADEEP	0.01	65.50%	0.01	71.80%	0.01	0.00	0.01
PONDICHERRY	0.14	56.20%	0.20	73.30%	0.11	0.07	0.18

Source: Basic Statistics: States, September 1994, CMIE

Types of Child Labour

Children in India are engaged in a wide variety of activities: paid and unpaid, formal and informal. Children's activities vary from urban to rural areas and also between boys and girls.

a) Unpaid domestic work
b) Unpaid non-domestic work
c) Wage labourers
d) Self-employed
e) Bonded labour

Unpaid Domestic Work

Children in both rural and urban areas are engaged in unpaid domestic work which frees the adults for other tasks. Cooking, washing, caring for younger siblings are some of the tasks performed by children within the home. These activities are also termed 'invisible work'. It is generally girls who are engaged in domestic work. Though these activities may appear to be harmless, they are generally full-time activities which deny the children who perform them of their right to education.

Unpaid Non-Domestic Work

Young children in rural areas, generally boys, help in cultivation, protecting crops from birds, collecting fodder, etc. Gradually they are involved with full-time agricultural work. Children also help their parents in cottage industries like weaving, pottery and metalware. They may be working within the family, that is, on family farms or family enterprises or they may be working outside the family on plantations or handicrafts sector as part of family labour. When children work as part of family labour they are not paid separately. Such children are also denied the opportunity of education.

Children also very often work as apprentices to artisans. Apprenticeship is very often merely a way of avoiding action under minimum age legislation. The system of apprenticeship is rampantly misused to extract maximum work out of children without paying them.

Wage Labour

Children work as wage labourers both in rural and urban organised and unorganised sector. They work in restaurants and road-side eateries as cooks, waiters and cleaners, in garages as mechanics and helpers, in households as full-time and part-time domestic servants, on plantations, in mines, in industries like match, glass, carpet weaving, slate, diamond cutting, gem polishing, lock making etc. as skilled and unskilled workers.

Employers prefer to hire children because they can be paid lesser wages. Children are generally paid on a piece-rate basis. This puts a lot of pressure on the child to work much faster than their strength permits.

Self-Employed Children

Some children are also self-employed as newspaper vendors, shoeshine boys, hawkers, unregistered porters at markets and railway stations and car cleaners. These children are generally harassed by the police and by older workers. A study conducted on the street children of Bombay shows that the largest number of working children are self employed as rag pickers, metal and scrap collectors or vendors selling edible and non-edible items.[11]

Note: In the 1971 census no distinction is made between 'main' work and 'marginal' work. In the 1981 census 'main' workers have been defined as those who have worked for more than 6 months. The 1981 census figures given above relate to 'main' workers only.

Bonded Labour

Children are bonded in both rural and urban areas. Bonded labour is a manifestation of indebtedness of the poor. It estimated that there are 5.5 million bonded child labourers in India. Parents very often pledge children in exchange of a loan. The child repays the loan by working. However, the child is often bonded for life because of exorbitant interest rates and outright fraud.

A study conducted by the Rural Wing of the National Labour Institute found that bonded children are the only easily available commodity all over Medak district in Andhra Pradesh. It was found that in all the villages in Siddipet, Medak and Gogipet talukas that were surveyed, children were bonded to moneylenders and landlords. In some villages, landlords depended entirely on the labour of bonded children.

Gangrade and Gathia's study of carpet weavers in Varanasi reveals that "to keep production cost low, the middlemen often suggest to the families to engage children under 12 years of age. They even pay advances of Rs. 400 to Rs. 500 for some family function and thus tie the child to work for them indirectly.[12]

Thus children are openly traded as commodities. Bidi workers in Vellore openly say that when everything else has gone, the only commodity that they can trade is their children and mortgaging children to the bidi entrepreneurs is a common phenomenon. They work for long hours without wages. Whenever wages are paid, a part is deducted against the loan.

Thousands of children in North Arcot are pledged to the agents of bidi entrepreneurs for sums ranging from Rs. 500 to Rs. 5000. Till the loans are repaid, the children are in bondage to the agent. Many of them are beaten black and blue for minor offences. It is estimated that there are more than 8000 pledged children working in North Arcot alone.

Child Labour in India is concentrated largely in agriculture, followed by services and industry. Table 10 shows that agriculture and allied activities such as livestock, forestry, fisheries, plantations etc. account for over 85 percent of the total child labour force as per the 1971 and 1981 census data. Manufacturing/Servicing sector has shown an increase from 6.08 percent to 8.64 percent between 1971 and 1981. Mining and quarrying, trade and commerce, construction, transport, storage and communication have shown a slight increase from 3.13 percent to 3.56 percent during the same period.

Consequences of Child Labour

Child labour has far reaching repercussions on the physical, mental and emotional well-being of children. It prevents the full realisation of a child's personality. Being the most vulnerable section of the population, they are exposed to all sorts of exploitation.

Long hours of work and difficult working conditions have a negative effect on the physical and mental development of children. In 1980 the Operation Research Group undertook an all-India sample survey of working children in about 40,000 households all over the

Table 10

Children Working in Different Areas of Employment in India 1971 and 1981 Census

S.No.	Nature of Activity	Child Workers in the Age Group (0-14) Years			
		1971 Census		1981 Census	
		N0. (Thousands)	Percentage	NO. Thousand	Percentage
1.	Cultivators	3,870	36.05%	4,013	35.93%
2.	Agricultural Labourers	4,586	42.72%	4,774	42.75%
3.	Livestock, Forestry, Fishing Hunting, Plantations, etc.	885	8.24%	704	6.30%
4.	Mining and Quarrying	24	0.22%	27	0.24%
5.	Manufacturing, Processing Serving, Repairs etc.				
	a Housing Industry	338	3.15%	425	3.81%
	b Others	315	2.93%	540	4.84%
6.	Construction	59	0.55%	79	0.71%
7.	Transport, Storage and Communication	42	0.39%	34	0.30%
8.	Trade and Commerce	211	1.97%	346	3.10%
9.	Other Services	405	3.77%	326	2.92%
	TOTAL	**10,735**	**100.00%**	**11,168**	**100.00%**

Source: Census of India, 1971 and 1981

Note: In the 1971 census no distinction is made between 'main' work and 'marginal' work. In the 1981 census 'main' workers have been defined as those who have worked for more than 6 months. The 1981 census figures given above relate to 'main' workers only.

country. Nearly 70 percent of the children working in rural areas and 65 percent in urban areas work for more than 7 hours a day. Working children, coming from poor families, are already malnourished. When they are forced to work long hours, the problem of malnutrition is worsened, leading to deterioration of the health of the child worker, which ultimately shortens his life span.

Children in rural areas working on mechanised farms are exposed to modern machines which they cannot cope with. Accidents are, therefore, common occurrences. Children working on farms using pesticides and chemical fertilisers may also be adversely affected. However, there is not much documentation on the health hazards of working in the agrarian sector on children.

More research has been undertaken on the health hazards faced by working children in urban areas. Neera Burra has classified health hazards faced by working children into three: (1) Intrinsically hazardous occupations (2) Hazards to health from the environment (3) Hazards arising from being vulnerable.[13]

Intrinsically hazardous occupations are those jobs which by their very nature can harm the health and well-being of the child and may even cause death. One may mention among them work in mines, in chemical factories, on construction sites, making fireworks, matches, glass, balloons, locks. In such jobs the worker comes into contact with harmful substances like chemicals or fire and where the likelihood of accidents is relatively high. These occupations would be hazardous for all workers, both adults and children. But since children are still in the process of growing and attaining their full physical stature, their growth is likely to be affected. Other occupations like rag-picking involve working in rubbish dumps where the danger of contracting tetanus would be great.

Employers prefer to use children in trenches and mines, which are too narrow for adults. These jobs may have the specific risk of silicosis and infections transmitted from rats and mice. According to an ILO report, about 28,000 children are employed in private mines in Meghalaya. Children work in trenches 90 cm wide and 1 m high, where adults could only crawl. As soon as their size is no longer profitable, they are retrenched.

In the lock industry of Aligarh children work on handpresses, on buffing and polishing machines and in electroplating and spray painting units. The work of polishing is perhaps the most hazardous. The face of the worker is within 10 inches of rotating machines and he directly inhales emery powder and metal dust. If a piece slips from the hand of a worker, it can severely injure another worker. More than 60 percent of the workers in polishing units are less than 14 years of age. Children as young as 8 and 9 can be seen working late in the night. Electroplating is another extremely hazardous process in which more than 70 percent of workers are children. Electroplating work is hazardous because the chemicals used are extremely dangerous such as potassium cyanide. trisodium phosphate, sodium silicate, hydrochloric acid, sulphuric acid, sodium hydroxide, etc. Children use these solutions with bare hands for the better part of a 12-hour day if not longer. Moreover, an electric current passes through these chemical tanks and children often get shocks. The floors of these units are wet and accidents take place often. In the spray painting units children inhale substantial quantities of paint and paint thinners, with grave consequences for their lungs. The hand pressers used for cutting different components is also dangerous because children are made to work on them for long hours. A lapse of concentration caused by exhaustion is the main cause of accidents and children often lose the tips of their fingers on machines. Tuberculosis, bronchitis, asthma and pneumoconiosis are the diseases that affect children working in the lock industry.[16]

In the balloon factories of Dahanu in Maharashtra, children are engaged in mixing rubber with chemicals, coloration of balloons and testing balloons with gas. A thick pall of dust and chemicals pervades the rooms which are small, cramped and ill-ventilated. Medical reports state that inhalation of such acids continuously over a period of time can burn the respiratory lining and cause pneumonia, broncho-pneumonia, cough, breathlessness and even heart failure.[14]

Thousands of children are employed in manufacturing *agarbattis* in Nagpur. The children prepare the base by mixing the chemicals with water and kneading it to a dark semi-solid mass called 'masala'. They are not provided with any gloves and do the mixing with their bare hands. They then roll the masala onto sticks and dust them with a dry powder. Later they are dipped in different perfumes and packed. After a few years of work, children develop rheumatic symptoms like pain in the wrists and elbows. Because of the constant inhalation of chemical dust, they develop breathing problems. They also develop skin and eye diseases and their necks and backbones ache constantly since they are required to bend for hours together.

The working conditions in the slate industry of Mandsaur district, Madhya Pradesh, both in the mines and in the factories is extremely hazardous because of the high degree of dust generated. Children working in this industry are exposed to the risk of contracting silicosis and dying an early death.

Many occupations may not be hazardous in themselves but the environment makes them such. In many other cases, an intrinsically hazardous industry becomes more dangerous because of lack of safety measures and because of unhygienic surroundings. The employer, whose sole interest is profit, is not interested in improving the surroundings in which the child works. The workplaces are overcrowded and ill-ventilated, lack basic health care and sanitation facilities and preventive measures against industrial accidents. Given the lack of precaution, the delicate nature of children and their long hours of work, their eye-sight is damaged in gem polishing, diamond-cutting, carpet-weaving, zari embroidery, etc.[16]

Surveys have shown that the existing working conditions in the carpet industry of Mirzapur-Bhadoi are unsuited for long hours of arduous work. Children have to squat for long hours in cramped positions because the plinth area is too small to comfortably accommodate the child labourers. Pits where the children work are not properly ventilated and lighting is insufficient. The loomsheds are generally congested and the air laden with wool fluff. Tuberculosis, night-blindness and poor vision are common among children in this industry.

The prevalence of the piece-rate system, where payment depends on the output, also puts extreme pressure on the child to work beyond its physical capacities. This in turn intensified the hazards. Table 11 gives an overview of the occupational hazards faced by working children.

Table 11
Occupational Hazards

Occupation	Related Diseases/Disabilities
Tile Industry	Tuberculosis, skin discoloration and allergic eruptions
Slate industry	Tuberculosis, silicosis, respiratory diseases
Match Industry/ Fireworks Industry	Tuberculosis, respiratory diseases, skin disease such as dermatitis, severe eye-strain, night blindness and premature blindness

Powerloom Industry	Byssinosis, fibrosis, bronchitis and tuberculosis
Glass Industry	Puneumoconiosis, tuberculosis, bums, life span reduced by a third due to intense heat and dust, and night blindness
Pottery Industry	Asthmatic bronchitis, tuberculosis,silicosis
Brass Industry	Acid burns, tuberculosis and other respiratory tract problems
Bidi Industry	Chronic bronchitis and tuberculosis
Diamond Industry	Severe eye strain, tuberculosis,and other lung diseases
Carpet Weaving Industry	Tuberculosis and other long diseases, eye strain and nightblindness
Lock Industry	Tuberculosis and other respiratory tract diseases, asthma and acute headaches
Balloon Industry	Pneumonia, broncho-pneumonia, cough, breathlessness and even heart failure
Zari Industry	Eye diseases, spondylitis and lead poisoning
Agarbatti Industry	Rheumatism of wrist and elbows, breathing problems, skin and eye diseases

A third type of hazard arises not from the nature of the occupations but the fact that children are vulnerable and are unable to fight for their rights. Children may be engaged in jobs that are considered non-hazardous environment for adults but the vulnerability of a child makes them hazardous. [17] Occupations like domestic work, working in *dhabas*, hawking, shoe-shining may be safe for adults, but the fact that children are at the mercy of the employer and do not have the support of their parents or anyone else results in a hazardous and exploitative situation. For example, children working in homes and *dhabas* work for long hours and are often severely punished for small mistakes. Children left on the streets to fend for themselves are exploited and abused by anti-social elements who misuse them for a variety of illegal activities.

Working children are unable to participate in leisure or recreational activities and therefore lose the psycho-social benefits. Ill-equipped yet forced to play adult roles from a tender age, they soon pick up habits like smoking, drinking and using drugs. They are also hurled into undesirable and anti-social activities like gambling and stealing.

Above all, a child who is working full-time does not have the time to go to school. Studies on child labour commissioned by the Planning Commission of India reiterate this fact. Working children are broadly divided into three types: (1) Children who are illiterate (2) Children who have studied till the primary level (3) Children who are still attending school. In the Brassware industry of Moradabad, 70 percent of child workers surveyed are illiterate, 22 percent have studied till the primary level and only 7 percent are still attending school. In the slate pencil industry of Mandsaur, 62 percent of the child workers are illiterate, 37 percent have studied till the primary level and none of the children from the sample were attending school. In the slate industry of Markapur, 53 percent of the child workers were illiterate, 44 percent had studied till the primary level and only 3 percent were still attending school.[18]

The working child remains illiterate with little chances of upward mobility or freeing himself of his oppressive and exploitative environment.

Thus child labour not only exposes the child to health hazards but also deprives him of the opportunity of mental and emotional development. It snatches away from the child the simple joys of childhood. In the absence of leisure facilities, schooling, adequate rest and nourishment, the child loses the opportunity to develop and realise his potential.

Notes

1. M. M. Rehman, *Society, Economy and Education of the Deprived.(Delhi: Anupam Publication; 1992)* p.297
2. Mahavir Jain, *Child Labour in India. A Select Bibliography* (Noida: National Labour Institute, 1994) p. 18
3. "India has the Largest Labour Force in the World", *Labour Gazettee,* Vol. LIX, No. 5, January 1980, p.328
4. A. N. Singh, *Child Labour in India: Socio-Economic Perspective* (Delhi: Shipra Publication, 1990), p.13
5. Ministry of Labour, *Report of the Committee on Child Labour* (Nasik: Government of India Press, 1979), p.9
6. Myron Weiner. The Child and the State in India: Child Labour and Education Policy in Comparative Perspective (Oxford: Oxford University Press, 1991) pp 13-14.
7. ibid.
8. Nerra Burra, "Issues Emerging from the Experiences of some Developing Countries of Asia", *Child and Education,* Digest 28 (Paris: UNESCO-UNICEF Cooperative Programme, 1989) p. 9-10.
9. *ibid.* p. 17
10. Neera Burra, " Child Labour in India: Poverty, Exploitation and Vested Interests "Social Action,Vol. 36; July-September 1986. p.252
11. Child Labour in the Lock Industry of Aligarh. (Noida: National Labour Institute; 1992) p p .7-10.
12. Geeta Menon, "Health Problems of Working Children: Some Observations", in Usha S. Naidu and Kamini Kapadia (eds.), *Child Labour and Health: Problems and Prospects* (Bombay: TISS, 1985) p. 212.
13. Weiner, op. cit. p.14.
14. Neera Burra, Seminar . op.cit. p.25.
15. Hazel D' Lima and Rima Gosalia, *Street Children of Bombay* (Noida: National Labour Institute, 1992) p. 36.
16. K. D. Gangrade and A Joseph Gathia. *Women and Child Workers in the Unorganised Sector* (New Delhi: Concept Publishing, 1983).s
17. Neera Burra " Health Hazards. *Seminar,* No 350, October 1988, p.25
18. Planning Commission, *Studies on Child Labour Commissioned by the Planning Commission, Government of India—Salient Features of Nine Studies* (New Delhi: Government of India, 1992) pp. 23, 40.

Annexure-I

Regression 1: Child Labour with No. of Poor Persons (Rral)

S. No.	State	Rural Child Labour	Rural No. of Poor Persons
1.	Andhra Pradesh.	1.8000	18.0200
2.	Bihar	1.0300	36.0000
3.	Gujarat	0.5600	10.1500
4.	Himachal Pradesh.	0.0970	1.1100
5.	J&K	0.2500	1.5400
6.	Karnataka	1.0100	13.1700
7.	Kerala	0.0780	9.5100
8.	Madhya Pradesh.	1.6300	24.8800
9.	Maharashtra	1.4500	22.7800
10.	Manipur	0.0018	0.3200
11.	Orissa	0.6800	16.0400
12.	Rajasthan	0.7700	9.1300
13.	Tamil Nadu	0.8300	18.0700
14.	Tripura	0.0240	1.1800
15.	Uttar P.radesh	1.3000	45.6900
16.	West Bengal	0.5200	23.6500

Regression Output:

Constant	0.2552
Std Error of Y Est	0.4334
R Squared	0.4874
No. of Observations	16.000
Degrees of Freedom	14.0000
X. Coefficient(s)	0.0136
Std Err of Coef.	0.0087

Annexure II

Regression 2: Child Labour with No. of Poor Persons (Urban)

S. No.	State	Urban	
		Child Labour	No. of Poor persons
1.	Andhra Pradesh	0.1400	4.4600
2.	Bihar	0.0440	4.0200
3.	Gujarat	0.0500	3.0800
4.	Himachal P.	0.0012	0.0500
5.	Jammu & Kashmir	0.0170	0.5000
6.	Karnataka	0.1240	4.7200
7.	Kerala	0.0130	2.4500
8.	Madhya Pradesh	0.0670	5.0900
9.	Maharashtra	0.1100	6.9500
10.	Manipur	0.0020	0.0960
11.,	Nagaland	0.0006	0.0040
12.	Orissa	0.0290	1.3100
13.	Punjab	0.0000	1.1500
14.	Rajasthan	0.0410	2.4400
15.	Tamil Nadu	0.1500	7.1700
16.	Tripura	0.0010	0.0600
17.	Uttar Pradesh	0.1250	9.8000
18.	West Bengal	0.0740	5.0200

Regression Output:

Constant	0.0021
Std Err of Y Est	0.0262
R Squared	0.7726
No. of Observations	18.0000
Degrees of Freedom	16.0000
X Coefficient(s)	0.0163
Std. Err of Coef.	0.0022

Annexure III

Regression 3: Child Labour with No. of Poor Persons (Total)

S. No.	State	Child Labour	No. of Poor persons
1.	Andhra Pradesh	1.9400	22.4800
2.	Bihar	1.0740	40.0200
3.	Gujarat	0.6100	13.2300
4.	Himachal Pradesh	0.0982	1.1600
5.	Jammu & Kashmir	0.2670	2.0400
6.	Karnataka	1.1340	17.8900
7.	Kerala	0.0910	11.9600
8.	Madhya Pradesh	1.6970	29.9700
9.	Maharashtra	1.5600	29.7300
10.	Manipur	0.0038	0.4160
11.	Nagaland	0.0156	0.0040
12.	Orissa	0.7090	17.3500
13.	Rajasthan	0.8110	11.5700
14.	Tamil Nadu	0.9800	25.2400
15.	Tripura	0.0250	1.2400
16.	Uttar Pradesh	1.4250	55.4900
17.	West Bengal	0.5940	28.6700

Regression Output:

Constant	0.2100
Std Err of Y Est	0.4326
R Squared	0.5673
No. of Observations	17.0000
Degrees of Freedom	15.0000
X Coefficient(s)	0.0307
Std Err of Coef.	0.0069

Annexure IV

Regression 4: Child Labour with Number of Unemployed. Persons (Rural)

S. No.	State	Rural	
		Child Labour	Unemployed Persons
1.	Andhra Pradesh	1.8000	1 8300
2.	Bihar	1.0300	1.5400
3.	Gujarat	0.5600	0.4600
4.	Himachal Pradesh	0.0970	0.0240
5.	Jammu & Kashmir	0.2500	0.1800
7.	Kerala	0.0780	0.8900
8.	Madhya Pradesh	1.6300	1.6600
9.	Maharashtra	1.4500	1.1500
10.	Manipur	0.0018	0.0010
11.	Orissa	0.6800	0.7900
12.	Rajasthan	0.7700	0.4700
13.	Tamil Nadu	0.8300	2.8500
14.	Tripura	0.0240	0.0250
15.	Uttar Pradesh	1.300	1.0700
16.	West Bengal	0.5200	2.1600

Regression Output

Constant	0.5138
Std. Err of Y Est	0.5657
R Squared	0.1270
No. of Observations	16.000
Degress of Freedom	14.0000
X Coefficient(s)	0.2459
Std Err. of Coef.	0.1724

Annexure V

Regression 5: Child Labour with Number of Unemployed Persons (Urban)

S. No.	State	Urban	
		Child Labour	Unemployed Persons
1.	Andhra Pradesh	0.1400	0.3800
2.	Bihar	0.0440	0.1900
3.	Gujarat	0.0500	0.3300
4.	Himachal Pradesh	0.0012	0.0060
5.	Jammu & Kashmir	0.0170	0.0260
6.	Karnataka	0.1240	0.5200
7.	Kerala	0.0130	0.3200
8.	Madhya Pradesh	0.0670	0.2100
9.	Maharashtra	0.1100	0.5600
10.	Manipur	0.0020	0.0006
11.	Orissa	0.0290	0.1300
12.	Punjab	0.0000	0.1100
13.	Rajasthan	0.0410	0.1400
14.	Tamil Nadu	0.1500	1.0200
15.	Tripura	0.0010	0.0070
16.	Uttar Pradesh	0.1250	0.4000
17.	West Bengal	0.0740	0.6800

Regression Output:

Constant	0.0122
Std Err of Y Est	0.0137
R. Squared	0.6652
No. of Observations	17.0000
Degrees of Freedom	15.0000
X. Coefficient(s)	0.1554
Std. Err of Coef.	0.0285

Annexure VI

Regression 6: Child Labour with Number of Unemployed Persons (Total)

S. No.	State	Total	
		Child Labour	**Unemployed Persons**
1.	Andhra Pradesh	1.9400	2.2100
2.	Bihar	1.0740	1.7300
3.	Gujarat	0.6100	0.7900
4.	Himachal Pradesh	0.0982	0.0300
5.	Jammu & Kashmir	0.2670	0.2060
6.	Karnataka	1.1340	1.4100
7.	Kerala	0.0910	0.9800
8.	Madhya Pradesh	1.6970	0.6000
9.	Maharashtra	1.5600	1.7100
10.	Manipur	0.0038	0.0016
11.	Orissa	0.7090	0.9200
12.	Rajasthan	0.8110	0.6100
13.	Tamil Nadu	0.9800	3.8700
14.	Tripura	0.0250	0.0320
15.	Uttar Pradesh	1.4250	1.4700
16.	West Bengal	0.5940	2.8400

Regression Output:

Constant	0.5135
Std Err of Y Est	0.5907
R. Squared	0.1704
No. of Observations	16.0000
Degrees of Freedom	14.0000
X Coefficient(s)	0.2353
Std Err of Coef.	0.1388

Annexure VII

Regression Data : Child Labour and Illiteracy, 1981

State	Literates Rural	Literates Urban	Literates Total	Rural Child Labour	Urban Child Labour	Total Child Labour
ANDHRA PRADESH	24.659	41.51	28.810	1.800	0.140	1.940
ARUNACHAL PRADESH	0.369	0.012	0.382	0.018	0.000	0.018
BIHAR	36305	0.281	36.587	1.030	0.044	1.074
GOA	0.229	0.073	0.301	0.007	0.002	0.009
GUJARAT	10.995	2.612	13.607	0.560	0.050	0.610
HIMACHAL PRADESH	1.670	0.063	1.733	0.097	0.001	0.098
KARNATAKA	13.605	3.011	16.616	1.010	0.124	1.134
KERALA	3.507	0.547	4.054	0.078	0.013	0.091
MADHYA PRADESH	24.733	3.134	27.867	1.630	0.067	1.697
MAHARASHTRA	18.492	4.863	23.354	1.450	0.110	1.560
MANIPUR	0.478	0.188	0.596	0.002	0.002	0.004
NAGLAND	0.302	0.024	0.326	0.015	0.001	0.016
ORISSA	12.052	0.926	12.977	0.680	0.029	0.709
RAJASTHAN	16.768	2.515	19.282	0.770	0.041	0.811
SIKKIM	0.137	0.015	0.152	0.008	0.001	0.008
TAMIL NADU	15.297	3.687	18.984	0.830	0.150	0.980
TRIPURA	0.827	0.033	0.860	0.024	0.001	0.025
UTTAR PRADESH	52.621	7.500	60.122	1.300	0.125	1.425
WEST BENGAL	19.771	3.752	23.523	0.520	0.074	0.594
ANDAMAN	0.047	0.010	0.057	0.001	0.000	0.001
LAKSHWADEEP	0.006	0.004	0.010	0.000	0.00	0.000
PONDICHERRY	0.108	0.072	0.180	0.002	0.002	0.004

Annexure VIII

Regression 7: Illiterates (Rural) With Child Labour(Rural)

Regression Output:

Constant	0.13
Std Err of Y Est	0.36
R Squared	0.67
No. of Observations	22.00
Degrees of Freedom	20.00
X Coefficient(s)	0.04
Std Err of Coef.	0.01

Annexure IX

Regression 8: Illiterates (Urban) With Child Labour(Urban)

Regression Output

Constant	0.01
Std Err of Y Est	0.03
R. Squared	0.78
No. of Observations	22.00
Degrees of Freedom	20.00
X Coefficient(s)	0.02
Std Err of Coef.	0.00

Annexure X

Regression 9: Illiterates (Total) With Child Labour(Total)

Regression Output:

Constant	0.12
Std Err of Y Est	0.37
R Squared	0.70
No. of Observations	22.00
Degrees of Freedom	20.00
X Coefficient(s)	0.03
Std Err of Coef.	0.01

IV
Child Labour in Select Indian Industries

There is a high concentration of child labour in several industries in India. These include slate, diamond cutting, gem polishing, powerloom, carpet weaving, lock making, pottery, metalware, match and glass.

Over the years there has been a decline in the employment of children in the organised sector because children employed in the organised sector are protected under the child labour laws. Today most of the working children are employed in the unorganised sector of the industries. They participate in practically all the operations.

The employment of children in these industries is not just a result of poverty but because the employer has a vested interest in employing children. Children constitute a cheap and uncomplaining workforce.

Children in these industries toil for long hours in hazardous operations and sub-standard hygenic conditions. Some industries in which children are employed in large numbers are being analysed in this chapter to get an exact picture of how exploitative and pervasive the practice of child labour has become. These industries are:

1. Match Industry of Sivakasi
2. Glass Industry of Firozabad
3. Carpet Industry of Mirzapur-Bhadoi
4. Brass Industry of Moradabad

Various indicators, *viz*, working conditions, wages, occupational hazards, are being used to illustrate the exploitative nature of this phenomenon.

Match Industry of Sivakasi

Tamil Nadu accounts for 66 per cent of the total match units in India. Sivakasi, in the state's Ramanathapuram district, is its epicentre. There are over 6000 match units in the area. According to figures provided by the All India Chamber of Match Industries, the production in Sivakasi amounted to as much as 77 percent of the entire national production of matches in 1977-78. The production of matches in this area is non mechanised.

Out of an estimated population of 1 lakh workers in the match and fireworks industries, the Gurupadaswamy report puts the figure of child labour in Sivakasi at 50,000. A study conducted by UNICEF in 1993, puts the figure of child labour at 80,000. However, according to unofficial sources, there are 1,25,000 children working in the Sivakasi belt. The International Committee of Jurists has said that Sivakasi has one of the largest concentration of child labour in the world.

A combination of economic and political factors are responsible for the extent and perpetuation of child labour in Sivakasi. The underdeveloped drought prone conditions of the district has made possible the recruitment of children in this growing cottage and small-scale sector competing with a multinational match industry. Children who work in match factories come from families dependent to a large extent on agriculture. However, only 7 per cent of the net area sown in the Ramanathapuram district has assured irrigation facilities. The remaining area depends on the erratic rainfall for water. Due to paucity of water in the region, only a small proportion of the cultivated area can sustain more than one crop a year. The drought conditions greatly facilitate the employment of children. The child becomes the worst victim of this underdevelopment. Most child labour comes from households dependent on agriculture and whose income is irregular. Children are therefore used to supplement family income.

Apart from cultivation, the only work that adults are engaged in is stone quarrying, which is physically back-breaking and ill-paid. By the time adults reach the age of 35-40, they are infirm and fall prey to tuberculosis and other diseases. There are also cases of families getting completely impoverished due to recurrent droughts, forcing them to move to towns. Once they migrate the entire family becomes totally dependent on the match factories for their survival. There being no creches in the factories, children hover around their mothers and play with matchsticks and splints. Unknowingly, the toddlers pick up the skill while at play and by the time they are 2 or 3-years-old, they have joined the workforce. In this way the child gets trapped in a no-exist situation even before she can speak coherently.

The industrial policy of the government is also to some extent responsible for the magnitude of child labour in Sivakasi because of the various incentives given to small and cottage industries. Match production in India flourished after the first world war when the Government of India imposed revenue duty on the import of matches. During this time, the Swedish Western India Match Company (WIMCO) established several match factories in India, which led to the eventual death of 21 Indian companies. Around this time small scale manufacturers' associations began to lobby for protection and prevāiled upon the government to impose excise duty on mechanised production. In 1943, the government evolved two categories for the purpose of levy and excise duty. Subsidies were granted to the cottage and small-scale sector. Producers of low volume were thus protected and this concession led to a phenomenal growth of the small and cottage sector industries. The non-mechanised sector today produces more matches than the mechanised sector. In 1978, the non-mechanised sector accounted for 70.24 percent of total production. In 1979, the Janata Government gave further benefits to the small and cottage sectors. In keeping with the growth of these industries, there has been a massive inflow of migrant workers, of whom children constitute a significant proportion. In 1980, however, the Central Government reduced the duty on the mechanised sector. This policy also forced employers to continue to pay exploitative wages, besides perpetuating child labour, to compete with the mechanised sector.[1]

Working Conditions of Children in Match Industry

Children are employed in almost all stages of match production. They are engaged in mixing and steaming chemicals in the boiler room; stamping frames of match splinters in trays of wet phosphorus and drying them on hot sheets of metal in a huge furnace; filling frames with sticks; placing and storing the frames in racks; filling match boxes into packages of dozen. Each stage of the process has its inherent hazards.

The ages of children working in match factories range between 3-1/2 to 15 years. In many factories some activities are fully undertaken by children below 7 years of age. Girls outnumber boys in this industry. A study conducted by Helen. R Seker reveals that girls account for almost 90 per cent of total child labour force employed in this industry. When parents were asked why they sent their girl children to work, 70 percent replied that their household incomes were low and they needed additional income. Since most of them wanted their male children to go to school, the burden of earning this additional income fell on the girl child.[2]

Children either work in small cottage units or are brought by organised transport to the small-scale units scattered in the neighbouring villages or in Sivakasi town. Between 3.00 and 5.00 a.m. every morning children in these villages, some as far as 30 kms away from their place of work, are woken-up and loaded into buses or vans belonging to the industries in Sivakasi town. In most cases, over 200 of them are loaded into a single bus. The buses drop them back to their respective villages between 6.00 and 9.00 p.m. The children, who put in nearly 12 hours of work, are therefore away from their homes for over 15 hours. Each of these villages has an agent who enrols children and ensures that the children are awake when the transport arrives.[3]

The working conditions in the industries are unsafe and detrimental to the health of the children. The workplaces are congested, improperly illuminated, full of chemical odour and poorly ventilated. There is lack of drinking water and toilet facilities in most workplaces. Children have to often carry heavy wooden scales and iron bars, weighing four kgs each, to be exposed to the sun or the chemical-dripping room.[4]

Every stage of the process of producing matches is hazardous. Children mixing chemicals in boiler rooms get lungfulls of toxic fumes, suffer from high degrees of intense heat and run the risk of being badly injured in fire accidents. Children who stamp frames on the metal sheets too suffer intense heat, toxic fumes and excessive strain on the arms and shoulders because they have to remove and place the heavy frames with great rapidity. Delay of even a second can cause the entire frame to go up in flames which could cause instant death. The strain often makes children feel dizzy and faint. Children also sit on their haunches, bending forward for hours, filling sticks into boxes with great frenzy. If the children speak to one another to relieve the monotony and drudgery of work, the supervisors hit them and sometimes even cut their wages. Most children get so tired of working in the factories that they do not get sleep at night, keep getting fever, throat congestion, cough and cold. They are given an aspirin at the factory everyday.[5]

Minimum safety standards are generally not maintained in these units. There is a high risk of fire and explosion in raw material stores, paste making, match-coating and box-filling processes. Fire accidents occur when match-heads rub against the friction side in course of putting the box together too quickly. Also, in the case of labelling, where the worker is required to put labels and bandrolls on filled boxes, slight friction can lead to fire. In the name of first-aid kit, only a tube of Burnol is kept. In several units, the building layout and design is inadequate. In most of the manufacturing units, one working hall opens into another. Usually the room where splints are paraffined and coated are connected to working halls, chemical store and chemical mixing room. When wax is heated on hot plates, a lot of smoke gets released. Chemicals are also mixed at 60-70 C. Smoke released from both processes spreads to other working areas in the absence of adequate ventilation. Several processes like frame filling, box filling, labelling, packing are carried out in the same shed. Thus, when fire breaks out, it spreads to other work sections too. Casualties in fire accidents are a common phenomenon. In a Sivakasi factory in 1981, one such fire took a toll of 32 people, including 6 children.

Children work for twelve hours on an average, daily, under tiring conditions for six to seven days a week, without a break for months together. The Factories Act, 1948, prohibits work during night by children but there are instances of children working till as late as 10.00 pm. Many children who have been working in these units for several years now earn less because they are not able to work as quickly. Some of them can no longer bear to continue working in this industry.

The children are paid on a piece rate basis. Thus they work feverishly to ensure maximum output. Despite working for over twelve hours a day, the average wage per week is Rs. 38 but incomes vary from upto Rs. 70 to as little as Rs. 12 per week. In some cases the status of the child worker is that of a helper to an adult, who is usually her sister or mother, and whatever work the child does is counted as the adult's work. The child worker is not paid for this.

Management claims that the workers are paid bonus twice a year, but a study conducted by the Child Labour Cell of the National Labour Institute reveals that only 40 percent of the children interviewed received bonus twice a year, 10 percent once a year and 20 percent did not receive any bonus. 30 percent of the children received neither wage nor bonus as their labour had been pledged by parents in return for an advance payment from the employers and the amount had not been fully recovered. This is one of the ways by which the employer retains the labour force.

A study on child labour in match industry of Sivakasi, commissioned by the Planning Commission, has listed anaemia and respiratory diseases amongst the occupational hazards of working in this industry.

A report submitted by the Area Development Programme for Ramanathapuram (prepared by UNICEF) said that nearly all workers are exposed to airborne concentration of substances. Diseases are only detected after cumulative poisons accumulate.

A UNICEF-aided paediatric and gynaecological study observed that among children working in match factories, skin diseases such as dermatitis are very common. There is a high incidence of tuberculosis and non-specific diseases of the upper respiratory passage. Working for long hours in dark, ill-ventilated rooms is a cause of severe eye-strain, night blindness and premature blindness. The report noted that 49 percent of the children had anaemia and the major complaint of children was recurrent abdominal pain.

Educational Status of Working Children in Match Industry

Most children working in match factories have either not been to school or have dropped out very easily. The Planning Commission-sponsored study, conducted on a sample of 490 working children of Sivakasi, found that 50 percent of the children are illiterate and only 43 percent children have studied upto the primary level. Out of the sample, only 11 percent of the working children are still attending school.[6]

With regards to education, the girl child is discriminated against. Parents of 52 percent of the children interviewed by Seker stated that it was no use educating their girls. This is reflected in the educational status of the siblings. Among the male siblings in the age group 0-14, 71.4% were sent to school; 17.8 percent were working in the industries and 10.8 percent were too young to work or go to school. On the other hand, of the female siblings in the age group of 0-14, 22.7 percent were in school, 65.9 percent were working and 11 percent were neither going to school nor to factories.

An industry which brings light into millions of households condemns a large number of children to toil endlessly in hazardous jobs at less than minimum wages. It epitomises the abhorrent and inhuman character of the practice of child labour.

Carpet Industry of Mirzapur-Bhadoi

The Mirzapur-Bhadoi belt in the state of Uttar Pradesh is the most important carpet producing area in India. A major share of the total export of carpets from India is from this region. Mirzapur-Bhadoi accounts for about 85 to 90 percent of the total value of carpets exported from India.

Children are employed in various processes in the carpet industry like sorting, weaving, knotting, washing and dyeing. But nearly 80 percent of the children are engaged in knotting and weaving of carpets.[7] These activities are treated as hazardous. Employment of children below 14 years is prohibited under the Child Labour (Prohibition and Regulation) Act, 1986. Despite this children continue to be employed in the carpet industry in a clandestine manner.

Exact figures on the number of child workers employed in carpet industry are not available. Current official estimates place the number at 75,000. But this estimate is far lower than the actual figure. A study conducted in this belt by B.N. Juyal, for the ILO and the Ministry of Labour, Government of India, puts the figure as high as 4,20,000, with 3,50,000 children employed in weaving process and the rest in other processes. The magnitude of child labour can also be estimated on the basis of the ratio between adult and child workers. As per the All-India Carpet Manufacturers Association, total number of weavers is 5,00,000. According to a primary census made in five different segments, the ratio between adult and child workers works out as 1:2.254. In an estimated population of 5,00,000 weavers, child weavers should number 3,46,000.[8]

The employment of children in this industry in such large numbers is due to several reasons. The tender thin fingers of the children are specially dexterous in piercing together the tightly drawn weft strings, the density of which increases in superior qualities. The industry also exploits the naturally sharper eye-sight of the young workers in weaving intricate and exquisite designs.

The children working in this industry can be divided into four categories:

1. Children working on own-family looms.
2. Children assisting adult family members, again without any direct remuneration.
3. Children treated as *chelas* or unpaid learners.
4. Children treated as wage-earners.

Children belonging to the fourth category can be further sub-divided into two categories:

a) Children from neighbouring areas who work at carpet-weaving units during the day and return to their homes at night.
b) Children, who have been sent from distant places like Palamu in Bihar, who work and live at carpet units.

Contrary to the prevailing notion that most children work on their family looms, hired child workers or wage earners constitute 70 percent of child workforce. It is a common practice to masquerade child workers as trainees or even family members because the working of children in family-owned units is not prohibited.

The carpet-weaving industry in this belt is estimated to have grown four-fold since 1975. This phenomenal growth of the industry led to an increase in the magnitude of child labour, largely in the wage sector, mostly of the migrant type. Not only the magnitude, but also the grid for drawing in child labour has expanded in recent years. The grid has expanded from Palamau in South Bihar to as far as Saharsa and Purnea in north-east Bihar, Santhal Parganas in the east of Bihar and adjoining Malda in West Bengal. The other main labour recruitment zone is the Vindhya-Kaimur plateau extending upto Sindi-Sarguja and Shahdol in Madhya Pradesh. Around Bhadoi, a lot of children are also brought from the Manikpura-Kawri area of Banda, Uttar Pradesh. Large-scale induction of labour from Nepal is also taking place in the last 2-3 years, as the demand for Tibetan-Nepali carpets has come from the European market. This development has also brought in, for the first time, a significant number of female weavers, adult as well as very young girls, from Nepal. Otherwise there are very few girls in the industry and they mostly work in familial setting.

Working Conditions of Children in Carpet Industry

A large number of recruitment agencies or middlemen have sprung up to induct children. Children are often bought from poverty-stricken families at tender ages for paltry sums. Another way of inducting child workers is to keep the child as security for a loan. Once 'bought' or 'pledged' they are kept captive and forced to work in inhuman conditions. The cruel and inhuman practice of keeping children captive was once again brought to light when the Bandhua Mukti Morcha rescued 27 bonded child labourers from the captivity of a loom owner.

The working hours of the children are long; with no adequate rest intervals or paid weekly holiday. The working hours of children range from 10 to 16 hours per day. Surveys have shown that most child workers begin work at around 6.00 am and finish their work by 7.00 p.m. The Factories Act, 1948, prohibits work during night by children but this law is blatantly violated.

In an interview conducted by A.N. Singh of 309 working children in Varanasi district, a majority of children, that is, 264 (85.4 percent) said that they work at night whereas 42 (13.6 percent) did not work at night and the rest, that is 3 (1.6 percent) did not disclose anything. Out of the 264 children who worked at night, 76 (28.8 percent) said they worked every night, 111 (42 percent) worked for two hours at night, 74 (28 percent) for three hours and 3 (1.1 percent) worked for fours hours daily during night.[9]

The existing working conditions are unsuited for long hours of arduous work. The plinth area is too small to comfortably accommodate the workers. Children have to squat for long hours in cramped position. Pits where the children work are not properly ventilated and lighting is insufficient. The loom sheds are generally congested and the air laden with woolfluff.

Violence and threats are casually used by employers to discipline children. Out of the 309 children interviewed by Singh, 35.8 percent said they regularly received threats from their employers. Similarly, 27.7 percent children said they were beaten by their employers. A large number of children rescued during raids have borne marks of physical torture.

The child labourers may be given cooked food from the employer's own kitchen, generally in the case of small units, or they may be required to cook themselves. Even in the latter case, the ration is generally given by the employers. In a survey conducted by Prembhai on working children, 60.5 percent children disclosed that they received only small quantities of food, not sufficient to fill their stomachs, 39.5 percent children reported that though they received adequate quantity of food, it was of poor quality.[10]

Sheo Nath, one among the five bonded child labourers rescued by civil and police officials, was lured to work in a carpet weaving factory by the owners who promised to pay him. Rs. 3000 per month and give him daily meals consisting of milk, rice, pulses and vegetables. However, Sheo Nath was made to work round-the-clock and was given only 'bajra ka ghatta' to survive on.[11]

Children working in carpet units are also used by loom-owners for domestic work, tending animal and agricultural work.

The wage pattern in carpet weaving varies from area to area. For example, in village Piprish, the piece rate system prevails, whereas in Sukhra children are paid a daily wage, which ranges from Re 1 to Rs. 10 per day. Food and other expenses incurred on the workers are deducted from their wages.

In the survey conducted by Prembhai on migrant child workers in Mirzapur district, 48 per cent received only food and no wages, 37 percent received only Re 1 per day and 8.7 percent of them earned Rs. 2 per day. A very small section, that is, 1.6 percent, were paid Rs. 3 per day, 3.5 percent children earned Rs. 4 and only 0.6 percent earned as much as Rs. 5 per day, as wages, in addition to food.

The main source of health hazard faced by children in this industry is exposure to airborne contaminants, especially fluff and dust of wool/cotton to which the children, especially migrant children, are exposed 24 hours since they live and sleep in the vacant corners of the loomshed itself. Investigations point to shockingly high incidence of tuberculosis. At a health camp organised mainly for working children studying at eight out of ten special schools being run by the *Saghan Kshetra Vikas Samiti*, 25 to 30 percent children tested positive for tuberculosis. In Piprish village, a number of young persons, about 30 years of age, who had started as child weavers, were being treated for tuberculosis. Night-blindness and poor vision have also assumed the proportions of an occupational disease among workers in this industry. The carpet-weavers also complain that they become incapable of working outdoor in sunshine. They develop some kind of phobia in terms of comparing carpet-weaving to jail work.

Surveys conducted by medical teams on child labourers in this industry reveal that about 50 percent child labourers are anaemic and/or suffering from worm infestation. Scabies is highly prevalent and constant contact with woollen fibres can cause allergies. The consequence of squatting cramped in damp pits for long hours results in boils, swelling of lower limbs and aching joints. Fever, cough and cold tend to be chronic probably on account of fluff and dust in the air.

Educational Status of Working Children in Carpet Industry

A sample survey conducted on 608 children reveals that 69 percent of the children in the sample are illiterate. Of the literate children, only 17 percent have been educated upto the secondary level. The rest of them are educated below or till the primary level. The survey also throws light on schooling status of working children. About 69 percent children have never attended school, while about 23 percent have dropped out. Only a small number, that is, 8 percent of the child workers, are attending formal school.[12]

The carpet industry of Mirzapur-Bhadoi earns large amount of foreign exchange for India (about Rs. 700 crores per year). This is achieved by violating the most basic rights of these children—their health, education and their very future. Their employment is an open and blatant violation of the law which prohibits employment of children under 14.

A campaign carried out in major carpet importing countries in Europe (particularly Germany and U.K.) against the purchase of carpets produced by children has aroused consumer awareness and threatens to affect the export of carpets to these countries. Moreover, a bill introduced by United States Senator Tom Harkins with the intention of prohibiting the import into the USA of products which use child labour in the manufacture has alarmed exporters and manufacturers because carpets from India are listed as such products. To ward off a ban on Indian carpets, a system of labelling carpets produced without child labour has been initiated. This issue is discussed in the next chapter.

Glass Industry of Firozabad

The glass industry of Firozabad produces 99 percent of India's glass bangles and is also the epicentre of the glass-blowing industry. On the basis of types of glass products produced here, glass industry of Firozabad can be classified into the following categories:

1. Glass-ware Industry
2. Glass Bangle Industry
3. Glass Block Making Industry

4. Glass Beads Industry
5. Glass Pottery Industry

At present there are about 600 glass manufacturing industries in the district. Work in the glass industry is carried out at 2 levels: (1) Factory level (2) Household level.

Two types of furnaces are used for making glass at Firozabad-pot furnace and tank furnace. The temperatures in pot furnaces range between 700°C to 800°C. But in the tank furnaces, the temperature is as high as 1800°C.

Children are employed in large numbers in this industry. The combination of heat, dust and intense noise in the factories has severe repercussions on the health of workers. The net result is that the health of the worker is cut short by 10 to 15 years. Adults, who are rendered incapable of working at the prime of their life, are forced to depend on their children for survival. This explains in large measure the prevalence of child labour in the glass industry.

Labour laws are openly flouted in Firozabad. Children under the age of 14 are prohibited from working under the Factories Act. The State Government has also declared, under Section 87 of the Factories Act, the glass industry as dangerous operations factories. Yet most factories employ children. It is estimated that 30,000 children are employed in the glass industry at the factory level. In addition, the number of children engaged in this industry at household level is estimated to be about two-and-a-half times more than the number of children working at factory level. Thus, over a lakh children work in this industry. The ratio of child workers to the total workers employed in glass industry is 35 to 40 percent and varies from industry to industry.[13]

Children are employed in almost all the processes of bangle-making and glass blowing. They carry molten glass on a seven-foot rod called 'labya' from the furnace to the adult worker and back to the furnace. Nearly 85 percent of the total child labour force is engaged in this activity.[14] In the bangle industry, children are also engaged in processes like 'judai' (joining the ends), 'chhatai' (sorting), 'katai' (engraving of different patterns with the help of abrasive wheels), 'pakai' (heating), packaging and sorting. Children are also engaged in marking the trademark on the products, cleaning the glass apparatus, shining the manufactured glass products and helping the main workers in other operations of glass manufacturing production.

A sample survey, sponsored by the Planning Commission, among 500 working children engaged in this industry, shows that 81 percent of the working children are male. Age-wise classification of working children indicates that bulk of the children (68 percent) in the sample are in the age-group of 11-14 years. The proportion of working children in the age group of 7 to 11 years is 28.4 percent. Children even in the age group of 4 to 7 years are working in the glass industry, though their proportion is very small (3.6 percent).[15]

Working Conditions of Children in Glass Industry

Children along with adult workers, assemble early morning at *mandis* or labour markets, waiting eagerly for the contractors representing the factories. Many children come from-far-flung villages. The contractors choose some workers for a day or two. These auctions of labour are held daily. Each factory has four or five contractors working for it.

Inside the factories the working conditions are appalling. Children sit in front of furnaces where the temperature is about 700 C. In many factories where children draw molten glass from tank furnaces, in which the temperature is between 1500 C to 1800 C, their bodies are 6 to 8 inches from the opening of the furnace. Since they are small in size, they have to put their arm right inside the furnace in order to draw adequate quantities of molten glass. As a result, the body almost touches the furnace.

The processes involved in '*judai,* '*katai*' and '*pakai*' are highly hazardous and involve back-breaking work. As the worker holds the glass close to the whirling wheel on which 'katai' is done, the glass dust, the heat of the whirling wheel and sometimes the whirling wheel itself touches the finger of the worker, injuring him.

'*Pakai*' (baking) is done on three-tiered ovens. On steaming asbestos sheets pulled out of the furnace, children speedily arrange bangles for '*pakai*'. Another worker puts them in the oven. Children involved in this process are close to the furnace for long hours.

'*Judai*' (joining the ends to form a ring) is done on acetyle or kerosene flames in dingy huts. The worker inhales both the glass fumes, acetyle flames and other pollutants. The rooms are full of soot and there is no ventilation as the flames could be extinguished by breeze. Almost 50 percent of this work is done by children. It involves tremendous eye strain as the workers sit in front of the lamps working continuously for almost 12 hours without removing their eyes from the flame.

Glass blowing work is generally done by adults but children sit in front of the blow glass workers, closing the mould after the molten glass is put into it. Their job is to line the mould with paper and close it after the blow glass worker puts the blown glass into it. As soon as the child closes the mould, even before he has time to remove his hands, the mould catches fire because of the paper inside it. The whole process takes a few seconds from the time the worker brings the molten glass on a 'labya' to the glass blower and the blown glass is put into the mould. After that, children carry the product to another worker who cuts it and then it is taken away for further heating. Children hold the heavy 'labias' in such a way that the burning glass is just 2 feet away from their bodies and a foot away from the bodies of other child workers. The workers are constantly on the move with blazing material in hand in the congested space. Factory floors are strewn with broken glass and naked electric wires can be seen everywhere. The noise in the factories is deafening and there is hardly any space to move without bumping into someone. It is not surprising that industrial accidents are frequent though government officials and factory owners deny it. It is alleged that fatal and near-fatal accident victims are thrown into the furnaces to destroy evidence. Children are the common victims because their bodies cannot take the trauma of such accidents easily. If in case of an accident, a worker does not report for work, he does not get wages for that period.

The working conditions in glass blowing, decorative glass and glass bangle units are to some extent different. However, the environmental stresses, such as heat and overcrowding near the platform of the furnaces, in all the three types of factories is more or less the same.

Though night work for children is prohibited under Section 63 of the Factories Act, 1948, children continue to work at night and even children as young as 7 and 8 years work in the night shift.

Children work for 10-14 hours daily. The study sponsored by the Planning Commission reveals than an alarming 40 percent of the children work for more than 8 hours a day. These children can compete with adults in putting in as many hours of work but the costs for these children as incurred in terms of ill health, loss of childhood, education and leisure far outweigh benefits (paltry wages) that acrue to them. Exploitation is evident as an adult working day is defined as constituting 8 hours. It is inhuman to make children work relentlessly for such long hours in the environs of a glass factory.

In bigger factories, workers, including child workers, are paid on a time-rate basis. In smaller units workers are paid on piece-rate basis. Any breakage is adjusted against the wages of the workers. As it happens, children often end up losing a whole day's earning for breaking glass accidentally. It takes a while before a child starts earning a reasonable wage.

The survey conducted on a sample of 500 children shows that the average monthly earning of a child labourer is Rs. 331, which is too little considering the hazardous and back-breaking work done by the children. A classification of working children on the basis of wages shows that 30 percent of the working children get wages of Rs. 4 per day while 69.2 percent earn below Rs. 13.40 per day. Only 9 percent of the working children earn above Rs. 20 per day and only 2.6 percent earn a little more than Rs. 32 per day.

The combination of heat, dust and noise has intense repercussions on the health of the workers. Tuberculosis is rampant amongst workers in this industry and the life of a worker is cut short by 10 to 15 years. According to a local doctor, children suffer from heat strokes, dehydration and occular diseases. Cataract develops very early. Vision also becomes poor. The workers also inhale soot, fumes and dust from the dry glass mixture (silica dust and soda ash among other chemicals) powder kept in the open. Other than tuberculosis, asthma, bronchitis, cough and other dust-related diseases are common. So are burns and cuts on hands and feet. For '*jhalai*' and '*judai*,' the children crouch over the kerosene flames for hours. Besides the constant inhaling of fumes, the children's eye-sight suffer and their physical growth is retarded. Night blindness is another common occupational hazard in this industry. A survey done by the Indian Council for Medical Research in 1989 revealed that 70 percent of the town's population has respiratory problems.

Educational Status of Working Children in Glass Industry

As per the study conducted on 505 working children, as many as 45.4 percent children in the sample are illiterate, 49 percent have attended school till the primary level and only 10.02 percent are educated upto the secondary level. An analysis of the schooling status of the working children shows that 45.40 percent have never attended school, 34.60 percent have attended but dropped out and only 20 percent of the working children are still attending school.

Child labour seems to be a crucial part of the glass industry of Firozabad because it is cheap labour. Factory owners and bureaucrats justify child labour on the ground that if these children are not allowed to work, they would starve. It is true that children in these industries, like elsewhere in India, work because their families are poor. But child labour cannot be justified in the name of poverty in a region where adult unemployment is so high.

Brassware Industry of Moradabad

Moradabad is one of the most important regions of production of metalware in the country. It is known throughout India and in many parts of the world for its decorative brassware: vases, planters, plates, coffee tables and various other objects d'art. Moradabad brassware fetches Rs. 700 crores per year in the export market.

There are three categories of manufacturing units in Moradabad: large manufacturing units, small manufacturing units and artisan-run units. According to the District Industries Centre, there are 3000 units registered as small-scale units with a capital of less than 35,00,000 whereas other sources indicate the existence of 3000 unregistered small-scale units.[16] About 1.5 lakh workers are directly engaged in the metalware industry, of whom 45,000 are children.

The main reason behind the use of children in this industry is that children are paid less than adults and hence production costs are kept low. Illiteracy among parents, lack of awareness about the hazards of employing children alongwith economic compulsions helps in ensuring the employment of these children. Children are involved in a variety of processes like casting (as furnace attendants), scraping and electroplating.

About three decades ago, the brassware industry was a cottage industry where artisans worked with the help of family members and virtually no hired labour was used. The skilled craftsman was in control of the industry to an extent that he purchased the raw materials himself, fashioned the goods and then sold them. But gradually work became more specialised, requiring different types of skills and processes which could not be carried out at home. Rise in prices of raw materials and the difficulty in keeping brass objects from tarnishing resulted in erosion of the domestic market. On the other hand, demand for items such as planters, dinner plates and tea services etc. from the international market increased, specially from the United States and European countries. Export of Moradabad brassware has increased from Rs. 50 crore to over Rs. 700 crore in the last 12 years. This led to an advent of modernisation in this industry. Techniques earlier applied were no longer adequate. Factories sprang up in response to the new pattern of demand. This resulted in hiring labour from outside. Between 1959-74, population of the self-employed dropped from 66 percent to less than 1 percent. Most artisans were reduced to wage earners. The growth of industry created a demand for a large workforce and this demand was met by workers from rural areas of Moradabad and from eastern Uttar Pradesh and Bihar.[17]

Children of artisans were always involved with the work of their family members on a part-time or full-time basis. However, the changing pattern of the industry resulted in a substantial increase in the share of children in the workforce. But this increase did not occur in a uniform way. For example, in the larger factories of Moradabad virtually no children are employed. This, according to factories owners, was due to two reasons. The first and most important one was that the new technology was not suitable for the height and strength of children. The size of the machine and the nature of the process involved, such as removing the round ignotes from the furnace, pressing them into shape, reheating and pressing the unfinished wares several times, seemed to be beyond the physical capacity of children. The other reason proffered by factory owners is that child labour is banned under the Factories Act and they did not want to risk prosecution on that account. Nevertheless, children are employed in most multi-process units and workshops. Factory owners subcontract the jobs of moulding, polishing and electroplating to workshops where child labour is freely used and abused.

It is generally made out that child labour in the brassware industry of Moradabad is a part of family labour because Child Labour Act of 1986 does not apply to those children who work as part of family labour. Almost all children work as wage labour.

A survey conducted among 606 working children in this industry shows that majority of child workers are in the age group of 6 to 14 years. Caste-wise classification of working children shows that 76 percent of the children are from other backward classes, 4 percent children are from schedule caste and 20 percent are from upper caste.[18]

Working Conditions of Children in Brassware Industry

Children are recruited by middlemen who usually belong to the same village and get a commission for bringing child workers. Parents are given an advance, which is adjusted against the wages of the children to induce them to send their children to work.

Children work in dingy workshops with very poor sanitary facilities and are exposed to serious hazards. The work involves plenty of metal debris which falls from the moulds or is scrapped from the rough product. The air is laden with dust which is constantly breathed in by the children. Children sit in the same positions for 6 to 7 hours continuously.

Fifty percent of workers involved in moulding in the box furnace workshops are children. Their main job is to rotate the wheel which fans the underground furnace. This is the first job given to a new child recruit. Another category of children heat the oblong ignot on top of the furnace, break it into small pieces with a small hammer and melt the required amount of brass. When the molten brass is ready, the child lifts the graphite crucible containing the raw material with his bare hands and long tongs and passes it to the adult worker. Often the job of the child who rotates the wheel also includes that of removing the crucible from the furnace and vice versa. Both the child who rotates the wheel and the child who removes the crucible help grind the hot black mixture into a fine powder with their bare hands and help remove the hot moulded metal from the moulds. On an average, children do this work for continuously 10 hours a day.[19]

The other process in which large number of children are working is polishing the semi-finished goods. Here out of 25,000 workers, 12,000 are children. Children apply chemicals on the wares to be polished, put emery powder on the used buffs so that they could be used again.[20]

There are about 10,000 workers engaged in welding, of whom 7,000 are children. Children generally work as helpers to adults. While the adults wear protective glasses to shield their eyes from flying sparks, children sitting close to the adults and watching them do not use protective glasses. The workshops where welding is carried out are very small and there is not enough space on the workshop floor. Cylinders often explode, causing injury to children. Children working in welding workshops are very young, mostly in the age group of 6 to 9 years. They work for 8 to 10 hours per day, with one weekly holiday.[21]

Salaries, daily wages and piece rates are the three modes of payment in this industry. The number of salaried employees is negligible. Wages are generally paid on piece rate basis and in some workshops daily wage system is followed. The wage that a child earns depends on the degree of his skill. Children on an average earn Rs. 174 per month.[22]

The two most hazardous processes in the brassware industry are moulding and polishing and it is in these two processes that child labour is all pervasive. Electroplating and welding are equally hazardous. The work in the box mould furnace workshops is extremely dangerous where the child has to rotate the wheel to keep the furnace burning. After the temperature has reached a certain level, the child tests it by opening the top of the underground furnace and throwing a little powder into it. Once the raw material and the molten glass is ready, flames shoot up from the mouth of the furnace. The child lifts the crucible of molten brass from the furnace and hands it to the adult worker. Moulding is a very delicate operation and if there is a slight mistake or accident the child can get very badly injured and can even lose his limbs. Children are not provided with any protective gear and stand barefoot on top of the furnace. If a drop of molten brass falls on the child's foot, there will be a hole in it. The child is not only in danger of getting badly hurt but the constan inhalation of fumes and gases from the furnace leads quite often to tuberculosis and other respiratory tract problems. The combination of poor nutrition and bad working conditions reduces the life of workers by half. They become too ill to work by the time they reach adulthood.

Children who work on polishing machines are also at considerable risk. They inhale all the metal dust and their bodies often bear the marks of acid burns. The room where this work is done is filled with vapours rising from the acid tubs. The stench is tremendous and the eyes burn. Those working in these units get chest diseases and often suffocate to death. Local doctors are reluctant to talk of health hazards for fear of getting into trouble. It is apparent that majority of child workers in the brassware industry are engaged in intrinsically hazardous occupations.

Educational Status of Child Workers in Brassware Industries

The study conducted on a sample of 606 children reports that 70 percent of child workers are illiterate and 23 percent have attended school till the primary level. In the sample, only 7 percent of the working children are still attending school.

Hidden behind the sparkle of brassware goods manufactured in this industry lies the tale of children being exploited by their parents, workshop owners and exporters.

The above analysis of child labour in select industries reveals that children are employed in large numbers in these industries because the employers have a vested interest in employing children as cheap and docile labour. Children work for long hours under appalling conditions in these industries and are exposed to several occupational hazards. Labour laws are openly flouted in these industries. Children in these industries work at the cost of their physical, social and mental well-being. The analysis of these industries highlights the inhuman nature of the practice of child labour and the blatant violation of the rights of the children working in these industries.

NOTES

1. Smitu, Kothari, *"There is Blood on these Matchsticks"-Child Labour in Sivakasi* (Economic and Political Weekly, Vol XVIII, No 47,July 2, 1983, p.1194.
2. Halen Seker, *No light in their Lives-Girl Child in the Match Industry of Sivakasi* (Noida: National Labour Institute, 1993) p.9.
3. Smitu, Kothari, *op.cit* p. 1191.
4. *Child Labour in Match Industry of Sivakasi* (Noida: Child Labour Cell, 1993) p.9.
5. Vishwapriya Iyengar "Pyre of Childhood:Child Workers in the Match Factories of Sivakasi" in Manju Gupta and Klauss Voll (eds.)., Young Hands at Work, (New Delhi; Atma Ram and Sons, 1987) p. 29.
6. Planning Commission, Child Labour in Match Industry of Sivakasi(Planning Commission, unpublished, 1992) p.40
7. B. N. Juyal, *Child Labour and Exploitation in the Carpet Industry—A Mirzapur-Bhadoi Case Study* (New Delhi: Indian Social Institute, 1986) p.27.
8. B. N. Juyal, Child Labour in the Carpet Industry in Mirzapur-Bhadoi-ASituational Analysis and Evaluation of the Government of India's National Child Labour Project, (New Delhi: ILO, 1993) p.5.
9. A. N. Singh, *Child Labour in India-Socio-Economic Perspectives* (New Delhi: Shipra Publications, 1990).pp. 132-136
10. Prembhai, Report to the Supreme Court on the Carpet Weavers of Mirzapur-Bhadoi (Unpublished, 1984) p.150.
11. M. F. Ahmad, "Five U.P Child Labourers Rescued", The Times of India, April 14, 1994
12. G.P.Mishra and P.N.Pande, Child Labour in Carpet Industry of Mirzapur—study sponsored by Planning Commission. Unpublished 1992) pp. 82-90
13. *ibid*; pp.19-20
14. Neera Burra, "Glass Factory of Ferozabad II-Plight of Workers" (Economic and Political Weekly, Vol XXI, No 47, November 22, 1986, p.2033.
15. G.P.Mishra and P.N.Pande, *op cit.*, p. 95.
16. *Child Labour in the Brassware Industry of Moradabad,* (Noida: Child Labour Cell, 1992).p.1.

17. *Ibid;* p.67.
18 *Planning Commission, Child Labour in Brassware Industry of Moradabad—Study sponsored by Planning Commission (Unpublished, 1992)* p.20, 23.
19. *Child Labour in the Brassware Industry of Moradabad, op. cit,* p.12.
20 *Ibid*
21. *Planning Commission, Child Labour in Brassware Industry of Moradabad, op. cit,* p.24
22. *Ibid.*

V

National Legislation and Action against Child Labour in India

The problem of child labour can be traced to the Industrial Revolution which began in the mid 18th and 19th century. Though children always participated in economic activities, their workplace was an extension of home and children were not given hazardous tasks. However, with the advent of industrialization, the family-based economy was destroyed and a large number of labourers displaced due to mechanisation of agriculture. Labour now became a marketable commodity. Extreme poverty led to the entry of the child into the labour market and exploitation of children became common. In India, too, children were employed in cotton and jute mills and coal mines. Gradually, legal measures were introduced to tackle the problem of child labour and the state assumed the responsibility of protecting children.

Action Taken before Independence

The Indian Government adopted constitutional, statutory and developmental measures to deal with the problem of child labour. The origin of statutory protection of the child worker in India can be traced back to the Indian Factories Act,1881. The Act prohibited employment of children under seven years of age and also in two separate factories on the same day. It limited the working hours of children to nine hours a day and stipulated that at least four holidays be given in a month. However, this Act covered only factories employing 100 persons or more. In 1891 this Act was revised. The Indian Factories Act, 1891, increased the minimum age limit to nine years and the hours of work were reduced to seven hours for children between 7 and 14 years. It also prohibited work at night between 8 p.m. and 5 a.m[1]. In 1901, the Mines Act was passed, which prohibited the employment of children under 12 years of age and employment dangerous to children's health and safety. In 1911. a new factories act was passed which reduced the working hours of children in factories to 6 hours a day. The Act prohibited work between 7 pm and 5.30 a.m. by children. It further provided that all child workers should possess age and fitness for employment certificate.[2] However, these measures provided very little protection to child workers. These measures were quite inadequate because they paid very little attention to the unorganised sector of industries.

In the period between 1920 and 1930 some more progress was made in protecting children. The formation of the International Labour Organisation in 1919 and the establishment of the All India Trade Union Congress in 1920 gave an impetus to reform laws relating to condition of labour in general and child labour in particular. During this period, measures were taken to give increased protection to children working in factories, mines and ports. By the Factories Act, 1922, the scope of factory was extended to cover any premise where 20 or more persons were employed and mechanised power was used. The local governments were empowered to extend the provisions to any premise where 10 or more persons were employed. This Act defined a child as a person who had not completed 15 years of age. It reduced the working hours of children to six and and necessitated the granting of a half an hour interval for children employed for more than five-and-a-half hours. Children were required by this Act to have a medical certificate along with a certificate of re-examination for continuing work[3]. The Indian Mines Act, 1923, raised the minimum age for employment from 12 to 13 years in mines. The Indian Ports (Amendment) Act, 1931, prescribed the minimum age for employment of children in handling goods in ports as 12 years.[4]

In the period between 1931 and 1949, more concerted efforts were made to deal with child labour. The scene was set with the publication of the report of the Royal Commission for Labour, which recommended extensive reforms. The Tea Districts Emigrant Labour

Act, 1932, was passed to check the migration of labour to the tea cultivating districts. One of its provisions laid down that no child under 16 should be employed or allowed to migrate to districts with tea plantations, unless the child is accompanied by his parents or other adult relative on whom the child is dependent[5]. In 1933, the Children (Pledging of Labour) Act was passed which prohibited the pledging of a child for the purpose of getting certain work done[6]. Factory legislation also underwent changes as a result of the Report of Royal Commission of Labour. The Factories Act of 1934 evolved elaborate provisions regularising employment in respect of various age groups working in factories. It prohibited employment of children under 12, restricted employment of children between 12 and 15 years to five hours a day and imposed certain restrictions on children between 15 and 17 years.[7]

The ILO in 1937 adopted a convention fixing a minimum age at which children were to be employed in certain occupations. The Employment of Children Act, 1938, was passed to implement this convention. It prohibited employment of children under 15 in hazardous occupations like railways and ports. It also dealt with employment in industrial establishments not covered by the Factories Act. Though the 1938 Act banned child labour in hazardous industries, it made an exception in favour of family labour.

Before independence, the law relating to the employment of children in various sectors had failed to achieve its goal—the elimination of the evils of child labour. A Labour Investigating Committee, instituted to examine the state of Indian labour in depth, in its report in 1946 pointed out that the main cause for this failure was the inadequacy of the inspecting staff to enforce the provisions of law.[8]

Action Taken after Independence

After Independence, the Factories Act, 1948, was passed, raising the minimum age for employment in factories to 14 years. The Act prohibited the employment of children between 14 and 17 years at night (between 10 pm and 6.00 am), between 14 and 15 years for not more than four-and-a-half hours in any day. It lays down that a child cannot be employed in two shifts and cannot be allowed to work in more than one factory on the same day. The Act required workers between the age of 14 and 18 years to obtain a certificate of fitness from a certifying surgeon and periodic examination. They were not allowed to work on machines that are considered dangerous. However, the Factories Act did not apply to such factories where there are less than 10 workers with power and less than 20 workers without the aid of power.[9]

The minimum Wages Act, passed in 1948, specified that the expression "adult", "adolescent" and "child" will have meaning assigned to them. It defined "child" as a person who has not completed his 15th year. However, this definition did not have any particular significance since the Act did not contain any important regulatory or prohibitory provision applicable only to child labour, except that it provides that in fixing or revising minimum rates of wages, different minimum rates of wages may be fixed for adults, adolescents, children and apprentices.[10]

At the time of the framing of the Indian Constitution the issue of child labour was not overlooked. In fact, it was brought to the forefront by the framers of the Constitution, who consciously incorporated provisions to ensure well-being of children. The protection of children below the age of 14 years was incorporated in the Constitution as a guaranteed and enforceable right in Part III of the Indian Constitution dealing with Fundamental Rights. Under Part III, Article 24 states: "No child below the age of 14 years shall be employed to work in any factory or mine or engaged in any hazardous employment". Even Article 23 deals with child labour since it prohibits traffic in human beings and beggars and other similar forms of forced labour. It is relevant in this context since children constitute a substantial part of "forced labour" prohibited under Article 23.

The framers of the Indian Constitution also incorporated provisions relating to child labour in Part IV of the Constitution dealing with Directive Principles of State Policy. Under Part IV, Article 39, Clause (c) provides that the health and strength of workers, men and women and tender age of children should not be abused and the citizens should not be forced by economic necessity to enter vocations unsuited to their age and strength. Similarly, Clause (f) of the same article states that the State shall, in particular, direct its policy towards securing that children are given opportunity and facilities to develop in a healthy manner and in conditions of freedom and dignity and that childhood and youth are protected against exploitation and against moral and material abandonment. Article 45 contains another directive which cannot be separated from the issue of child labour. It was laid down as far back as 1950 that the State shall endeavour to provide by the year 1960 free and compulsory education for all children until they complete the age of 14 years. The Government of India has not honoured this pledge even at the end of the century.

Reading of Article 24, along with the guidelines contained in Articles 39 and 45, makes it abundantly clear that employment of children is prohibited by the Constitution. Yet the practice of child labour continues unabated, in defiance of the constitutional mandate and vision.

In 1951, the Plantations Labour Act was passed to prevent the employment of children under 12 years in plantations. In 1952, the Mines Act was passed, which prohibited the employment of children under 15 in mines. An adolescent could be employed for underground work as adult on the satisfaction of 2 conditions—first, he must have completed 16 years of age and secondly, he must have a certificate of fitness from a surgeon.[11]

In 1954, the Factories Act was again amended to prohibit the employment of adolescents under the age of 17 years at night. "Night" under this Act meant a period of 12 consecutive hours which included the hours between 10 pm and 7 am. By the Merchant Shipping Act, 1958, children under 15 were prohibited to be engaged or carried to sea to work in any capacity in any ship except in certain specific cases.[12]

In 1961, the Motor Transport Workers Act was passed to prohibit the employment of children under 15 in motor transport undertakings. In the same year, the Apprentice Act was passed for regulating and controlling of trainees. This Act was amended in 1973. The Act prohibited the undergoing of apprenticeship training of a person under 14. In 1966, the *Beedi* and Cigar Workers (Conditions of Employment) Act, was passed. It prohibited the employment of children under 14 in any industrial premise manufacturing *beedis* or cigars. Young persons between 14 and 18 were also prohibited to work at night between 7 pm and 6 am in such establishments.[13]

In 1978, the Employment of Children Act, 1938 was further amended so as to extend the prohibition of employment of a child below 15 years in railway premises, such as cinder-picking or clearing of an ashpit or building operation, in catering establishments at a railway station or in occupations relating to construction of a railway station or any other work done in close proximity to or between the railway lines. These occupations were not covered before 1978[14]

The various central laws mentioned above were not laws on child labour. They either related to employment in general or were confined to certain specified employments. These laws were not passed with a focus on child labour in general but with reference to regulate employment in a particular industry as and when the need arose.

In addition to these Central Acts, the states passed various shops and commercial establishment acts for their respective states. In these acts, the minimum age of employment on shops and commercial establishment varies from 12 to 15 years.

Child labour has been a subject of various committees, commissions and boards. In 1968, a National Commission on Labour Welfare was instituted. The National Commission on Labour observed that child labour was an economic problem and its practice amounted to a denial of opportunity to children for their proper physical development and education. The Commission noted that although the economic difficulties faced by the poor and their children were real, it was necessary to provide children education in their more receptive years. It recommended combination of work with education and flexible employment hours which would not inhibit education.[15]

A National Children's Board was established in 1975, with the Prime Minister as its president to create greater public awareness towards the needs of children and to plan and review periodically the progress made in protecting and promoting the welfare of children, including working children.

In 1976, the Government set up a one-man Commission headed by Harbans Singh, former Member, Board of Revenue, to investigate the problems of child labour in various factories and industries in Ramanathapuram District of Tamil Nadu. The report was submitted in 1977 and was not made public.

The report states that 40 to 45 percent of the total labour force employed in the match industry, are children. Girls outnumber boys by three to one. Children are employed longer than the stipulated hours of work, namely four-and-a-half hours per day. The children spend nearly 16 hours away from home. Accidents are a common occurrence in the area. "The provisions of both the Factories Act and Employment of Children Act are being violated with impunity". The Commission admits that factory owners face only "nominal" punishment if caught violating the provisions of the above acts.[16] Accepting that banning child labour would not necessarily result in the stoppage of work by children altogether, the report suggests that working hours should be reduced, wages increased and coupled with incentives for production. However, none of the conclusions and recommendations suggest radical measures to end the scourge of child labour. In fact, the report is more concerned about the match industry's health than that of the children. The bias is clear when it points out that child labour is an economic problem and should be tackled accordingly without causing hardships to the parents or the industries.[17]

Work of the Ministry of Labour

The Ministry of Labour appointed a 16-member Committee under the Chairmanship of M.S. Gurupadswamy in 1979 to investigate the causes leading to child labour and examine the problems arising out of the employment of children. The Committee made an in-depth study on the nature and extent of the problem, adequacy of existing laws and the supportive measures necessary to help the working children and eliminate child labour in the long run.

The Committee formulated a questionnaire to elicit information on the various issues connected with child labour from the public, Members of Parliament and state legislatures, representatives of trade unions, employers organisations, prominent social workers, university teachers, education experts, etc.

The Committee noted that the "existing situation in respect of child labour in India can still be summarised as one of continuing drift. Though there is little evidence of children at work in the organised sector of industry in certain pockets of the country, the over-all position is as had been observed by the Whitley Commission nearly 50 years ago. Bulk of the children continue to be employed in the rural environment. While most of them work without wages, there is an increasing number amongst them of children employed for wages and also of many working on jobs which are hazardous. They handle dangerous chemicals (pesticides, fertilizers, etc.) and they are also employed on machines with sharp edges and blades. Definite efforts are called for to prohibit their working in such occupations. Quite a large number of children residing in rural areas are also employed in cottage industries where again the regulation by law is minimal, and the positive adjuncts which ought to be there to help the working children are not at all institutionalised. There is still large scale migration of children from rural areas to urban areas. These children take to employment in smaller establishments in cities under varying exploitative conditions. The regulation by law of employment of children covers only fringe of these occupations and ironically even where regulation has been sought, the enforcement is extremely half-hearted and tardy".[18]

The Committee observed that the existing legal framework for employment of children is dispersed and patchy. This has been one of the prime reasons for a missing focus in the efforts which have so far been made to regulate the employment of children in some of the sectors of economic activity. The Committee was unable to locate in most cases, the precise rationale for the varying definitions of the term 'child' for the purpose of employment. Of the 10 major Acts which include provisions relating to employment of children, five have defined 'child' as below 15 years of age, three provide for the age of 14 and one provides the ages between 12 and 14. The Committee also noticed variations in the adoption of some Acts by different state governments. The reference to employment of children in many of these enactments is so mixed up in the quagmire of other matters and requirements that the kind of emphasis which is intended in respect of children is more or less lost. In most cases data on child labour was not forthcoming from state governments. There was hardly any administrative mode available of any prosecution having been made for violation of the provisions in Acts relating to employment of children. The annual reports relating to administration of such laws also contained hardly any mention about this aspect.[19]

Considering the situation, the Committee strongly put forth the view that there is a paramount need for urgent action on the part of the Government to bring the law relating to children in proper focus. To avoid any ambiguity in respect of the basic objectives in this direction, it called for consolidation of existing laws relating to prohibition and regulation of employment of children into a single comprehensive one. The new legislation should adopt uniform definitions of the expressions 'child' and 'adolescent' and prescribe 'hours of work', 'conditions of work' etc. The Committee recommended that the minimum age for entry to any employment should be 15. The new law should also have the flexibility of extending to other occupations, such as, mechanised agriculture, horticulture, forestry, fisheries, etc.

The Committee emphasised that enactment of a law is only a first step. What is really important is its enforcement. The Committee found several inadequacies in the existing set up for the implementation of various laws. It reiterated that the task of enforcement cannot be entirely handled by the government machinery. It called for greater involvement of the society at large and voluntary organisations and trade unions in particular. It also called for more stringent penalties for violation of provisions relating to child labour. It recommended the constitution of advisory boards both at the Centre and State levels to keep a constant surveillance on the conditions of working children. Various supportive measures were suggested by the Committee to deal with the problem of child labour. These included removal of poverty and unemployment, ensuring minimum wages, meaningful education policy whereby the curriculum takes note of the actual environmental needs, medical and health support, providing supplementary nutrition to working children, housing facilities, recreation and cultural activities and protection from health hazards.

In pursuance of one of the recommendations of the Committee on child labour, the Central Advisory Board on Child Labour was set up in March, 1981 to review the implementation of existing legislation, suggest legislative as well as welfare measures for working children, review the progress of welfare measures for working children recommend the industries and areas where there must be a progressive elimination of child labour. It was reconstituted in 1987 under the chairmanship of Minister of Labour to render advice on the problems of child labour.

Child Labour (Prohibition and Regulation) Act, 1986

The Child Labour (Prohibition and Regulation) Act was passed in December, 1986. This Act repealed the Employment of Children's Act, 1938, but repealed its Schedules A and B. All rules made in this Act were in addition to the Factories Act, 1948, the Plantation Labour Act, 1951 and the Mines Act, 1951.

The Act was passed to prohibit the employment of children in hazardous jobs and to regulate the conditions of work for children in other jobs of non-hazardous nature.

The Act bans the employment of children, that is, a person who has not completed his fourteenth year of age, in occupations connected with:

(1) Transport of passengers, goods or mail by railway;
(2) Cinder picking, clearing of an ash pit or building operation in the railway premises;
(3) Work in catering establishment at a railway station;
(4) Work relating to the construction of a railway station or when any work is done in close proximity to or between the railway lines;

(5) A port authority within the limits of any port.

It also bans the entry of children in the following processes. *Beedi* making, carpet weaving; cement manufacturing including bagging of cement; cloth printing, dyeing and weaving; manufacture of matches, explosive and fireworks; mica cutting and splitting; shellac manufacturing; soap manufacture; tanning; wool-cleaning; building and construction industry.[20]

Notifications were issued in 1989 and 1993 and the government also prohibited employment of children in the following occupations and processes: Work relating to selling of crackers and fireworks in shops with temporary licences, abattoirs slaughter houses; manufacture of slate pencils (including packing), manufacture of products from agate, manufacturing processes using toxic metals and substances such as lead, mercury, manganese, chromium, cadmium, benzene, pesticides and asbestos; hazardous processes as defined in Section 2 and 'dangerous operations' as notified under Section 87 of the Factories Act, 1948; printing; cashew and cashewnut descaling and processing and soldering processes in electronic industries.[21]

The Act regulates the conditions of work of children in employment where they are not prohibited from working. It lays down that no child shall be allowed to work more than 6 hours per day with a rest interval for at least one hour after 3 hours of work. Every child employed in an establishment shall be given a weekly holiday. No child will be allowed to work between 7 pm and 8 am and no overtime will be permitted.

The Act states that the government can make rules for the health and safety of children who are permitted to work in any establishment. These rules provide for matters like cleanliness, ventilation, disposal of waste, dust and fume, lighting, drinking water, sanitary facilities, safety precautions, etc.

The 1986 Act provides for more stringent penalties for violation of the Act. It provides that whoever employs a child in contravention of Section 3, that is, in prohibited employment, shall be punished with imprisonment of not less than 3 months but which extends to one year or with fine which shall not be less than Rs. 10,000 but which extends to Rs. 20,000 or both. For other violations, that is violation of regulatory provisions, the punishment laid down is imprisonment of one month or imposition of fine upto Rs. 10,000 or both. It also provides that any person, besides a police officer or an inspector, can file a complaint regarding commission of offences.These complaints have to be filed with a court not inferior to that of a Metropolitan Magistrate or a Magistrate of the first class.

While the 1986 Act provides a uniform definition of 'child' by replacing the definition in all other acts by defining a 'child' as a person who has not completed his fourteenth year of age, it has resulted in lowering the age of a child's entry from 15 to 14 into some employments like motor transport, merchant shipping and factories. The Minimum Wages Act, 1948, Merchant Shipping Act, 1958 and the Motor Transport Workers Act, 1961, had defined 'child' as a person below 15 years of age. The 1986 Act also does not include Section 3(2) of the 1938 Act which prohibited night employment of persons below 7 years of age.

The 1986 Act does not ban child labour in the family. However, it restricts the definition of family to parent, children, brother and sister as against the much broader definition of the 1938 Act. Section 3 of the Act also does not prohibit the employment of children in hazardous occupation or processes provided the process is carried out by the occupier (person who has ultimate control over the establishment or workshop) with the aid of his family or to any school established by or receiving assistance or recognition from the government. This provision is susceptible to abuse. It has offered protection to several carpet-weaving units, match units, glass units etc. to continue exploitation of children under the guise of the family. Moreover, once an occupation or process has been identified as hazardous for children, there is no justification or rationale in exempting family-based units from employing children.

The 1986 Act does not include several processes which are hazardous for children. The Act does not include industries like lock industry, balloon industry, pottery industry and several others in its list of prohibited occupations and processes even though children are forced to work in these industries with dangerous chemicals and machines. The agricultural sector, which constitutes 80 percent of child labour, also appears to be outside the regulatory reach of the Act. This Act also does not specify the minimum age of employment of children in occupations and processes other than the prohibited ones.

The word "occupier" in the 1986 Act is defined as a person who has ultimate control over the affairs of the establishment or workshop. This definition needs to be expanded to include agents and contractors who are responsible for employing children.

It is important to note that the 1986 Act omits Section 3 (B) of the Employment of Children Act, 1938, requiring that a notice be sent to the inspector before any of the prohibited processes are started in any workshop, regarding the name and situation of the workshop, the name of the person in actual management the address for communication, and the nature of processes to be carried on in the workshop. As a result of this omission, the burden of tracking down such processes is now shifted to an under-staffed and ill-equipped Labour Inspectorate or private individuals. Second, the provision of a mandatory notice would have acted as a deterrent to some extent against employing children.[22]

While the 1986 Act does prohibit child labour in certain sectors and regulates the conditions of working children in other employments, it does not include provisions for education, healthcare, nutrition, etc.

Inspite of all these laws children continue to work in prohibited occupations and there is very little regulation of child labour in non-prohibited areas of employment. One of the major reasons appears to be ineffective implementation of child labour laws in our country.

Over the years there has been a shift in the employment of children from the organised sector into the unorganised sector. Owners of small-scale establishments keep the number of workers employed by them below 10 so that their establishment does not fall within the purview of the Factories Act, 1948 or let out or subcontract several processes to family-based units since the 1986 Act exempts such units. This is common in several industries such as match industry of Sivakasi, glass industry of Firozabad and carpet-weaving industry of Mirzapur-Bhadoi.

It is difficult to enforce labour laws in the unorganised sector because the units are unregistered and large in number and scattered over a wide area. The number of labour inspectors is also extremely low. There are other practical problems as well. When the inspectors visit an area where there is a concentration of units employing child labour, he may find children physically present and at work only in the first one or two units visited. In all the other units child workers are made to disappear or hidden away on learning of the inspectors visit. Where the inspector does manage to find children employed in a particular establishment in violation of the law and takes up prosecution, he then faces many legal difficulties. When the unit is small, the claim often made in court is that the child workers are the children of the family and are therefore covered by the exemption under the Child Labour(P and R) Act. In other larger units, it is often claimed by the employer that the children are present only for the purpose of meeting their parents or bringing their lunch etc. Since there is usually no documentary evidence to prove that the child is working in a unit, prosecution becomes difficult. Another aspect, crucial in prosecution, is the age of the child. Most laws relating to child labour specify the minimum age of entry into employment to be 14 years. However, since birth certificates are not common in the rural areas or among the poorer people in India, a medical certificate of the child's age is required to be kept by the employer. Where this is not available, the inspector has to get the child medically examined at the employer's cost. All this requires time and money. Even when convicted, the employers are let off by the courts with nominal fines.[23]

Another significant reason responsible for lack of enforcement of child labour is the prevailing attitudes and perceptions of the parents of working children, employers, law-makers, law-enforcers and society at large. It is widely believed that there is nothing wrong in employing children, it in fact helps to alleviate the poverty of the child's family and helps impart skills to children for their future lives.

The government proposes to amend the Child Labour (P and R) Act, 1986, in order to strengthen and streamline the prohibitory and regulatory provisions of the Act to ensure effective implementation. The following amendments are on the anvil.

- Section 16 is to be amended for more effective implementation of Act. The Act is proposed to be amended to provide for summary trial by Executive Magistrates in case of violation of the prohibitory provisions, which are proposed to be made a cognizable offence.
- Section 17 is to be amended to shift the burden of proof of the age of the children employed from the prosecution to the employer in line with similar provisions existing in the Factories Act and the *Beedi* and Cigar Workers Act. Thus the burden shall be on the accused to prove that child labourers working with the accused is not under the prescribed age.
- Section 20 is to be amended so that the more stringent penalty of the Child Labour (P and R) Act will be made applicable in case of violations of four Central Acts, namely, the *Beedi* and Cigar Workers (Conditions of Employment) Act, 1966, Bonded Labour System (Abolition) Act, 1976, Plantation Labour Act, 1951 and Contract Labour (Regulation and Abolition) Act, 1970.
- Section 2(iv) defining establishments is proposed to be amended

to extend the scope of the protective provisions to progressively cover more activities in which child labour is likely to be engaged. This is an enabling provision to add additional types of work places, if necessary. This enabling provision is currently absent in the definition.

- Section 2(vi) casts a responsibility on tne "Occupier" of the establishments to comply with its provisions in employments such as carpet, *beedi*, matches etc. While children are employed in large numbers, they may not be directly under the main principal employer. Section 2 (vi) is sought to be amended, casting responsibility on the principal employers clearly by amplifying the present definition of the term "Occupier".
- In order to discourage employers from engaging children because of existing lower rates of wages fixed for children, amendment to the Minimum Wages Act is also proposed by a reference doing away with the present provisions under the Act which permitted different rates of minimum wages to be fixed for child workers.

These recommendations are aimed at giving the Act more teeth. Though these recommendations are commendable, it is doubtful if they will be effectively enforced. The proposal to make the use of child labour a cognizable offence is praiseworthy but the past record of law enforcement shows that the guilty are generally let off.

The proposal to provide equal wages to children has been viewed with scepticism. In a country where even adult workers do not get minimum wages, it is difficult to imagine how this proposal to provide equal wages to children will be implemented.

Above all, the government has opted for a go-slow and conservative approach in its proposed amendments by not prohibiting child labour in hazardous industries in family-based and government-aided and recognized schools. It is therefore not surprising that the Cabinet approval of these amendments in 1994 failed to evoke any great elation amongst the crusaders for abolition of child labour. Moreover, legislation by itself cannot bring about a radical transformation in the prevalence of child labour.

National Policy on Child Labour

Keeping in mind the fact that legislation alone would not be sufficient to deal with the problem of exploitation of child labour, the government announced a three-prolonged National Policy on Child Labour in August 1987. The action plan of this policy has been set out under the following headings;

1. Legislative Action Plan.
2. The focussing of general development programmes for benefitting child labour wherever possible.
3. Project-based plan of action in areas of high concentration of child labour engaged in wage and quasi-wage employment.

Under the Legislative Action Plan a Child Labour Technical Advisory Committee has been set up to advise the Central Government on addition of occupations and processes to the schedule contained in the Child Labour (Prohibition and Regulation) Act, 1986. The provisions of the Factories Act, 1948; the Mines Act, 1951 and the Child Labour (P and R) Act, 1986 are to be enforced to ensure that children are not employed in hazardous employment and to regulate their work in non-hazardous employments. The State and Central government departments are to review the situation in order to ensure that child labour is not employed in prohibited occupations and in non-prohibited employments the provisions set out for their health and safety, for the maintenance of registers and for regulating the period of work or overtime or of weekly holidays and days of rest are enforced in all establishments.[24]

Since National Development Programmes exist with very wide coverage, in order to have an impact on child labour it was decided to focus general development programmes for the benefit of child workers in areas such as education , health, nutrition and coverage by anti-poverty programmes.

The National Education Policy aims at universalizing primary education by the year 2000 (modified target) through an expansion of formal and non-formal education system. Non-formal education centres for child labour are to be set up with the involvement of voluntary agencies and panchayati raj institutions. Non-formal education centres are expected to play an important role in enrolling and retaining working children, particularly girls. Part time and vocational courses will also be imparted at these centres. Such non-formal education centres for working children would aim to educate children upto class V level, with arrangements for continuance of non-formal education upto class VIII level wherever possible. Incentives and assistance will be given to child labour belonging to disadvantaged classes like SC/ST families whose children work for wage quasi-wage employment. There is a provision for micro planning for non-formal education centres for child labour, especially for those belonging to disadvantaged sections. Efforts will also be made to link the non-formal educational institutions with open schools or with the formal education system in order to enable working children to continue their education.

Since health is a state subject, state governments will be recommended to undertake intensive medical inspection of children in those areas where child labour is prevalent. The state governments will be persuaded to extend the coverage of the school health services programme to child labour. There is also provision to arrange for health screening at non-formal education centres for child labour.

Families which have child labour will be included in poverty-alleviation programmes like IRDP/NREP/RLEGP etc. to enable them to raise themselves above the poverty line. Proposals from state governments, non-governmental organisations and voluntary organisations for taking up nutritional and other programmes in child labour areas will be funded on a priority basis.

Under the project based plan of action, specific sectors of employment where the incidence of child labour is high have been identified. These are:

(1) The match industry in Sivakasi, Tamil Nadu.
(2) The diamond polishing industry in Surat, Gujarat.
(3) The precious stone polishing industry in Jaipur, Rajasthan.
(4) The glass industry in Firozabad, Uttar Pradesh.
(5) The brassware industry in Moradabad, Uttar Pradesh.
(6) The handmade carpet industry in Mirzapur-Bhadoi, Uttar Pradesh.
(7) The lock industry in Aligarh, Uttar Pradesh.
(8) The handmade carpet industry in Jammu and Kashmir.
(9) The slate industry in Mandsaur, Madhya Pradesh
(10) The slate industry in Markapur, Andhra Pradesh

Projects for children working in the handmade carpet industry in Jammu and Kashmir and diamond polishing in Surat, Gujarat, originally included in the NCLP, could not be started. In addition, a project for the children working in the tile industry in Jaggampet, Andhra Pradesh, has been sanctioned. Four more projects have been sanctioned in March, 1994. They are :

(1) Carpet-weaving industry in Garhwa, Bihar.
(2) *Beedi* industry in Sambalpur district, Orissa.
(3) Brass imdustry in Jamnagar, Bihar
(4) Tribal children, agriculture and chemical industry in Thane district, Maharashtra.

The main thrust of the National Child Labour Project is to reduce the incidence of child labour in the project area, thereby encouraging the elimination of child labour progressively. In each of the project areas the strategy is to evolve a package comprising the following elements:

1. Stepping up the enforcement of Child Labour (P & R) Act, 1986 and the Factories Act, 1948.
2. Coverage of families of child labour under the income employment generation programmes under the overall aegis of anti-poverty programmes.
3. Where there is a concentration of SC/ST families with child labour, a concentration of special component and tribal sub-plans by the state governments in each project area.
4. Formal and non-formal education of child labour and adult education of the parents of the working children.
5. Coordinating the activities of different departments/ministries of the Central and State governments to benefit child labour.
6. Setting up of special schools for child workers together with provisions of vocational education/training in such special schools, supplementary nutrition, a stipend for the children taken out from prohibited employments and health care for all children attending such special schools.

The first phase of the special project-based plan was expected to cover 30,000 working children.

At the national level, the programme is carried out under the auspicies of the Ministry of Labour. For initiating a new National Child Labour Project in any area/industry, the concerned state government is required to submit a detailed proposal to the Central government (Ministry of Labour). A Central Monitoring Committee has been set up for overall supervision and evaluation of various child labour projects under the National Child Labour policy. Representatives of concerned Central Ministers/State governments and projects are included in the Committee.

During the Seventh Plan period, the outlay on these projects was Rs. 493 lakhs. The outlay envisaged for the Eighth Plan is Rs. 15 crores. For the year 1995-96, the Planning Commission had allotted Rs. 34.40 crores with assurance of more funds, depending upon performance.

The Ministry of Labour has been financing, since 1981-82, voluntary organisations by way of grant-in-aid for taking up action-oriented projects for the benefit of child labour and women labour. Voluntary agencies are being financially assisted to the extent of 75 percent for taking up welfare projects for working children under the grant-in-aid scheme. During 1994-95, financial assistance was given to 11 voluntary organisations in the field of child labour for implementation of projects for the welfare of working children to provide non-formal education, supplementary nutrition, health care and vocational skills/training

The initiation of the project-based plan of action, under the auspices of the NCLP, is indeed a step in the right direction. However, the project-based plan of action does not cover several areas and industries where the incidence of child labour is high and the working conditions hazardous. Among such industries are:

(1) Balloon industry of Dhanu district, Maharashtra
(2) Zari industry of Lucknow and Delhi
(3) Pottery industry in Khurja
(4) Powerloom industry of Bhiwandi, Mumbai etc.

Moreover, the scope and implementation of the project-based plan of action has left a lot to be desired. The first phase of the project-based plan was expected to cover 30,000 working children. However, so far only 14,800 children have been covered under the 12 NCLP projects under implementation in 8 states.[25] A major activity undertaken under the NCLP is establishment of special schools to provide basic facilities like non-formal education, vocational training, supplementary nutrition, etc. to the children withdrawn from employment. However, so far only 167 schools have been sanctioned under 13 projects, covering only 14,500 children.[26]

Sivakasi National Child Labour Project

A study conducted into the working of the Sivakasi National Child

Labour Project concluded that the project had not achieved much success in eliminating child labour from the industry. Though the main thrust of the project was to reduce the incidence of child labour, the number of working children has not perceptibly decreased in the past few years. Inspections by factory inspectors have made an impact in reducing child labour from the bigger factories. However, a large number of children continue to be employed in the smaller units to which the Factories Act does not apply. Despite the shortage of inspectors, however, the number of inspections and prosecutions have increased. In the period from 1987 to 1992, 107 prosecutions were launched, in 1993, 66 prosecutions were launched and upto 30 June 1994, 64 prosecutions were launched. While the earlier prosecutions all ended in acquittals, several cases in the recent past have ended in conviction. However, only the minimum penalty has been imposed.[27] In the area of non-formal education, 100 non-formal education centres were started but were subsequently wound up. The only activity that has been taken up under non-formal education is the establishment of special schools. There were 26 special schools with 1800 children being run by 11 voluntary organisations up till March 1994. The number of special schools has since increased to 33 and the number of children to 2150. Between 1988 and 1994, 1313 children passed out of the special schools, out of whom 714 were enrolled into formal school. While there is no doubt that the individual children studying in the special schools have benefited as a result of the special schools, the schools do not appear have to have had an impact on the overall problem of child labour since the numbers by all accounts have not decreased. The reason may lie in the smallness of the effort compared to the magnitude of the problem and the fact that a simultaneous drive on the formal school front was not taken up.[28]

Mirzapur-Bhadoi National Child Labour Project

An evaluation of the National Child Labour Project in the carpet industry of Mirzapur-Bhadoi also concludes that special schools, a key component of the NCLP, have not made an impact on the overall numbers of working children in this industry. The children withdrawn from the industry and placed in special schools have been replaced by others, particularly migrant child labourers. In terms of composition of the beneficiaries' of the programme, a majority of children enrolled in the special schools had been working in a family setting and not as hired labour.[29]

Markapur National Child Labour Project

The NCLP of Markapur, Andhra Pradesh, also does not appear to have achieved much success in achieving its objective of elimination of child labour from the slate industry. A major shortcoming is the lack of a project document meant exclusively for Markapur. Enforcement of relevant acts prohibiting employment of children is extremely poor. No information is available on inspections and prosecutions for employment of children under the Mines Act or Factories Act. As regards the employment and income support activities are concerned, it was reported in a study done by the University of Hyderabad that 150 child labour families had been identified for grant of bank loans for self employment schemes. It appears, however, that none of these persons received the loans. No concerted effort appears to have been made by the project management to ensure that child labour families were covered under income generation schemes.[30]

Under the formal and non-formal education scheme, the project document envisaged the establishment of 20 special schools for child workers removed from work and opening of additional primary schools. In all, 13 special schools with a total strength of 1000 children have been started under the NCLP; 400 of the children are in a residential school and 600 children in 12 day schools. The special schools follow the formal school syllabus, and have not, so far, introduced any novel or innovative teaching methods. It has, however, a good vocational training programme. However, the Hyderabad University study, earlier referred to, mentions that there are some complaints that children admitted into the residential schools are not actually child workers and that it does not admit Schedule Caste children. No information is available on whether additional primary schools have been opened in the area or on whether the school enrolment and retention rate has increased.[31]

The Labour Ministry has been indicted by the Parliamentary Standing Committee on Labour and Welfare for being "not at all serious" in implementing its recommendations to abolish child labour in the country.

Task Force on Child Labour

A Task Force on child labour was instituted on the recommendation of the Central Advisory Board on Child Labour under the Chairmanship of Dr. L. M. Singhvi to recommend the institutions and mechanisms necessary for implementing the Child Labour (Prohibition and Regulation) Act, 1986 and Legal Action Plan contained in the NCLP. The Task Force submitted its report in December 1989. The recommendations of the Task Force comprise 3 categories, *viz.*,

(i) General Recommendations
(ii) Recommendations on the Child Labour (P and R) Act, 1986
(iii) Recommendations on the National Policy on Child Labour.

The Task Force made 11 general recommendations. Chief among these 11 are:[32]

- Highest priority must be accorded to the child. To accomplish this there should be a joint committee of the houses of parliament and similar committees in state legislatures to represent the unrepresented constituency of the child.

- There should be a single ministry or department for child welfare at the centre and states in order to reduce the existing multiplicity of authorities to the minimum and optimising operational coherence and coordination.

- There should be a statutory system of Child Labour Ombusdman or Child Labour Commission entrusted with the task of investigation, resolution of grievances and disputes and giving authoritative directions to employers and others.

- A child code, including within its scope a child labour code, must be formulated. Such a code would reflect the vision of goals as well as long-term and immediate strategies.

The Task Force made the following recommendations with respect to the Act of 1986[33].

- A timetable with mandatory outer limits for Act to come into force should be provided in the Act.

- A uniform definition of child with reference to age is useful. However, the lowering of age limit from 15 to 14 in certain occupations by the 1986 Act is undesirable.

- An enabling provision should be enacted to Section 3 of the 1986 Act to check malpractices employed in the exploitation of child labour under the guise of an occupier carrying a process with the aid of his family or children producing goods in schools receiving assistance or recognition from government.

- Maximum permissible punishment should be increased to simple imprisonment upto 3 months and the maximum permissible fine which may be imposed should be increased to Rs. one lakh with a proviso that in case of a second or subsequent conviction a sentence of imprisonment shall be mandatory.

With respect to the National Policy and Action Plan the Task Force recommended that a White Paper should be published explaining the historical background, analysing the present situation, giving reliable statistical and other data and projecting its own perceptions and policies in terms of targets, allocations and types of programmes and other activities it has envisaged. It also called upon the government to provide proper educational and vocational training facilities. While seeking to prohibit and regulate child labour, the task force emphasised that one of the most important prerequisite for the success of any child labour policy is a massive national programme for public civic education on child labour. According to the Task Force report, it is necessary that public opinion is created and public interest is sustained in respect of the problems of child labour.

On 15th August, 1994, former Prime Minister P. V. Narasimha Rao made a call to eliminate child labour in hazardous employments by the year 2000 A.D. Following the call made by the P.M, the National Authority for Elimination of Child Labour, headed by the Union Labour Minister, was constituted on 26 September 1994 and

Rs. 850 crore have been earmarked for schemes to eliminate child labour in hazardous employments. This programme, however, appears to be extremely unrealistic since it hopes to cover 2 million children in five years.

The programme has made little headway because of a resource crunch and an ongoing tussle between the ministries of labour and human resource development over the issue of setting up special schools.

The programme envisaged that two million children working in hazardous occupations would be withdrawn and rehabilitated in a five-year period through special schools having facilities such as non-formal education, vocational training, stipend, nutrition and health checks.

Since the programme was launched the Labour Ministry has received Rs. 33 crore in 1995-96, Rs. 40 crore in 1996-97 and an adhoc grant of Rs. 18 crore for 1997-98 pending the final decision of the cabinet. In June 1996, the Labour Ministry had prepared a Rs. 2170 crore proposal for starting 300 projects but none of them were approved.

Moreover, the ministries of Labour and Human Resource development have been at loggerheads over the running of special schools. The human resource development ministry does not want the labour ministry to run the special schools. If wants the labour ministry to only identify the children to be rehabilitated and hand them over to it.[34]

Supreme Court Order on Child Labour*

In order to check exploitation of child labour in hazardous industries, the Supreme Court on December 10, 1996 directed that all offending employers must pay a compensation of Rs. 20,000 for every such child, under the provisions of the Child Labour (Prohibition and Regulation) Act, 1986.

The court stated: "The inspectors, appointed under Section 17 of the Act would see that for each child employed in violation of the Act, the employer concerned pays Rs. 20,000 which would be deposited in a fund known as the Child Labour Rehabilitation-cum-Welfare Fund. The liability of the employer would not cease even if

*Supreme Court Order On Writ Petition (C)N0. 465 of 1986. M.C. Mehta V. State of Tamil Nadu and Others, December, 1986

he would desire to disengage the child presently employed by him. The Court said that the income generated from the corpus funds would be used to assure the child's education in a suitable institution with a view to making him a "better citizen". The Court has also asked the state to see that an adult member of the working child's family get a job in lieu of the child's job. In case this was not possible, a sum of Rs. 5,000 should be contributed to the fund for each child, the court said. Employment given or payment made (whatever the case may be) would cease if the child is not sent by parents to school.

The judgement was delivered by a three judge bench comprising Justice Kuldip Singh, Justice B. L. Hansaria and Justice S. B. Majumdar while deposing of a public interest litigation (writ petition) filed by environmentalist lawyer M. C. Mehta against the State of Tamil Nadu.

The court order identified nine major industries as hazardous. They include the match industry of Sivakasi; the diamond polishing industry of Surat; the precious-stone polishing industry of Jaipur; Ferozabad's glass industry; brassware industry of Moradabad; the handmade carpet industry of Mirzapur-Bhadoi; lock industry of Aligarh; and the slate industry of Markapur, A. P. and Mandsaur, M.P.

The court noted : "We have the fond hope that the closing years of the 20th century will see us keeping the promise made to our children by our constitution about half a century ago." Recalling Rabindranath Tagore's memorable lines from the Gitanjali, the court hoped: "Let the child of the 21st century find himself into that heaven of freedom."

Acknowledging that poverty was the main cause of child labour, the court said that unless an alternative source of income was assured to the family, the question of abolition of child labour would really remain a "will-of-the-wisp." Noting that creating employment for a large number of adults would "strain" the state's resources, the court said that it was not issuing any direction to do it presently. "Instead, we leave the matter to be sorted out by an appropriate government."

The court directed the states to conduct a survey on child labour which was to be completed within six months. The Secretary to the Minister of Labour, Government of India was required to appraise the court within one year about the compliance of the directions.

The court has held labour inspectors responsible for ensuring that children withdrawn from hazardous industries are provided proper education. In jobs of non-hazardous nature, inspectors are responsible for ensuring that children work for not more than six hours a day and receive education for at least two hours each day and cost of education should be borne by the employer.

The court's judgement was based on a report by a three-member legal experts committee headed by Supreme Court Bar Association president R. K. Jain which inspected the hazardous fireworks industry in Sivakasi. The other members of the committee were Indira Jaisingh and K. C. Dua.

Additional funds to the tune of Rs. 2,000 crore will be required for complying with the Supreme Court judgement, according to tentative estimates prepared by the labour ministry. About Rs. 500 crore will be required just to meet one directive of the Supreme Court under which either the State government would have to provide a job to the adult member of the family of the child withdrawn from work or alternatively it would have to contribute Rs. 5,000 to the district-level child labour welfare-cum-rehabilitation fund.

The Supreme Court judgement is an important step in dealing with the problem of child labour. However, the court directive is not an answer to the problem of child labour since eradicating undesirable practices by law is generally ineffective in India, as witnessed from the poor record in implementation of existing laws, directives and conventions on the subject. It will be difficult to implement the order because most children in the hazardous industries work in the unorganized sector. The court has also ignored the plight of children in agriculture and services sector, thereby excluding from its scope a majority of child workers.

Assistance from ILO

The ILO has been assisting the Indian government to tackle the problem of child labour. Two ILO projects, namely Child Labour Action and Support Programme (CLASP) and International Programme on the Elimination of Child Labour (IPEC) are being currently implemented under the technical cooperation programme of the ILO.

The IPEC programme is global in scope and provides technical advisory services to all ILO members on request. The programme seeks to eliminate child labour by stimulating governments to establish and apply national policies and laws in line with international standards on child labour, launching programmes to protect and rehabilitate child workers which will serve as models for replication; generating a climate of awareness, concern and demand for action regarding child labour.

The ILO and the Government of India signed a Memorandum of Understanding (MOU) on IPEC in the second quarter of 1992 reaffirming that national efforts in the country would be aimed at the eventual elimination of child labour and that this objective could be attained only through vigorous action by state governments, involvement of NGOs and trade unions. IPEC in India pursues the goal of progressive elimination of child labour through a comprehensive approach based on the ILO Convention No. 138. The direct target groups of the IPEC are:

- Bonded child labourers
- Children employed in formal and informal manufacturing sectors, for example, factories, industrial enterprises, cottage industries, home production, etc.
- Children working in agricultural sector
- Children working in commercial trade and services industries, for example, street vending, restaurants, garbage collection, etc.

A National Steering Committee with representatives of employers organisations, trade unions and NGOs and with the Secretary, Ministry of Labour, Government of India, as Chairperson has been established by the Ministry of Labour. Its function amongst others is to select action programme proposals for inclusion in the national programme under IPEC. Assistance is provided to NGOs for undertaking flexible programmes suiting local requirements.

Some of the highlights of the IPEC programme in India are[35]:

- Release and rehabilitation of bonded child labourers and children working in hazardous and abusive circumstances.
- Raising public awareness against child labour.
- Assisting in policy making at the national and state levels.
- Training NGOs on the design, management and evaluation of child labour projects.

- Training of labour and factory inspectors on enforcement of child labour laws.
- Sensitizing employers and employers' organisations against child labour.
- Enrolling working children in regular schools after weaning them away from the workplace.
- Activising dysfunctional and non-functional government schools in areas where working children are concentrated.
- Sensitizing trade unions, their leaders and their worker members on child labour.
- Eliminating child labour in selected areas and workspots.

The labour ministry and the ILO signed a memorandum of understanding (MoU) on January 29, 1997 for the continuance of IPEC beyond December 31, 1996. The allocation under the programme since its inception has been of the order of $ 4.15 million. A total of 118 projects benefitting over 81,000 children in 15 states have been implemented with IPEC assistance through trade unions, employers' bodies and NGOs.

It has been alleged the IPEC funds are being used badly and the project has degenerated into an educational programme from being an initiative to abolish child labour. It has also been suggested that there is an overlap between IPEC's child labour projects and the government's NCLP initiative of 1987. The NGOs say that IPEC's very name states its aim as child labour elimination. So it should leave welfare activities to the government and concentrate on more radical agenda. The government's own initiative of 1987 includes non-formal education for working children, nutrition and a small stipend for children working in hazardous industries. The NGOs say that since the government and multilateral agencies are already funding this exercise, there is no reason for doing more of the same the IPEC money. However, ILO officials insist that IPEC is a demonstration programme, aimed only at showing what can be done about the child labour problem. The idea is to make "myriad interventions" by enhancing enforcement officers' skills, creating awareness, offering non-formal education for child workers and so on. Besides, ILO officials claim that about half the children directly targeted by IPEC have stopped work[36].

The other ILO programme, CLASP, originated in response to the initiatives taken by the Indian government in the mid-1980s to deal with the problem of child labour. With the passing of the Child Labour (P and R) Act, 1986, and the adoption of NCLP in 1987, there was a sudden spurt of child labour activities in the country resulting in an increased demand on the government to provide technical expertise and leadership in the matter. The ILO felt that it could play an important role in strengthening the technical expertise and capacity of the government in tackling the problem of child labour. The programme is aided by the Government of Germany. The agreement between the German Government and the Government of India was signed in November 1992 and CLASP became operational thereafter.

The aim of CLASP is to enhance the central government's policy, planning and implementation capacity; to increase its capability to provide support for ongoing and future projects by state governments and NGOs; mobilise greater support and sustain a community-wide movement on behalf of working children; and facilitate a more efficient use of government resources. Assistance taken under the programme is used for the purpose of supporting ongoing activities under the NCLP. The total allocation under the programme is US $ 8.30 lakhs. Upto December 1994, expenditure had been incurred to the extent of US $ 2.40 lakhs[37].

Some of the important activities undertaken under this programme are [38].

- Conduct of baseline surveys in NCLP areas
- Establishment of data bank on child labour
- Conduct of project design workshops
- Preparation of project documents for new NCLPs
- Preparation of guidelines for NCLP managers
- Preparation of guidelines for labour inspectors
- Training of teachers, state government officials
- Organisation of study tours for child labour elimination functionaries to NCLP areas
- Conduct of seminars for officials and NGOs
- Preparation of model education curricula for special schools run under NCLP
- Development of pedagogic methodologies

- Production of appropriate materials
- Undertaking study of the utility of vocational training amongst children.

Since the inception of the project, several workshops have been held. The first of these was a consultation workshop held in September 1993 on curriculum development for non-formal education. In January 1994, a workshop for training of teachers' trainers was held to arrive at a common training format for training the teachers of the special schools for child workers in the NCLP. A workshop on design, management and evaluation of NCLP was held in Mandsaur, Madhya Pradesh, in July 1994 to assess the progress made on the Mandsaur NCLP and give it fresh directive.

When CLASP was conceived as a project, it was not foreseen that another ILO project, IPEC, would come into operation. As a result, there are several activities of project that overlap. For example, both CLASP and IPEC are engaged in building capacity of the government in combating child labour, training inspectors, creating awareness, interacting with NGOs etc.

Assistance from UNICEF

The UNICEF has also been assisting the Indian Government to deal with the problem of child labour. UNICEF acknowledges the need to seriously address child labour as a key component of its policy to advocate implementation of the Convention on the Rights of the Child and achievement of goals for improving the development and well-being of children.

UNICEF believes that child labour can be eliminated if appropriate policies are implemented. According to UNICEF policy, child labour can be eliminated in a phased manner and within a specified period of time. The initial focus should be on the elimination of child labour in hazardous industries, in prostitution and the elimination of bonded child labour, as children working under such conditions are immediately at risk.

UNICEF India believes that the main strategy to eliminate child labour would include strong legislation and its enforcement, specific measures to release and rehabilitate children from labour, accompanying social policies, such as education and rural development, and activities to raise public awareness on the issue of child labour. UNICEF assists Central and State Governments to develop and implement programmes and action plans for the release and rehabilitation of children from labour in various industries and occupations. In addition to supporting government programmes on child labour, UNICEF also seeks to develop and strengthen alliances with NGOs, industry, external agencies, trade unions, media and academics to promote the elimination of child labour.

UNICEF focusses on programmes to rehabilitate children released from labour into the educational system and to improve the livelihoods of their families through support from anti-poverty programmes. Through its state offices, UNICEF seeks to provide assistance in key states for the development of intersectoral programmes for the release and rehabilitation of child labourers. For example, in Tamil Nadu, a Joint Committee convened by the Chief Minister conducted research and developed an integrated strategy for combating child labour in the fireworks and match industry in Sivakasi. The strategy involves introduction of compulsory primary education in the state and targetting rural development and income generation schemes to the children's families.

UNICEF recognizes that reliable data is required to assist advocacy and monitoring in the context of child labour. UNICEF has provided financial assistance under a Master Plan of Operation for child labour programmes. UNICEF supports the Child Labour Cell, established at the National Labour Institute, for monitoring and research activities.

India's Response to International Action and Programmes On Child Labour

The ILO has been promoting protective action in respect of working children through the mechanism of international labour standards in the form of conventions and recommendations. These conventions are expected to act as benchmarks for member countries of ILO.The ILO has so far adopted 14 conventions relating to child labour. India has so far ratified 6 of the conventions. Table 1 gives a list of the conventions ratified by India. India ratified the Convention on the Rights of the Child in November 1992. Though India has ratified 6 ILO conventions, it has not implemented its commitment to the principles contained in these conventions.

The Indian Government has come under pressure to deal with the problem of child labour from Western countries, particularly the United States of America and Germany. There has been a campaign in the West to ban the import of products produced by children. The carpet industry of India, which employs a large number of children, has become the focal point of this campaign.

The US Congress has warned that it would not allow the import of merchandise produced by children to enter the American market. Senator Tom Harkins has introduced the Child Labour Deterrence Act. This bill prohibits the transfer of any goods manufactured by children. The Harkins Bill is due to be passed this year. Representative Barney Frank introduced the Child Labour Deterrences Act in July 1995. It is similar to the legislation already circulating in the Senate introduced by Harkins. The legislation introduced by Frank would put a halt to the importation of manufactured and mined goods produced by children under the age of 15.

TABLE II
INTERNATIONAL CONVENTIONS RATIFIED BY INDIA

Name of The Convention	Month and Year
Right of night work of young persons (industry) convention, 1919 of ILO	July, 1921
Minimum age of (trimmers & stokers) convention, 1921 of ILO	November, 1922
Medical Examination of young persons (C) convention, 1921 of ILO	November, 1922
Right to night work of young persons (industry) convention (revised), 1948 of ILO	February, 1950
Employment of children under minimum age convention, 1919 of ILO	September, 1955
Minimum age (underground) work) convention, 1965 of ILO	March, 1975
Convention of the rights of the child, 1989	November, 1992

It also requires the development and maintenance of a list of industries that use child labour. Companies violating the prohibition against importing these products would be subject to stiff penalties. Similar legislation has been introduced in Germany.

The Western nations are demanding a label system for guaranteeing that carpets and other products are not made by children. This has come as a big blow to the export-oriented industries which employ children on a large scale, particularly the carpet industry. To ward off a ban on Indian carpets, the Indian Government has announced the Kaleen label, offered to carpets made without child labour. Carpet exporters have backed the Kaleen label. According to Abdul Hadi, Secretary of the All India Carpet Manufacturers Associations, all its 400 members have endorsed the Kaleen label. Holland became the first country to endorse the Kaleen certification in March 1996. However, NGOs in India have dismissed the Kaleen label on the ground that a government-backed certificate would be unconvincing. They have set up the Rugmark label, which comprises representatives from the carpet industry, South Asia Coalition on Child Servitude (SACCS), the Carpet Manufacturers Association without Child Labour, the Indo-German Export Promotion Project (IGEP) and UNICEF. It has been lobbying among importers and consumers abroad not to buy carpets without the Rugmark label. The carpet industry has not taken to Rugmark. So far, only 100 of the country's 4000-odd carpet exporters have applied for it and only 20 have been granted the label. However, many large importers, stores and mail-order companies are now insisting on Rugmark. The National Consumer League, a leading consumer rights group in the US, has also announced its support for the Rugmark[39]. However, carpet looms are so scattered that it will be very difficult to monitor them. The registering of looms began only in 1992. There are at least 150,000 looms and listing them is going to be difficult.

The Western nations are also campaigning to put labour standards, particularly child labour, on the agenda of the newly created World Trade Organisation by introducing a social clause. They would like trade curbs to be imposed on developing countries like India where young children are employed in jobs which are often dangerous, instead of going to school. India has campaigned against such a linkage and has accused the rich countries of trying to erect barriers to free trade in the guise of labour standards. The Indian Commission on Labour Standards, created in August 1994, has suggested that instead of a flat rejection of a linkage between labour standards and trade or a complete surrender, India should press rich industrialized countries to help funds the costs of wiping out child labour by the turn of the century.

There is no doubt that the rich countries want a linkage not so much for the sake of improving the lot of labour in Third World nations but for protecting their own trading share. However, we cannot overlook deplorable labour practices in the name of protecting our share in international trade. Moreover, threats to introduce a social clause has sensitised the government to the plight of children slaving to earn a livelihood. India needs to take constructive steps to end the exploitation of children. Exporters of products made by children need to take measures to eradicate child labour to ensure the survival of their businesses because it may not be long before measures by Western nations like Harkins Bill come into force and put them out of their business.

The Government of India has adopted constitutional, statutory and developmental measures to deal with the problem of child labour. Several parts of the constitution, directly or indirectly, prohibit the practice of child labour. However, the goals of the constitution are far from being realized. Several laws have also been passed to deal with problem of child labour. However, despite these laws children continue to work in prohibited occupations and there is very little regulation of child labour in non-prohibited areas of work. This is largely due to ineffective implementation of child labour laws in India. The government has also launched developmental programmes for the benefit of child labour. However, the scope and implementation of these programmes has left a lot the be desired. These programmes have not had much success in reducing the incidence of child labour.

Notes

1. Ministry of Labour, *Report of the Committee on Child Labour* (Nasik: Government of India Press, 1979) p. 20.
2. *Ibid.*, p. 21.
3. *Ibid.*
4. *Ibid.*
5. *Ibid.*, p. 22
6. *Ibid.*
7. *Ibid.*
8. Jinesh Chandra Kulshreshtha, *Child Labour in India* (New Delhi: Ashish Publishing House, 1978) p. 55.
9. *The Factories Act,* 1948 (New Delhi: Government of India, 1948) p. 21.

10. Jinesh Chandra Kulshreshtha, *op. cit.*, p. 56.
11. Ministry of Labour, Report of the Committee on Child Labour, *op. cit.*, p. 24.
12. *Ibid.*
13. *Ibid.*
14. *Ibid.*
15. *Report of the National Commission on Labour*, (New Delhi, Government of India, 1968) p. 385.
16. Smitu Kothari, "There's Blood on Those Matchsticks. Child Labour in Sivakasi" *Economic and Political Weekly*, Vol. XVIII, No. 27, July 1983, p. 1200.
17. *Ibid.*
18. Ministry of Labour, Report of the Committee on Child Labour, *op. cit.*, p. 19.
19. *Ibid.*, p. 36-37.
20. *Child Labour (Prohibition and Regulation) Act, 1986 and Child Labour (Prohibition and Regulation) Rules,* 1988 (New Delhi: Government of India, 1995) pp. 19-20.
21. *Ibid.*, p. 21
22. Ministry of Labour, *Report of the Task Force on the Implementation of the Child Labour (Prohibition and Regulation) Act, 1986 and the Legal Action Plan Contained in the National Child Labour Policy* (New Delhi: Government of India, 1989) p. 26.
23. Meena Gupta, "Special Problems of Enforcement of Child Labour Laws and Regulation", *Awards Digest: Journal of Labour Legislation*, Vol. XVIII, No. 3-6, March-June 1992, pp. 42-43.
24. Ministry of Labour, *National Policy on Child Labour. Workshop of District Collectors/ Heads on Elimination of Child Labour in Hazardous Occupations* (New Delhi: Government of India, 1995) pp. 2-3.
25. Ministry of Labour, *Children and Work, Workshop of District Collectors/Heads on Elimination of Child Labour in Hazardous Occupations* (New Delhi: Government of India, 1995) p. 20.
26. Ministry of Labour, *Child Labour in India* (Unpublished, 1994) p. 15.
27. Meena Gupta, *The Sivakasi National Child Labour Project*—A Status Paper (New Delhi: ILO, 1994) pp. 4-5.
28. *Ibid.*, pp. 5-8.
29. B. N. Juyal, *Child Labour in the Carpet Industry in Mirzapur-Bhadoi. A Situational Analysis and Evaluation of Government of India's NCLP* (New Delhi: ILO, 1993) pp. 9-10.
30. Meena Gupta, The Markapur National Child Labour-Project *A Status Paper* (New Delhi: ILO, 1994) pp. 4-6.
31. *Ibid.*
32. Ministry of Labour, *Report of the Task Force on the Implementation of the Child Labour (Prohibition and Regulation) Act, 1986 and the Legal Action Plan Contained in the National Child Labour Policy, op. cit.*, pp. 43-47.
33. *Ibid.*
34. Sawhney Inder, "Child Labour Rehab Projects in Limbo", *The Times of India*, October 10, 1997.
35. International Labour Organisation, *IPEC Programme Document* (Geneva: ILO, 1993) pp. 10-12.
36. Shefali Misra, "IPEC in the Dock", *Business Standard*, March 4, 1994.
37. Ministry of Labour, Children and Work. Workshop of District Collectors/Heads on Elimination of Child Labour in Hazardous Occupations, *op. cit.*, p. 9.
38. *Ibid.*, pp. 9-10.
39. "Free the Children or Face the Music", *Business World* 15-31 July, 1995, pp. 56-57.

VI
Children—Focus of Development

This study has examined the magnitude of child labour, which continues unabated in gross violation of the rights of the child. The following conclusions emerge from the preceding analysis of child labour as a human rights issue.

The growing incidence of the problem of child labour has made it a cause for international and national concern. Several efforts have been made at the global level to deal with the problem, the most recent being the Convention on the Rights of the Child adopted by the UN General Assembly in 1989. The Convention, guided by the principle of "first call for children", recognizes the exceptional vulnerability of children and declares that childhood is entitled to special care. Other UN agencies, for example, ILO, UNICEF and UNESCO, work towards providing children a fair deal in society. While these efforts are commendable, there is a wide gap between theory and practice. Children continue to be a sizeable section of the workforce despite national and international legislation prohibiting it.

In India, the rights of the child have been relegated to the background. The incidence of child labour has been increasing in the country. Child labour in India is concentrated in rural areas. Out of the total child workforce in India, 91.4 per cent work in rural areas and 8.86 per cent in urban areas.

There are several factors responsible for the growing incidence of child labour in India. One important cause responsible for the prevalence of child labour is poverty. Children are forced to work to supplement the family income. Unemployment is also another cause responsible for child labour. However, child labour in turn accentuates poverty and unemployment. While millions of children work in India, adults are faced with the problem of unemployment and underemployment. Moreover, since children can be hired at low wages, child labour lowers the overall rate of wages in the labour market. Thus child labour both supplements and decreases family income. Employers find it profitable to employ children because children cost less and can be easily disciplined. Employers, therefore, have a vested interest in maintaining child labour.

Furthermore, inadequate educational facilities and lack of compulsory education for all children below the age of 14 years is also an important cause for the incidence of child labour in India. A sizeable section of the children who drop out of school find employment of some kind. The states where drop-out rates are high, incidence of child labour is also high. For instance, drop-out rates are very high in states of Bihar and Andhra Pradesh, which also have a high incidence of child labour. On the other hand, drop-out rate is the lowest in Kerala, which has the lowest incidence of child labour.

A statistical analysis of historical data used in this study demonstrates the correlation between the incidence of child labour and the various causal factors. The statistical analysis of causes of child labour in India points to a strong correlation between child labour and poverty and illiteracy.

Children in India are engaged in a wide variety of activities: paid and unpaid, formal and informal. Children's activities vary from urban to rural and also between boys and girls. The broad categories in which children are engaged are: (a) Unpaid domestic work, (b) Unpaid non-domestic work, (c) Self-employed, (d) Wage labourers, (e) Bonded labour. Child Labour in India is concentrated largely in agriculture, followed by services and industry.

Child labour has far reaching repercussions on the intellectual, physical and emotional development of children. They are engaged in occupations which have a deleterious impact on their physical well-being. Moreover, children who work fulltime do not have the time to go to school. Surveys indicate that a majority of child workers are illiterate. Working children are also unable to participate in leisure or recreational activities. They have to sacrifice the joys of childhood in trying to eke out a living. The continued practice of child labour in India has affected its image in the world community.

An analysis of child labour in select industries reveals that over the years there has been a decline in the employment of children in the organised sector because children employed in the organised sector are protected under the child labour laws. Most working children are employed in the unorganised sector of industries. The incidence of child labour is very high in the unorganised sector because the employers have a vested interest in employing children as cheap labour. Children also constitute a docile and uncomplaining workforce. It is common practice to masquerade child labourers as trainees or even family members because the working of children in family-based units is not prohibited. Factory owners also sub-contract several processes to small workshops where child labour is freely used. Children constitute more than half the working population in the industries examined.

Children are employed in almost all the stages of production in these industries. For example, in the match industry of Sivakasi, children are employed in almost all stages of match production. They are engaged in mixing, steaming chemicals in the boiler rooms, stamping frames of match splinters in trays of wet phosphorous and drying them on hot sheets of metal in huge furnaces, filling frames with sticks and filling match boxes. The ages of children working in match factories range between 4 to 14 years. In many factories some activities are fully undertaken by children below 7 years of age.

Children are forced to work long hours under appalling conditions in these industries. In the glass industry of Firozabad, children sit in front of furnaces where temperature is around 700°C. In many factories where children draw molten glass from tank furnaces, in which temperature is between 1500°C to 1800°C, their bodies are 6 to 8 inches from the opening of the furnace. Since they are small in size, they have to put their hand right inside the furnace in order to draw adequate quantities of molten glass. As a result, the body almost touches the furnace. The processes involved in glass industry are highly hazardous and involve back-breaking work. In this industry also children are employed in almost all the processes. Children work for 10-14 hours daily in the glass industry. The study sponsored by the Planning Commission reveals that an alarming 40 percent of the children work for more than 8 hours daily. In the brassware industry of Moradabad, children work in dingy workshops with very poor sanitary conditions and are exposed to serious hazards. The work involves plenty of metal debris which falls from the moulds or is scrapped from the rough product. The air is laden with dust which is constantly breathed in by the children. Children sit in the same position for 6 to 7 hours continuously. The two most hazardous processes in the industry are moulding and polishing and it is in these processes that child labour is all pervasive. If there is a slight mistake or accident the child can get very badly injured and can even lose his limbs. Children are not provided any protective gear and stand barefoot on top of the furnace. The combination of poor nutrition and bad working conditions in these industries reduce the life of workers by half. They become too ill to work by the time they reach adulthood.

Children are exposed to several occupational hazards in these industries. In the carpet industry of Mirzapur-Bhadoi, children are exposed to airborne contamination, especially fluff and dust of wool and cotton. Investigations point to a very high incidence of tuberculosis in the industry. In a survey conducted at a health camp for working children, 25 to 30 percent children tested positive for tuberculosis. Night blindness and poor vision have also assumed the propositions of occupational diseases. In the brassware industry of Moradabad, tuberculosis and other respiratory tract problems are rampant because of constant inhalation of vapours arising from acid tubs. A UNICEF-aided study observed that among children working in match factories, skin diseases such as dermatitis, tuberculosis and non-specific diseases of the upper respiratory passage are common. Working for long hours in dark, ill-ventilated rooms is a cause of severe eye strain, night blindness and premature blindness.

Labour laws are openly flouted in these industries. Under the Factories Act children are prohibited from working in the glass industry of Firozabad. Yet, all factories employ children. It is estimated that 30,000 children are employed in this industry at the factory level. In addition, the number of children working at the household level is estimated to be about two-and-a-half times more than the number of working children at the factory level. Children are prohibited from working at night but this rule is blatantly violated. In the match industry of Sivakasi there are instances of children working till as late as 10.00 pm. In the glass industry of Firozabad, children as young as 6 or 7 work in the night shift.

A majority of children working in these industries have either not been to school or drop-out easily. A study sponsored by the

Planning Commission on the working children of Sivakasi found 50 percent of children were illiterate. Out of the sample, only 11 percent of the working children were still attending school. As per the study conducted on working children in glass industry of Firozabad, as many as 45.4 percent children in the sample were illiterate and only 20 percent of the working children were still attending school.

The appalling working conditions, absence of minimum safety standards, long hours of work, low wages, hazardous nature of work and the poor educational status of working children are pointers to the exploitative nature of child labour. Child workers lead a miserable life of deprivation and exploitation. An analysis of child labour in the above industries shows that the continued and large-scale practice of child labour is a blatant violation of the rights of the child.

The Government of India has adopted constitutional, developmental and statutory measures to tackle the problem of child labour. Article 24 of the Indian Constitution prohibits the employment of children below the age of 14 years. Several others parts of the constitution also prohibit the employment of children. However, the Indian Government has failed to honour the commitment made by the framers of the Indian Constitution. The Indian Government has also ratified several international conventions relating to the rights of the child. However, it has failed to honour the basic principles of these conventions.

Several laws have also been passed in India to prohibit and regulate the employment of children, the latest being the Child Labour (Prohibition and Regulation) Act of 1986. The Act was passed to prohibit the employment of children in hazardous jobs and to regulate the conditions of work for children in other jobs of non-hazardous nature. However, the Child Labour Act of 1986 does not prohibit the employment of children in family-based units. This has resulted in gross misuse of the Act. Moreover, the Act does not exclude from its list of "hazardous jobs" several occupations and processes which are extremely hazardous.

Despite passing of several laws, children continue to work in prohibited occupations and there is very little regulation of child labour in non-prohibited areas of employment. This is mainly because of ineffective implementation of child labour laws in developing countries, particularly in India.

Since legislation alone is not sufficient to deal with the problem of child labour, the government has arrived at a National Policy on Child Labour. Under the NCLP, a project-based plan of action in areas of high concentration of child labour was initiated. Though the initiation of the project-based plan of action is commendable, its scope is very narrow since it does not cover several areas and industries where the incidence of child labour is high and the working conditions hazardous. Moreover, there is a lag between targets set by the plan and the actual achievements. The first phase of the project-based plan was expected to cover 30,000 working children. However, so far only 14,800 working children have been covered under the 12 projects. The NCLP has not had much impact on the overall number of working children in the industries targetted.

Despite preventive legislation and launching of several projects, the exploitation of children continues unabated. There is a lack of political will in India to deal with the issue of child labour. Rights of the child are relegated to the background because children do not constitute a vote bank. This is corroborated by the fact that in the 1996 elections no party manifesto spoke of eradicating child labour.

The Supreme Court has, in a landmark directive, ordered the creation of a corpus fund to check the exploitation of child labour in hazardous industries. It directed all offenders to pay a compensation of Rs. 20,000 for every such child under the provisions of the Child Labour (Prohibition & Regulation) Act, 1986. However, there is a great deal of scepticism regarding the realisation of the hope expressed by the Supreme Court bench, since India's record of implementing laws, directives and conventions is very poor.

Whether child labour should be banned or not in India is a question that has aroused a great deal of controversy. However, merely banning child labour is not the solution to the problem. The solution lies in adopting a multi-pronged approach. Child labour in India cannot be justified on the ground of poverty. There is a need for enacted legislation to be backed by effective enforcement. Priority must be given to eliminating child labour, especially in dangerous occupations and processes. It is necessary to take purposeful policy decisions if the existing situation has to be changed significantly. Poverty-alleviation and employment generation programmes need to be targetted at families in which children are employed. Merely rescuing children from the clutches of employers is not enough. It is necessary to rehabilitate them.

Abolition of child labour is closely linked with the introduction of compulsory education. The state must assume responsibility of sending children to school. It must fulfil its obligation of providing compulsory education to all till the age of 14 years and ensuring that children attend school. Moreover, the curriculum must be made relevant to the needs of the child.

Above all, public opinion must be mobilised against child labour. There can be no change in society unless the people who compose that society work towards initiating the change. The people must be made aware of the deleterious effects of child labour and the price that society will have to pay in future if it continues to abuse its children.

To sum up, child labour is an aberration that goes against tenets of civilized living. Children have only one opportunity to grow and develop. It is, therefore, necessary that children should be the focus of development. Child labour has far-reaching repercussions on the overall well-being of children. The practice of child labour amounts to a denial of the rights of children. India's record in protecting the rights of the child is dismally poor despite the enactment of several laws and ratification of international conventions.

Annexure I

The United Nations Convention on the Rights of the Child

PREAMBLE

The States Parties to the present Convention,

Considering that in accordance with the principles proclaimed in the Charter of the United Nations, recognition of the inherent dignity and of the equal and inalienable rights of all members of the human family is the foundation of freedom, justice and peace in the world,

Bearing in mind that the people of the United Nations have, in the Charter reaffirmed their faith in fundamental human rights and in the dignity and worth of the human person, and have determined to promote social progress and better standard of life in larger freedom,

Regarding that the United Nations has, in the Universal Declaration of Human Rights and in the International Covenants on Human Rights, proclaimed and agreed that everyone is entitled to all the rights and freedoms set forth therein, without distinction of any kind, such as race, colour, sex, language, religion, political or other opinion, national or social origin, property, birth or other status,

Recalling that, in the Universal Declaration of Human Rights, the United Nations has proclaimed that childhood is entitled to special care and assistance,

Convinced that the family, as the fundamental group of society and the natural environment for the growth and well-being of all its members and particularly children, should be afforded the necessary protection and assistance so that it can fully assume its responsibilities within the community,

Recognizing that the child, for the full and harmonious development of his or her personality, should grow in a family environment, in an atmosphere of happiness, love and understanding,

Considering that the child should be fully prepared to live an individual life in society, and brought up in the spirit of the ideals proclaimed in the Charter of the United Nations, and in particular in the spirit of peace, dignity, tolerance, freedom, equality and solidarity,

Bearing in mind that the need for extending particular care to the child has been stated in the Geneva Declaration on the Rights of the Child of 1924 and in the Declaration of the Rights of the Child adopted by the United Nations in 1959 and recognized in the Universal Declaration of Human Rights, in the International Covenant on Civil and Political Rights (in particular in articles 23 and 24), in the International Covenant on Economic, Social and Cultural Rights (in particular in its article 10) and in the statutes and relevant instruments of specialized agencies and international organizations concerned with the welfare of children,

Bearing in mind that, as indicated in the Declaration of the Rights of the Child adopted by the General Assembly of the United Nations on 20 November 1959, "the child, by reason of his/her physical and mental immaturity, needs special safeguards and care, including appropriate legal protection, before as well as after birth",

Recalling the provisions of the Declaration on Social and Legal Principles relating to the Protection and Welfare of Children, with Special Reference to Foster Placement and Adoption Nationally and Internationally (General Assembly resolution 41/85 of 3 December 1986) the United Nations Standard Minimum Rules for the Administration of Juvenile Justice ("The Beijing Rules") (General Assembly resolution 40/33 of 29 November 1985); and the Declaration on the Protection of Women and Children in Emergency and Armed Conflict (General Assembly Resolution 3318 (XXIX) of 14 December, 1914).

Recognizing that in all countries in the world there are children living in exceptionally difficult conditions, and that such children need special consideration.

Taking due account of the importance of the traditions and cultural values of each people for the protection and harmonious development of the child.

Recognizing the importance of international co-operation for improving the living conditions of children in every country, in particular in the developing countries.

Have agreed as follows:

PART I

Article 1

For the purpose of the present Convention, a child means every human being below the age of 18 years unless, under the law applicable to the child, majority is obtained earlier.

Article 2

1. The State Parties to the present Convention shall respect and ensure the rights set forth in this convention to each child within their jurisdiction without discrimination of any kind, irrespective of the child's or his or her parents' or legal guardians' race, colour, sex, language, religion, political or other opinion, national, ethnic or social origin, property, disability, birth or other status.
2. States Parties shall take all appropriate measures to ensure that the child is protected against all forms of discrimination or punishment on the basis of the status, activities, expressed opinions, or beliefs of the child's parents, legal guardians, or family members.

Articles 3

1. In all actions concerning children, whether undertaken by public or private social welfare institutions, court of law, administrative authorities or legislative bodies, the best interest of the child shall be a primary consideration.
2. State Parties undertake to ensure the child such protection and care as is necessary for his or her well-being, taking into account the rights and duties of his or her parents, legal guardians, or other individuals legally responsible for him or her, and, to this end, shall take all appropriate legislative and administrative measures.
3. States Parties shall ensure that the institutions, services and facilities responsible for the care or protection of children shall conform with the standards established by competent authorities, particularly in the areas of safety, health, in the number and suitability of their staff.

Article 4

States Parties shall undertake all appropriate legislative, administrative, and other measures for the implementation of the rights recognized in this Convention. In regard to economic, social and cultural rights, States Parties shall undertake such measures to the maximum extent of their available resources and, where needed, within the framework of international co-operation.

Article 5

States Parties shall respect the responsibilities, rights, and duties of parents or, where applicable, the members of the extended family or community as provided for by the local custom, legal guardians or other persons legally responsible for the child, to provide, in a manner consistent with the evolving capacities of the child, appropriate direction and guidance in the exercise by the child of the rights recognized in the present Convention.

Article 6

1. States Parties recognize that every child has the inherent right to life.
2. States Parties shall ensure to the maximum extent possible the survival and development of the child.

Article 7

1. The child shall be registered immediately after birth and shall have the right from birth to a name, the right to acquire a nationality, and as far as possible, the right to know and be cared for by his or her parents.
2. States Parties shall ensure the implementation of these rights in accordance with their national law and their obligations under the relevant international instruments in this field, in particular where the child would otherwise be stateless.

Article 8

1. States Parties undertake to respect the right of the child to preserve his or her identity, including nationality, name and family relations as recognized by law without unlawful interference.
2. Where a child is illegally deprived of some of all of the elements of his or her identity, States Parties shall provide appropriate assistance and protection, with a view to speedily re-establishing his or her identity.

Article 9

1. States Parties shall ensure that a child shall not be separated from his or her parents against their will, except when competent authorities subject to judicial review determine, in accordance with applicable law and procedures, that such separation is necessary for the best interests of the child. Such determination may be necessary in a particular case such as one involving abuse or neglect of the child by the parents, or one where the parents are living separately and decision must be made as to the child's place of residence.
2. In any proceedings pursuant to paragraph 1, all interested parties shall be given an opportunity to participate in the proceedings and

make their views known.

3. States Parties shall respect the right of the child who is separated from one or both parents to maintain personal relations and direct contact with both parents on a regular basis, except if it is contrary to the child's best interests.

4. Where such separation results from any action initiated by a State Party, such as the detention, imprisonment, exile, deportation or death (including death arising from any cause while the person is in the custody of the State) of one or both parents or of the child, that State Party shall, upon request, provide the parents, the child or, if appropriate, another member of the family with the essential information concerning the whereabouts of the absent member(s) of the family unless the provision of the information would be detrimental to the well-being of the child. States Parties shall further ensure that submission of such a request shall of itself entail no adverse consequences for the person(s) concerned.

Article 10

1. In accordance with the obligation of States Parties under Article 9, paragraph 1, applications by a child or his or her parents to enter or leave a State Party for the purpose of family reunification shall be dealt with by States Parties in a positive, humane and expeditious manner. States Parties shall further ensure that the submission of such a request shall entail no adverse consequences for the applicants and for the members of their family.

2. A child whose parents reside in different States shall have the right to maintain on a regular basis save in exceptional circumstances personal relations and direct contacts with both parents. Towards that end and in accordance with the obligation of States Parties under Article 9, paragraph 2, States Parties shall respect the right of the child and his or her parents to leave any country, including their own, and to enter their own country. The right to leave any country shall be subject not only to such restrictions as are prescribed by law and which are necessary to protect the national security, public order (*ordre public*), public health or morals or the rights and freedoms of others and are consistent with the other rights recognized in the present Convention.

Article 11

1. States Parties shall take measures to combat the illicit transfer and non-return of children abroad.

2. To this end, States Parties shall promote the conclusion of bilateral

or multilateral agreements or accession to existing agreements.

Article 12

1. States Parties shall assure to the child who is capable of forming his or her own views the right to express those views freely in all matters affecting the child, the views of the child being given due weight in accordance with the age and maturity of the child.

2. For this purpose, the child shall in particular be provided the opportunity to be heard in any judicial and administrative proceedings affecting the child, either directly, or through a representative or an appropriate body, in a manner consistent with the procedural rules of national law.

Article 13

1. The child shall have the right to freedom of expression; this right shall include freedom to seek, receive and impart information and ideas of all kinds, regardless of frontiers, either orally, in writing or in print, in the form of art, or through any other media of the child's choice.

2. The exercise of this right may be subject to certain restrictions, but these shall only be such as are provided by law and are necessary:

   (a) for respect of the rights of reputations of others; or

   (b) for the protection of national security or of public order (*ordre public*), or of public health or morals.

Article 14

1. States Parties shall respect the right of the child to freedom of thought, conscience and religion.

2. States Parties shall respect the rights and duties of the parents and, when applicable, legal guardians, to provide direction to the child in the exercise of his or her right in a manner consistent with the evolving capacities of the child.

3. Freedom to manifest one's religion or beliefs may be subject only to such limitations as are prescribed by law and are necessary to protect public safety, order, health, or morals or the fundamental rights and freedoms of others.

Article 15

1. States Parties recognize the rights of the child to freedom of association and to freedom of peaceful assembly.

2. No restrictions may be placed on the exercise of these rights other than those imposed in conformity with the law and which are necessary in a democratic society in the interests of national security or public safety, public order (*ordre public*), the protection of public

health or morals or the protection of the rights and freedoms of others.

Article 16

1. No child shall be subjected to arbitrary or unlawful interference with his or her privacy, family, home or correspondence, nor to unlawful attacks on his or her honour and reputation.
2. The child has the right to the protection of the law against such interference or attacks.

Article 17

States Parties recognize the important function performed by the mass media and shall ensure that the child has access to information and material from a diversity of national and international sources, especially those aimed at the promotion of his or her social, spiritual and moral well-being and physical and mental health. To this end States Parties shall:

(a) Encourage the mass media to disseminate information and material of social and cultural benefit to the child and in accordance with the spirit of Article 29;

(b) Encourage international cooperation in the production, exchange and dissemination of such information and material from a diversity of cultural, national and international sources;

(c) Encourage the production and dissemination of children's books;

(d) Encourage the mass media to have particular regard to the linguistic needs of the child who belongs to a minority group or who is indigenous;

(e) Encourage the development of appropriate guidelines for the protection of the child from information and material injurious to his or her well-being bearing in mind the provisions of Articles 13 and 18.

Article 18

1. States Parties shall use their best efforts to ensure recognition of the principle that both parents have common responsibilities for the upbringing and development of the child. Parents or, as the case may be, legal guardians have the primary responsibility for the upbringing and development of the child. The best interests of the child will be their basic concern.
2. For the purpose of guaranteeing and promoting the rights set forth in this Convention, States Parties shall render appropriate assistance to parents and legal guardians in the performance of their child-rearing responsibilities and shall ensure the development of

institutions, facilities and services for the care of children.

3. States Parties shall take all appropriate measures to ensure that children of working parents have the right to benefit from child care services and facilities for which they are eligible.

Article 19

1. States Parties shall take all appropriate legislative, administrative, social and educational measures to protect the child from all forms of physical or mental violence, injury or abuse, neglect or negligent treatment, maltreatment or exploitation including sexual abuse, while in the care of parent(s), legal guardian(s) or any other person who has the care of the child.

2. Such protective measures should, as appropriate, include effective procedures for the establishment of social programmes to provide necessary support for the child and for those who have the care of the child, as well as for other forms of prevention and for identification, reporting, referral, investigation, treatment, and follow-up of instances of child maltreatment described heretofore, and, as appropriate, for judicial involvement.

Article 20

1. A child temporarily or permanently deprived of his or her family environment, or in whose own best interests cannot be allowed to remain in that environment, shall be entitled to special protection and assistance provided by the State.

2. States Parties shall in accordance with their national laws ensure alternative care for such a child.

3. Such care could include, *inter alia*, foster placement, Kafala of Islamic Law, adoption or if necessary placement in suitable institutions for the care of children. When considering solutions, due regard shall be paid to the desirability of continuity in a child's upbringing and to the child's ethnic, religious, cultural and linguistic background.

Article 21

States Parties which recognize and/or permit the system of adoption shall ensure that the best interests of the child shall be the paramount consideration and they shall:

(a) ensure that the adoption of a child is authorized only by competent authorities who determine, in accordance with applicable law and procedures and on the basis of all pertinent and reliable information, that the adoption is permissible in view of the child's status concerning parents, relatives and legal guardians and that, if required, the persons concerned have given their informed consent to the adoption on the basis of such counselling as may be necessary;

(b) recognized that intercountry adoption may be considered as an alternative means of child's care, if the child cannot be placed in a foster or an adoptive family or cannot in any suitable manner be cared for in the child's country of origin;

(c) ensure that the child concerned by intercountry adoption enjoys safeguards and standards equivalent to those existing in the case of national adoption;

(d) take all appropriate measures to ensure that, in intercountry adoption, the placement does not result in improper financial gain for those involved in it;

(e) promote, where appropriate, the objectives of this article by concluding bilateral or multilateral arrangements or agreements, and endeavour, within this frame-work, to ensure that the placement of the child in another country is carried out by competent authorities or organs.

Article 22

1. States Parties shall take appropriate measures to ensure that a child who is seeking refugee status or who is considered a refugee in accordance with applicable international or domestic law and procedures shall, whether unaccompanied by his or her parents or by any other person, receive appropriate protection and humanitarian assistance in the enjoyment of applicable rights set forth in this Convention and in other international human rights or humanitarian instruments to which the said States are Parties.

2. For this purpose, States Parties shall provide, as they consider appropriate, co-operation in any efforts by the United Nations and other competent intergovernmental organizations or non-governmental organizations co-operating with the United Nations to protect and assist such a child and to trace the parents or other members of the family of any refugee child in order to obtain information necessary for reunification with his or her family. In cases where no parents or other members of the family can be found, the child shall be accorded the same protection as any other child permanently or temporarily deprived of his or her family environment for any reason, as set forth in the present Convention.

Article 23

1. States Parties recognize that a mentally or physically disabled child should enjoy a full and decent life, in conditions which ensure dignity, promote self-reliance, and facilitate the child's active

participation in the community.

2. States Parties recognize the right of the disabled child to special care and ensure the extension, subject to available resources, to the eligible child and those responsible for his or her care, of assistance for which application is made and which is appropriate to the child's condition and to the circumstances of the parents or other caring for the child.

3. Recognizing the special needs of a disabled child, assistance extended in accordance with paragraph 2 shall be provided free of charge, whenever possible, taking into account the financial resources of the parents or others caring for the child, and shall be designed to ensure that the disabled child has effective access to and received education, training, health care services, rehabilitation services, preparation for employment and recreation opportunities in a manner conducive to the child's achieving fullest possible social integration and individual development, including his or her cultural and spiritual development.

4. States Parties shall promote in the spirit of international co-operation the exchange of appropriate information in the field of preventive health care and of medical, psychological and functional treatment of disabled children, including dissemination of and access to information concerning methods of rehabilitation education and vocational services, with the aim of enabling States Parties to improve their capabilities and skills and to widen their experience in these areas. In this regard, particular account shall be taken of the needs of developing countries.

Article 24

1. States Parties recognize the right of the child to the enjoyment of the highest attainable standard of health and to facilities for the treatment of illness and rehabilitation of health. States Parties shall strive to ensure that no child is deprived of his or her right of access to such health care services.

2. States Parties shall pursue full implementation of this right and, in particular, shall take appropriate measures:

(a) To diminish infant and child mortality,

(b) To ensure the provision of necessary medical assistance and health care to all children with emphasis on the development of primary health care,

(c) To combat disease and malnutrition including within the framework of primary health care, through *inter alia* the application of readily available technology and through the provision of adequate nutritious foods and clean drinking water, taking into consideration the dangers and risks of environmental pollution,

(d) To ensure appropriate pre-and post-natal health care for mothers,

(e) To ensure that all segments of society, in particular parents and children, are informed, have access to education and are supported in the use of basic knowledge of child health and nutrition, the advantages of breast-feeding, hygiene and environmental sanitation and the prevention of accidents,

(f) To develop preventive health care, guidance for parents, and family planning education and services.

3. States Parties shall take all effective and appropriate measures with a view to abolishing traditional practices prejudical to the health of children.

4. States Parties undertake to promote and encourage international co-operation with a view to achieving progressively the full realization of the right recognized in this article. In this regard, account shall be taken of the needs of developing countries.

Article 25

States Parties recognize the right of a child who has been placed by the competent authorities for the purpose of care, protection, or treatment of his or her physical or mental health, to a periodic review of the treatment provided to the child and all other circumstances relevant to his or her placement.

Article 26

1. States Parties shall recognize for every child the right to benefit from social security, including social insurance, and shall take the necessary measures to achieve the full realization of this right in accordance with their national law.

2. The benefits should, where appropriate, be granted taking into account the resources and the circumstances of the child and persons having responsibility for the maintenance of the child as well as any other consideration relevant to an application for benefits made by or on behalf of the child.

Article 27

1. States Parties recognize the right of every child to a standard of living adequate for the child's physical, mental, spiritual, moral and social development.

2. The parent(s) or others responsible for the child have the primary responsibility to secure, within their abilities and financial capacities,

the conditions of living , necessary for the child's development.

3. States Parties in accordance with national conditions and within their means shall take appropriate measures to assist parents and others responsible for the child to implement this right and shall in case of need provide material assistance and support programmes, particularly with regard to nutrition, clothing and housing.

4. States shall take all appropriate measures to secure the recovery of maintenance for the child from the parents or other persons having financial responsibility for the child, both within the State Party and from abroad. In particular, where the person having financial responsibility for the child lives in a State different from that of the child, State Parties shall promote the accession to international agreements or the conclusion of such agreements as well as the making of other appropriate arrangements.

Article 28

1. States Parties recognize the right of the child to education, and with a view to achieving this right progressively and on the basis of equal opportunity, they shall, in particular:

(a) make primary education compulsory and available free to all;

(b) encourage the development of different forms of secondary education, including general and vocational education, make them available and accessible to every child, and take appropriate measures such as the introduction of free education and offering financial assistance in case of need;

(c) make higher education accessible to all on the basis of capacity by every appropriate means;

(d) make educational and vocational information and guidance available and accessible to all children;

(e) take measures to encourage regular attendance at schools and the reduction of drop-out rates.

2. States Parties shall take all appropriate measures to ensure that school discipline is administered in a manner consistent with the child's human dignity and in conformity with the present Convention.

3. States Parties shall promote and encourage international co-operation in matters relating to education, in particular with a view to contributing to the elimination of ignorance and illiteracy throughout the world and facilitating access to scientific and technical knowledge and modern teaching methods. In this regard, particular account shall be taken of the needs of developing countries.

Article 29

1. States Parties agree that the education of the child shall be directed to:

(a) the development of the child's personality, talents, and mental and physical abilities to their fullest potential;

(b) the development of respect for human rights and fundamental freedoms, and for the principles enshrined in the Charter of the United Nations;

(c) the development of respect for child's parents, his or own cultural identity, language and values, for the national values of the country in which the child is living, country from which he or she may originate, and for civilizations different from his or her own;

(d) the preparation of the child for responsible life in a free society, in the spirit of understanding, peace tolerance, equality of sexes, and friendship among all peoples, ethnic, national and religious groups and persons of indigenous origin;

(e) the development of respect for the natural environment.

2. No part of this Article or Article 28 shall be construed so as to interfere with the liberty of individuals and bodies to establish and direct educational institutions, subject always to the observance of the principles set forth in paragraph 1 of this article and to the requirements that the education given in such institutions shall conform to such minimum standards as may be laid down by the State.

Article 30

In those States in which ethnic, religious or linguistic minorities or persons of indigenous origin exist, a child belonging to such a minority or who is indigenous shall not be denied the right, in community with other members of his or her group, to enjoy his or her own culture, to profess and practice his or her own religion, or to use his or her own language.

Article 31

1. States Parties recognize the right of the child to fully participate in cultural and artistic life and shall encourage the provision of appropriate and equal opportunities for cultural, artistic, recreational and leisure activity.

Article 32

1. States Parties recognize the right of the child to be protected from economic exploitation and from performing any work that is likely be hazardous or to interfere with the child's education, or to be harmful to the child's health or physical, mental, spiritual, moral or

social development.

2. States Parties shall take legislative, administrative, social and educational measures to ensure the implementation of this article. To this end, and having regard to the relevant provisions of other international instruments, States Parties shall in particular:

(a) provide for a minimum age or minimum ages for admissions to employment;

(b) provide for appropriate regulation of the hours and conditions of employment; and

(c) provide for appropriate penalties or other sanctions to ensure the effective enforcement of this article.

Article 33

States Parties shall take all appropriate measures, including legislative, administrative, social and educational measures, to protect children from the illicit use of narcotic drugs and psychotropic substances as defined in the relevant international treaties, and to prevent the use of children in the illicit production and trafficking of such substances.

Article 34

States Parties undertake to protect the child from all forms of sexual exploitation and sexual abuse. For these purposes, States Parties shall in particular take all appropriate national, bilateral and multilateral measures to prevent:

(a) the inducement of coercion of a child to engage in any unlawful sexual activity;

(b) the exploitative use of children in prostitution or other unlawful sexual practices;

(c) the exploitative use of children in pornographic performances and materials.

Article 35

States Parties shall take all appropriate national, bilateral and multilateral measures to prevent the abduction, the sale of or traffic in children for any purpose or in any form.

Article 36

States Parties shall protect the child against all other forms of exploitation prejudicial to any aspects of the child's welfare.

Article 37

States Parties shall ensure that:

(a) No child shall be subjected to torture or other cruel, inhuman or degrading treatment or punishment. Neither capital punishment nor life imprisonment without possibility of release shall be imposed for offences committed by persons below 18 years of age;

(b) No child shall be deprived of his or her liberty unlawfully or arbitrarily. The arrest, detention or imprisonment of a child shall be in conformity with the law and shall be used only as a measure of last resort and for the shortest appropriate period of time.

(c) Every child deprived of his liberty shall be treated with humanity and respect for the inherent dignity of the human person, and in a manner which takes into account the needs of persons of their age. In particular, every child deprived of liberty shall be separated from adults unless it is considered in the child's best interest not to do so and shall have the right to maintain contact with his or her family through correspondence and visits, save in exceptional circumstances.

(d) Every child deprived of his or her liberty shall have the right to prompt access to legal and other appropriate assistance as well as the right to challenge the legality of the deprivation of his or her liberty before a court or other competent, independent and impartial authority and to a prompt decision on any such action.

Article 38

1. States Parties undertake to respect and to ensure respect for rules of international humanitarian law applicable to them in armed conflicts which are relevant to the child.
2. States Parties shall take all feasible measures to ensure that persons who have not attained the age of 15 years do not take a direct part in hostilities.
3. States Parties shall refrain from recruiting any person who has not attained the age of 15 years into their armed forces. In recruiting among those persons who have attained the age of 15 years but who have not attained the age of 18 years, States Parties shall endeavour to give priority to those who are oldest.
4. In accordance with their obligations under international humanitarian law to protect the civilian population in armed conflicts, States Parties shall take all feasible measures to ensure protection and care of children who are affected by an armed conflict.

Article 39

States Parties shall take all appropriate measures to promote physical and psychological recovery and social re-integration of a child victim of: any form of neglect, exploitation, or abuse; torture or any other form of cruel, inhuman or degrading treatment or punishment; or armed conflicts. Such recovery and re-integration shall take place on an environment which fosters the health, self-respect and dignity of the child.

Article 40

1. States Parties recognize the right of every child alleged as, accused of, or recognized as having infringed the penal law to be treated in a manner consistent with the promotion of the child's sense of dignity and worth, which reinforces the child's respect for the human rights and fundamental freedoms of others and which takes into account the child's age and desirability of promoting the child's reintegration and the child's assuming a constructive role in society.

2. To this end, and having regard to the relevant provisions of international instruments, States Parties shall, in particular, ensure that:

(a) No child shall be alleged as, be accused of, or recognized as having infringed the penal law by reason of acts or omissions which were not prohibited by national or international law at the time they were committed;

(b) Every child alleged as or accused of having infringed the penal law has at least the following guarantees:

(i) to be presumed innocent until proven guilty according to law;

(ii) to be informed promptly and directly of the charges against him or her, and if appropriate through his or her parents or legal guardian, and to have legal or other appropriate assistance in the preparation and presentation of his or her defence.

(iii) to have the matter determined without delay by a competent, independent and impartial authority or judicial body in a fair hearing according to law, in the presence of legal or other appropriate assistance and, unless it is considered not to be in the best interest of the child, in particular, taking into account his or her age or situation, his or her parents or legal guardians;

(iv) not to be compelled to give testimony or to confess guilt; to examine or have examined adverse witnesses and to obtain the participation and examination of witnesses on his or her behalf under conditional equity;

(v) if considered to have infringed the penal law, to have this decision and any measures imposed in consequence thereof reviewed by a higher competent, independent and impartial authority or judicial body according to law;

(vi) to have the free assistance of an interpreter if the child cannot understand or speak the language used;

(vii)to have his or her privacy fully respected at all stages of the procedures.

3. States Parties shall seek to promote the establishment of laws, procedures, authorities and institutions specifically applicable to children alleged as, accused of, or recognized as having infringed the penal law; and in particular:

(a) the establishment of a minimum age below which children shall be presumed not to have the capacity to infringe the penal law;

(b) whenever appropriate and desirable, measures for dealing with such children without resorting to judicial proceedings, providing that human rights and legal safeguards are fully respected.

4. A variety of dispositions, such as care, guidance and supervision orders; counselling; probation; foster case; education and vocational training programmes and other alternatives to institutional care shall be available to ensure that children are dealt with in a manner appropriate to their well-being and proportionate both to their circumstances and the offence.

Article 41

Nothing in this Convention shall affect any provisions that are more conducive to the realization of the rights of the child and that may be contained in:

(a) the law of a State Party; or

(b) international law inforce for that state.

PART II

Article 42

States Parties undertake to make the principles and provisions of the Convention widely known, by appropriate and active means, to adults and children alike.

Article 43

1. For the purpose of examining the progress made by States Parties in achieving the realization of the obligations undertaken in the present Convention, there shall be established a Committee on the Rights of the Child, which shall carry out the functions hereinafter provided.

2. The Committee shall consist of 10 experts of high moral standing and recognized competence in the field covered by this Convention. The members of the Committee shall be elected by States Parties

from among their nationals and shall serve in their personal capacity, consideration being given to equitable geographical distribution as well as to the principal legal systems.

3. The members of the Committee shall be elected by secret ballot from a list of persons nominated by States Parties. Each State Party may nominate one person from among its own nationals.

4. The initial election to the Committee shall be held no later than six months after the date of the entry into force of the present Convention and thereafter every second year. At least four months before the date of each election, the Secretary-General of the United Nations shall address a letter to States Parties inviting them to submit their nominations within two months. The Secretary-General shall subsequently prepare a list in alphabetical order of all persons thus nominated, indicating States Parties which have nominated them, and submit it to the States Parties to the present Convention.

5. The elections shall be held at meetings of States Parties convened by the Secretary-General at United Nations Headquarters. At those meetings, for which two-thirds of States Parties shall constitute a quorum, the persons elected to the Committee shall be those who obtain the largest number of votes and an absolute majority of the votes of the representatives of States Parties present and voting.

6. The members of the Committee shall be elected for a term of four years. They shall be eligible for re-election if renominated. The term of five of the members elected at the first election shall expire at the end of two years; immediately after the first election the names of these five members shall be chosen by the Chairman of the meeting.

7. If a member of the Committee dies or resigns or declares that for any other cause he or she can no longer perform the duties of the Committee, the State Party which nominated the members shall appoint another expert from among its nationals to serve for the remainder of the term, subject to the approval of the Committee.

8. The Committee shall establish its own rules of procedure.

9. The Committee shall elect is officers for a period of two years.

10. The meetings of the Committee shall normally be held at the United Nations Headquarters or at any other convenient place as determined by the Committee. The Committee shall normally meet annually. The duration of the meetings of the Committee shall be determined, and reviewed, if necessary, by a meeting of the States Parties to the present Convention, subject to the approval of the General Assembly.

11. The Secretary-General of the United Nations shall provide the necessary staff and facilities for the effective performance of the functions of the Committee under the present Convention.
12. With the approval of the General Assembly, the members of the Committee established under the present Convention shall receive emoluments from the United Nations resources on such terms and conditions as the Assembly may decide.

Article 44

1. States Parties undertake to submit to the Committee, through the Secretary-General of the United Nations, reports on the measures they have adopted which give effect to the rights recognized herein and on the progress made on the enjoyment of those rights:
(a) within two years of the entry into force of the Convention for the State Party concerned.
(b) threafter every five years.
2. Reports made under this article shall indicate factors and difficulties, if any, affecting the degree of fulfillment of the obligation under the present Convention. Reports shall also contain sufficient information to provide the Committee with a comprehensive understanding of the implementation of the Convention in the country concerned.
3. A State Party which has submitted a comprehensive initial report to the Committee need not in its subsequent reports submitted in accordance with paragraph 1 (b) repeat basic information previously provided.
4. The Committee may request from States Parties further information relevant to the implementation of the Convention.
5. The Committee shall submit to the General Assembly of the United Nations through the Economic and Social Council, every two years, reports on its activities.
6. States Parties shall make their reports widely available to the public in their own countries.

Article 45

In order to foster the effective implementation of the Convention and to encourage international co-operation in the field covered by the Convention;

(a) The specialized agencies, UNICEF and other United Nations organs shall be entitled to be represented at the consideration of the implementation of such provisions of the present Convention as fall within the scope of their mandate. The Committee may invite the specialized agencies, UNICEF and other competent bodies as it may consider appropriate to provide expert advice on the implementation of the Convention in areas falling within the scope of their respective mandates. The Committee may invite the specialized agencies, UNICEF and other United Nations organs to submit reports on the implementation of the Convention in areas falling within the scope of their activities.

(b) The Committe shall transmit, as it may consider appropriate, to the specialized agencies, UNICEF and other competent bodies, any reports from States Parties that contain a request, or indicate a need, for technical advice or assistance alongwith the Committee's observations and suggestions, if any, on these requests or indications.

(c) The Committee may recommend to the General Assembly to request the Secretary-General to undertake on its behalf studies on specific issues relating to the rights of the child.

(d) The Committee may make suggestions and general recommendations based on information received pursuant to article 44 and 45 of the Convention. Such suggestions and general recommendations shall be transmitted to any State Party concerned and reported to the General Assembly, together with comments, if any, from States Parties.

PART III

Article 46

The present Convention shall be open for signature by all States.

Article 47

The present Convention is subject to ratification. Instruments of ratification shall be deposited with the Secretary-General of the United Nations.

Article 48

The present Convention shall remain open for accession by any State. The instruments of accession shall be deposited with the Secretary-General of the United Nations.

Article 49

1. The present Convention shall enter into force on the thirtieth day following the date of deposit with the Secretary-General of the United Nations of the twentieth instrument of ratification or accession.

2. For each State ratifying or acceding to the Convention after the deposit of the twentieth instrument of ratification or accession, the Convention shall enter into force on the thirtieth day after the deposit by such State of its instrument of ratification or accession.

Article 50

1. Any State Party may propose an amendment and file it with the Secretary-General of the United Nations. The Secretary-General shall thereupon communicate the proposed amendment to States Parties with a request that they indicate whether they favour a conference of States Parties for the purpose of considering and voting upon the proposals. In the event that within four months from the date of such communication at least one-third of the States Parties favour such a conference, the Secretary-General shall convene the conference under the auspices of the United Nations. Any amendment adopted by a majority of States Parties present and voting at the conference shall be submitted to the General Assembly of the United Nations for approval.
2. An amendment adopted in accordance with paragraph (1) of this Article shall enter into force when it has been approved by the General Assembly of the United Nations and accepted by a two-third majority of States Parties.
3. When an amendment enters into force, it shall be binding on those States Parties still being bound by the provisions of this Convention and any earlier amendments which they have accepted.

Article 51

1. The Secretary-General of the United Nations shall receive and circulate to all States the text of reservations made by States at the time of ratification or accession.
2. A reservation incompatible with the object and purpose of the present Convention shall not be permitted.
3. Reservations may be withdrawn at any time by notification to this effect addressed to the Secretary-General of the United Nations who shall then inform all States. Such notification shall take effect on the date on which it is received by the Secretary-General.

Article 52

A State Party may denounce this Convention by written notification to the Secretary-General of the United Nations. Denunciation becomes effective one year after the date of receipt of the notification by the Secretary-General.

Article 53

The Secretary-General of the United Nations is designated as the depository of the present Convention.

Article 54

The original of the present Convention, of which the Arabaic, Chinese, English, French, Russian and Spanish texts are equally authentic, shall be deposited with the Secretary-General of the United Nations.

In witness thereof the undersigned plenipotentiaries, being duly authorized thereto by their respective Governments, have signed the present Convention.

Done at New York this 20th day of November, 1989.

Annexure II

Convention 138

Convention Concerning Minimun Age Admission to Employment

The General Conference of the International Labour Organisation,

Having been convened at Geneva by the Governing Body of the International Labour Office, and having met in its Fifty-eight Session on 6 June 1973, and

Having decided upon the adoption of certain proposals with regard to minimum age for admission to employment, which is the fourth item on the agenda of the session, and

Noting the terms of the Minimum Age (Industry) Convention 1919, the Minimum Age (Sea) Convention, 1920, the Minimum Age (Agriculture) Convention, 1921, the Minimum Age (Trimmers and Stokers) Convention, 1921, the Minimum Age (Non-Industrial Employment) Convention, 1932, the Minimum Age (Sea) Convention (Revised), 1936, the Minimum Age (Industry) Convention (Revised), 1937, the Minimum Age (Fishermen) Convention, 1959, and the Minimum Age (Underground Work) Convention, 1965, and

Considering that the time has come to establish a general instrument on the subject, which would gradually replace the existing ones applicable to limited economic sectors, with a view to achieving the total abolition of child labour, and

Having determined that this instrument shall take the form of an international Convention,

adopts this twenty-sixth day of June of the year one thousand nine hundred and seventy-three the following Convention, which may be cited as the Minimum Age Convention, 1973.

Article 1

Each Member for which this Convention is in force undertakes to pursue a national policy designed to ensure the effective abolition of child labour and to raise progressively the minimum age for admission to employment or work to a level consistent with the fullest physical and mental development of young persons.

Article 2

1. Each Member which ratifies this Convention shall specify, in a declaration appended to its ratification, a minimum age for admission to employment or work within its territory and on means of transport registered in its territory; subject to Articles 4 to 8 of this Convention, no one under that age shall be admitted to employment or work in any occupation.
2. Each Member which has ratified this Convention may subsequently notify the Director-General of the International Labour Office, by further declarations, that it specifies a minimum age higher than that previously specified.
3. The minimum age specified in pursuance of paragraph 1 of this Article shall not be less than the age of completion of compulsory schooling and, in any case, shall not be less than 15 years.
4. Notwithstanding the provisions of paragraph 3 of this Article, a Member whose economy and educational facilities are insufficiently developed may, after consultation with the organizations of employers and workers concerned, where such exist, initially specify a minimum age of 14 years.
5. Each Member which has specified a minimum age of 14 years in pursuance of the provisions of the preceding paragraph shall include in its reports on the application of this Convention submitted under Article 22 of the Constitution of the International Labour Organisation a statement—
(a) that its reason for doing so subsists; or
(b) that it renounces its right to avail itself of the provisions in question as from a stated date.

Article 3

1. The minimum age for admission to any type of employment or work which by its nature or the circumstances in which it is carried out is likely to jeopardise the health, safety or morals of young persons shall not be less than 18 years.
2. The types of employment or work to which paragraph 1 of this Article applies shall be determined by national laws or regulations or by the competent authority, after consultation with the organisations of employers and workers concerned, where such exist.
3. Notwithstanding the provisions of paragraph 1 of this Article,

national laws or regulations or the competent authority may, after consultation with the organizations of employers and workers concerned, where such exsit, authorise employment or workers as from the age of 16 years on condition that the health, safety and morals of the young person concerned are fully protected and that the young persons have received adequate specific instructions or vocational training in the relevant branch of activity.

Article 4

1. In so far as necessary, the competent authority, after consultation with the organisations of employers and workers concerned, where such exist, may exclude from the application of this Convention limited categories of employment or work in respect of which special and substantial problems of application arise.

2. Each Member which ratifies this Convention shall list in its first report on the application of the Convention submitted under Article 22 of the Constitution of the International Labour Organisation any categories which may have been excluded in pursuance of paragraph 1 of this Article, giving the reasons for such exclusion, and shall state in subsequent reports the position of its law and practice in respect of the categories excluded and the extent to which effect has been given or is proposed to be given to the Convention in respect of such categories.

3. Employment or work covered by Article 3 of this Convention shall not be excluded from the application of the Convention in pursuance of this Article.

Article 5

1. A Member whose economy and administrative facilities are insufficiently developed may, after consultation with the organisations of employers and workers concerned, where such exist, initially limit the scope of application of this Convention.

2. Each Member which avails itself of the provisions of paragraph 1 of this Article shall specify, in a declaration appended to its ratification, the branches of economic activity or types of undertakings to which it will apply the provisions of the Convention.

3. The provisions of the Convention shall be applicable as a minimum to the following: mining and quarrying; manufacturing; construction; electricity, gas and water; sanitary services; transport, storage and communication; and plantations and other agricultural undertakings mainly producing for commercial purposes, but excluding family and small-scale holdings producing for local consumption and not regularly

employing hired workers.

4. Any Member which has limited the scope of application of this Convention in pursuance of this Article—

(a) shall indicate in its reports under Article 22 of the Constitution of the International Labour Organisation the general position as regards the employment or work of young person and children in the branches of activity which are excluded from the scope of application of this Convention and any progress which may have been made towards wider application of the provisions of the Convention;

(b) may at any time formally extend the scope of application by a declaration addressed to the Director-General of the International Labour Office.

Article 6

This Convention does not apply to work done by children and young persons in schools for general, vocational or technical education or in other training institutions, or to work done by persons at least 14 years of age in undertakings, where such work is carried out in accordance with conditions prescribed by the competent authority, after consultation with the organisations of employers and workers concerned, where such exist, and is an integral part of—

(a) a course of education or training for which a school or training institution is primarily responsible,

(b) a programme of training mainly or entirely in an undertaking, which programme has been approved by the competent authority; or

(c) a programme of guidance or orientation designed to facilitate the choice of an occupation or of a line of training.

Article 7

1. National laws or regulations may permit the employment or work of persons 13 to 15 years of age on light work which is—

(a) not likely to be harmful to their health or development; and

(b) not such as to prejudice their attendance at school, their participation in vocational orientation or training programmes approved by the competent authority or their capacity to benefit from the instruction received.

2. National laws or regulations may also permit the employment or work of persons who are at least 15 years of age but have not yet completed their compulsory schooling on work which meets the requirement set forth in sub-paragraphs (a) and (b) of paragraph 1 of this Article.

3. The competent authority shall determine the activities in which employment or work may be permitted under paragraphs 1 and 2 of this Article and shall prescribe the number of hours during which and the conditions in which such employment or work may be undertaken.

4. Notwithstanding the provisions of paragraphs 1 and 2 of this Article, a Member which has availed itself of the provisions of paragraph 4 of Article 2 may, for as long as it continues to do so, substitute the ages 12 and 14 for the ages 13 and 15 in paragraph 1 and the age 14 for the age 15 in paragraph 2 of this Article.

Article 8

1. After consultation with the organisations of employers and workers concerned, where such exist, the competent authority may, by permits granted in individual cases, allow exceptions to the prohibition of employment or work provided for in Article 2 of this Convention, for such purposes as participation in artistic performances.

2. Permits so granted shall limit the number of hours during which and prescribe the conditions in which employment or work is allowed.

Article 9

1. All necessary measures, including the provision of appropriate penalties, shall be taken by the competent authority to ensure the effective enforcement of the provisions of this Convention.

2. National laws or regulations or the competent authority shall define the persons responsible for compliance with the provisions giving effect to the Convention.

3. National laws or regulations or the competent authority shall prescribe the registers or other documents which shall be kept and made available by the employer; such registers or documents shall contain the names and ages or dates of birth, duly certified wherever possible, of persons whom he employs or who work for him and who are less than 18 years of age.

Article 10

1. This Convention revises, on the terms set forth in this Article, the Minimum Age (Industry) Convention, 1919, the Minimum Age (Sea) Convention, 1920, the Minimum Age (Agriculture) Convention, 1921, the Minimum Age (Trimmers and Stokers) Convention, 1921, the Minimum Age (Non-Industrial Employment, Convention, 1932, the Minimum Age (Sea) Convention (Revised), 1936, the Minimum Age (Industry) Convention (Revised), 1937, the Minimum Age (Non-Industrial Employment) Convention (Revised), 1937, the Minimum Age (Fishermen) Convention, 1959, and the Minimum Age

(Underground Work) Convention, 1965.

2. The coming into force of this Convention shall not close the Minimum Age (Sea) Convention (Revised), 1936, the Minimum Age (Industry) Convention (Revised), 1937, the Minimum Age (Non-Industrial Employment) Convention (Revised), 1937, the Minimum Age (Fishermen) Convention, 1959, or the Minimum Age (Underground Work) Convention, 1965 to further ratification.

3. The Minimum Age (Industry) Convention, 1919, the Minimum Age (Sea) Convention, 1920, the Minimum Age (Agriculture) Convention 1921, and the Minimum Age (Trimmers and Stokers) Convention, 1921, shall be closed to further ratification when all the parties thereto have consented to such closing by ratification of this Convention or by a declaration communicated to the Director-General of the International Labour Office.

4. When the obligations of this Convention are accepted:

(a) by a Member which is a party to the Minimum Age (Industry) Convention (Revised), 1937, and a minimum age of not less than 15 years is specified in pursuance of Article 2 of this Convention, this shall *ipso jure* involve the immediate denunciation of that Convention,

(b) in respect of non-industrial employment as defined in the Minimum Age (Non-Industrial Employment) Convention, 1932, by a Member which is a party to that Convention, this shall *ipso jure* involve the immediate denunciation of that Convention.

(c) in respect of non-industrial employment as defined in the Minimum Age (Non-Industrial Employment) Convention (Revised), 1937 by a Member which is a party to that Convention, and a minimum age of not less than 15 years is specified in pursuance of Article 2 of this Convention, this shall *ipso jure* involve the immediate denunciation of that Convention,

(d) in respect of maritime employment, by a Member which is a party to the Minimum Age (Sea) Convention (Revised), 1936, and a minimum age of not less than 15 years is specified in pursuance of Article 2 of this Convention or the Member specifies that Article 3 of this Convention applies to maritime employment, this shall *ipso jure* involve the immediate denunciation of that Convention,

(e) in respect of employment in maritime fishing, by a Member which is a party to the Minimum Age (Fishermen) Convention, 1959 and a Minimum age of not less than 15 years is specified in pursuance of Article 2 of this Convention or the Member specifies that Article 3 of this Convention applied to employment in maritime fishing, this shall *ipso jure* involve the immediate denunciation of that Convention,

(f) by a Member which is a party to the Minimum Age (Underground Work) Convention, 1965, and a minimum age of not less than the age specified in pursuance of that Convention is specified in pursuance of Article 2 of this Convention or the Member specifies that such an age applies to employment undergropund in mines in virtue of Article 3 of this Convention, this shall *ipso jure* involve the immediate denunciation of that Convention, if and when this Convention shall have come into force.

5. Acceptance of the obligations of this Convention—

(a) shall involve the denunciation of the Minimum Age (Industry) Convention, 1919, in accordance with Article 12 thereof,

(b) in respect of agriculture shall involve the denunciation of the Minimum Age (Agriculture) Convention, 1921, in accordance with Article 9 thereof,

(c) in respect of maritime employment shall involve the denunciation of the Minimum Age (Sea) Convention, 1920, in accordance with Article 10 thereof, and of the Minimum Age (Trimmers and Stokers) Convention, 1921, in accordance with Article 12 thereof, if and when this Convention shall have come into force.

Article 11

The formal ratifications of this Convention shall be communicated to the Director-General of the International Labour Office for registration.

Article 12

1. This Convention shall be binding only upon those Members of the International Labour Organisations whose ratifications have been registered with the Director-General.
2. It shall come into force twelve months after the date on which the ratifications of two Members have been registered with the Director-General.
3. Thereafter, this Convention shall come into force for any Member twelve months after the date on which its ratification has been registered.

Article 13

1. A Member which has ratified this Convention may denounce it after the expiration of ten years from the date on which the Convention first comes into force, by an act communicated to the Director-General of the International Labour Office for registration. Such denunciation shall not take effect until one year after the date on which it is registered.

2. Each Member which has ratified this Convention and which does not, within the year following the expiration of the period of ten years mentioned in the preceding paragraph, exercise the right of denunciation provided for in this Article, will be bound for another period of ten years and, thereafter, may denounce this Convention at the expiration of each period of ten years under the terms provided for in this Article.

Article 14

1. The Director-General of the International Labour Office shall notify all Members of the International Labour Organisation of the registration of all ratifications and denunciations communicated to him by the Members of the Organisation.

2. When notifying the Members of the organisation of the registration of the second ratification communicated to him, the Director-General shall draw the attention of the Members of the Organisation to the date upon which the Convention will come into force.

Article 15

The Director-General of the International Labour Office shall communicate to the Secretary-General of the United Nations for registration in accordance with Article 102 of the Charter of the United Nations full particulars of all ratifications and acts of denunciation registered by him in accordance with the provisions of the preceding Articles.

Article 16

At such times as it may consider necessary the Governing Body of the International Labour Office shall present to the General Conference a report on the working of this Convention and shall examine the desirability of placing on the agenda of the Conference the question of its revision in whole or in part.

Article 17

1. Should the Conference adopt a new Convention revising this Convention in whole or in part, then, unless the new Convention otherwise provides—

(a) the ratification by a Member of the new revising Convention shall *ipso jure* involve the immediate denunciation of this Convention, notwithstanding the provisions of Article 13 above, if and when the new revising Convention shall have come into force;

(b) as from the date when the new revising Convention comes into force this convention shall cease to be open to ratification by the Members.

2. This Convention shall in any case remain in force in its actual form and content for those Members which have ratified it but have not ratified the revising Convention.

Annexure III

Recommendation 146

Recommendation Concerning Minimum Age for Admission to Employment

The General Conference of the International Labour Organisation,
Having been convened at Geneva by the Governing Body of the International Labour Office, and having met in its Fifty-eight Session on 6 June 1973, and
Recognising that the effective abolition of child labour and the progressive raising of the minimum age for admission to employment constitute only one aspect of the protection and advancement of children and young persons, and
Noting the concern of the whole United Nations system with such protection and advancement, and
Having adopted the Minimum Age Convention, 1973, and
Desirous to define further certain elements of policy which are the concern of the International Labour Organisation, and
Having decided upon the adoption of certain proposals regarding minimum age for admission to employment, which is the fourth item on the agenda of the session, and
Having determined that these proposals shall take the form of a Recommendation supplementing the Minimum Age Convention, 1973,
adopts this twenty-sixth day of June of the year one thousand nine hundred and seventy-three the following Recommendation, which may be cited as the Minimum Age Recommendation, 1973:

I. NATIONAL POLICY

1. To ensure the success of the National policy provided for in Article 1 of the Minimum Age Convention, 1973, high priority should be given to planning for and meeting the needs of children and youth in national development policies and programmes and to the progressive extension of the inter-related measures necessary to provide the best possible conditions of physical and mental growth for children and young persons.

2. In this connection special attention should be given to such areas

of planning and policy as the following:

(a) firm national commitment to full employment, in accordance with the Employment Policy Convention and Recommendation, 1964, and the taking of measures designed to promote employment-oriented development in rural and urban areas;

(b) the progressive extension of other economic and social measures to alleviate poverty wherever it exists and to ensure family living standards and income which are such as to make it unnecessary to have recourse to the economic activity of children;

(c) the development and progressive extension, without any discrimination, of social security and family welfare measures aimed at ensuring child maintenance, including children's allowances;

(d) the development and progressive extension of adequate facilities for education and vocational orientation and training appropriate in form and content to the needs of the children and young person concerned;

(e) the development and progressive extension of appropriate facilities for the protection and welfare of children and young persons, including employed young persons, and for the promotion of their development.

3. Particular account should as necessary be taken of the needs of children and young persons who do not have families or do not live with their own families and of migrant children and young persons who live and travel with their families. Measures taken to that end should include the provision of fellowships and vocational training.

4. Full-time attendance at school or participation in approved vocational orientation or training programmes should be required and effectively ensured up to an age at least equal to that specified for admission to employment in accordance with Article 2 of the Minimum Age Convention, 1973.

5. (1) Consideration should be given to measures such as preparatory training, not involving hazards, for types of employment or work in respect of which the minimum age prescribed in accordance with Article 3 of the Minimum Age Convention 1973, is higher than the age of completion of compulsory full-time schooling.

(2) Analogous measures should be envisaged where the progressional exigencies of a particular occupation include a minimum age for admission which is higher than the age of completion of compulsory full-time schooling.

II. MINIMUM AGE

7. (1) Members should take as their objective the progressive raising

to 16 years of the minimum age for admission to employment or work specified in pursuance of Article 2 of the Minimum Age Convention, 1973.

(2) Where the minimum age for employment of work covered by Article 2 of the Minimum Age Convention, 1973, is still below 15 years, urgent steps should be taken to raise it to that level.

8. Where it is not immediately feasible to fix a minimum age for all employment in agriculture and in related activities in rural areas, a minimum age should be fixed at least for employment on plantations and in the other agricultural undertakings referred to in Article 5, paragraph 3, of the Minimum Age Convention, 1973.

III. HAZARDOUS EMPLOYMENT OR WORK

9. Where the minimum age for admission to types of employment or work which are likely to jeopardise the health, safety or morals of young persons in still below 18 years, immediate steps should be taken to raise it to that level.

10. (1) In determining the types of employment or work to which Article 3 of the Minimum Age Convention, 1973, applies, full account should be taken of relevant international labour standards, such as those concerning dangerous substances, agents or processes (including ionising radiation), the lifting of heavy weights and underground work.

(2) The list of the types of employment or work in question should be re-examined periodically and revised as necessary, particularly in the light of advancing scientific and technological knowledge.

11. Where, by reference to Article 5 of the Minimum Age Convention, 1973, a minimum age is not immediately fixed for certain branches of economic activities or types of undertakings, appropriate minimum age provision should be made applicable therein to types of employment or work presenting hazards for young persons.

IV. CONDITIONS OF EMPLOYMENT

12. (1) Measures should be taken to ensure that the conditions in which children and young persons under the age of 18 years are employed or work reach and are maintained at a satisfactory standard. These conditions should be supervised closely.

(2) Measures should likewise be taken to safeguard and supervise the conditions in which children and young persons undergo vocational orientation and training within undertakings, training institutions and schools for vocational or technical education and to formulate standards for their protection and development.

13. (1) In connection with the application of the preceding Paragraph,

as well as in giving effect to Article 7, Paragraph 3, of the Minimum Age Convention, 1973, special attention should be given to—

(a) the provision of fair remuneration and its protection, bearing in mind the principle of equal pay for equal work;

(b) the strict limitation of the hours spent at work in a day and in a week, and the prohibition of overtime, so as to allow enough time for education and training (including the time needed for homework related thereto), for rest during the day and for leisure activities;

(c) the granting, without possibility of exception, save in genuine emergency of a minimum consecutive period of 12 hours' night rest, and of customary weekly rest days;

(d) the granting of an annual holiday with pay of at least four weeks, and, in any case, not shorter than that granted to adults;

(e) coverage by social security schemes, including employment injury, medical care and sickness benefit schemes, whatever the condition of employment or work may be;

(f) the maintenance of satisfactory standards of safety and health and appropriate instruction and supervision.

(2) Sub-paragraph (1) of this Paragraph applies to young seafarers in so far as they are not covered in respect of the matters dealt with therein by International Labour Conventions or Recommendations specifically concerned with maritime employment.

V. ENFORCEMENT

14. (1) Measures to ensure the effective application of the Minimum Age Convention, 1973, and of this Recommendation should include —

(a) the strengthening as necessary of labour inspection and related services, for instance by the special training of inspectors to detect abuse in the employment of work of children and young persons and to correct such abuses; and

(b) the strengthening of services for the improvement and inspection of training in undertakings.

(2) Emphasis should be placed on the role which can be played by inspectors in supplying information and advice on effective means of complying with relevant provisions as well as in securing their enforcement.

(3) Labour inspection and inspection of training in undertakings should be closely coordinated to provide the greatest economic efficiency and, generally, the labour administration services should work in close co-operation with the services responsible for the

education, training, welfare and guidance of children and young persons.

15. Special attention should be paid—

(a) to the enforcement of provisions concerning employment in hazardous types of employment or work; and

(b) in so far as education or training is compulsory, to the prevention, of the employment or work of children and young persons during the hours when instruction is available.

16. The following measures should be taken to facilitate the verification of ages:

(a) the public authorities should maintain an effective system of birth registration, which should include the issue of birth certificates;

(b) employers should be required to keep and to make available to the competent authority registers or other documents indicating the names and ages or dates of birth, duly certified wherever possible, not only of children and young persons employed by them but also of those receiving vocational orientation or training in their undertakings;

(c) children and young persons working in the streets, in outside stalls, in public places, in intinerant occupations or in other circumstances which make the checking of employer's records impracticable should be issued licences or other documents indicating their eligibility for such work.

Annexure IV

The Child Labour (Prohibition and Regulation) Act, 1986 and the Child Labour (Prohibition and Regulation) Rules, 1988

The Child Labour (Prohibition and Regulation) Act, 1986 (Act No. 61 of 1986)

[23rd December, 1986]

An Act to prohibit the engagement of children in certain employments and to regulate the conditions of work or children in certain other employments

Be it enacted by Parliament in the Thirty-seventh Year of the Republic of India as follows:

Comments

Social and beneficial legislation—Social legislation is designed to protect the interest of a class of society who, because of their economic conditions, deserves such protection. With a view to pass the test of reasonable classification there must exist intelligible differentiate between persons on things grouped together from those who have been left out and there must be a reasonable nexus with the object to be achieved by the legislation.

The Court must strive to so interpret the statute as to protect and advance the object and purpose of the enactment. Any narrow or technical interpretation of the provisions would defeat the legislative policy. The Court must, therefore, keep the legislative policy in mind in applying the provisions of the Act to the facts of the case.

PART I
Preliminary

1. Short title, extent and commencement—

(1) This Act may be called the Child Labour (Prohibition and Regulation) Act, 1986.
(2) It extends to the whole of India.
(3) The provisions of this Act, other than Part III, shall come into force at once, and Part III shall come into force on such date as the Central Government may, by notification in the official Gazette, appoint, and different dates may be appointed for different States and for different classes of establishments.

Comment

May and shall—Where the Legislature uses two words "may" and "shall" in two different parts of the same provision *prima facie* it would appear that the Legislature manifested its intention to make one part directory and another mandatory. But that by itself is not decisive. The power of the Court still to ascertain the real intention of the Legislature by carefully examining the scope of the statute to find out whether the provision is directory or mandatory remains unimpaired even where both the words are used in the same provision. In interpreting the provisions the exercise undertaken by the Court is to make explicit the intention of the Legislature which enacted the legislation. It is not for the Court to reframe the legislation for the very good reason that the powers to "legislate" have not been conferred on the Court.

In order to sustain the presumption of constitutionality of a legislative measure, the Court can take into consideration matters of common knowledge, matters of common report, the history of the times and also assume every state of facts which can be conceived existing at the time of the legislation.

2. Definitions—In this Act, unless the context otherwise requires,
(i) "appropriate Government" means, in relation to an establishment under the control of the Central Government or a railway administration or a major port or a control of the Central Government or a railway administration or a major port or a mine or oilfield, the Central Government, and in all other cases, the State Government;
(ii) "child" means a person who has not completed his fourteenth year of age;
(iii) "day" means a period of twenty-four hours beginning at midnight;
(iv) "establishment" includes a shop, commercial establishment, workshop, farm, residential hotel, restaurant, eating-house, theatre or other place of public amusement or entertainment;
(v) "family", in relation to an occupier, means the individual, the

wife or husbands as the case may be, of such individual, and their children, brother or sister of such individual;

(vi) "occupier", in relation to an establishment or a workshop, means the person who has the ultimate control over the affairs of the establishment or workshop;

(vii) "prescribed" means prescribed by rules made under Sec. 18;

(ix) "week" means a period of seven days beginning at midnight on Saturday night or such other night as may be approved in writing for a particular area by the Inspector;

(x) "workshop" means any premises (including the precincts thereof) wherein any industrial process is carried on, but does not include any premises to which the provisions of Sec. 67 of the Factories Act, 1948 (63 of 1948), for the time being, apply.

Comments

This section defines the various words and expressions occurring in the Act.

Interpretation of section—The Court can merely interpret the section; it cannot re-write, re-cast or re-design the section.

Ambiguous expression—Courts must find out the literal meaning of the expression in the task of construction. In doing so if the expressions are ambiguous then the construction that fulfills the object of the legislation must provide the key to the meaning. Courts must not make mockery of legislation and should take a constructive approach to fulfill the purpose and for that purpose, if necessary, iron out the creases.

PART II
Prohibition of Employment of Children in Certain Occupations and Processes

3. Prohibition of employment of children in certain occupations and processes—No child shall be employed or permitted to work in any of the occupations set forth in Part A of the Schedule or in any workshop wherein any of the processes set forth in Part B of the Schedule is carried on:

Provided that nothing in this section shall apply to any workshop wherein any process is carried on by the occupier with the aid of his family or to any school established by or receiving assistance or recognition from, Government.

Comment

This section imposes prohibition on employment of children in the occupation and processes specified in the Scheduled.

Proviso. A proviso is intended to limit the enacted provision so as to except something which would have otherwise been within it or in some measure to modify the enacting clause. Sometimes proviso may be embedded in the main provision and becomes an integral part of it so as to amount to a substantive provision itself.

4. **Power to amend the Schedule**—The Central Government, after giving by notification in the official Gazette, not less than three months' notice of its intention so to do, may, be like notification, add any occupation or process to the Schedule and thereupon the Schedule shall be deemed to have been amended accordingly.

Comment

This section empowers the Central Government to amend the Schedule so as to include therein any occupation or process considered necessary.

Construction of a section—It is an elementary rule that construction of a section is to be made of all parts together. It is not permissible to omit any part of it. For, the principle that the statute must be read as a whole is equally applicable to different parts of the same section.

5. **Child Labour Technical Advisory Committee**—

(1) The Central Government may, by notification in the official Gazette, constitute an advisory committee to be called the Child Labour Technical Advisory Committee (hereinafter in this section referred to as the Committee) to advise the Central Government for the purpose of addition or occupations and processes to the Schedule.

(2) The Committee shall consist of a Chairman and such other members not exceeding ten, as may be appointed by the Central Government.

(3) The Committee shall meet as often as it may consider necessary and shall have power to regulate its own procedure.

(4) The Committee may, if it deems it necessary so to do, constitute one or more subcommittees and may appoint to any such sub-committee, whether generally or for the consideration of any particular matter, any person who is not a member of the Committee.

(5) The term of office of, the manner of filling casual vacancies in the office of, and the allowances, if any, payable to, the Chairman and other members of the Committee, and the conditions and restrictions subject to which the Committee may appoint any person

who is not a member of the Committee as a member of any of its sub-committees shall be such as may be prescribed.

Comment

This section empowers the Central Government to constitute the Child Labour Technical Advisory Committee for giving advice in the matter of inclusion of any occupation and process in the Schedule.

PART III

Regulation of Conditions of Work of Children

6. **Application of Part**—The provisions of this Part shall apply to an establishment or a class of establishments in which none of the occupations or processes referred to in Sec. 3 is carried on.

Comment

This section lays down that provisions of this Part shall apply to an establishment in which none of the prohibited occupation or processes is carried on.

7. **Hours and period of work**—

(1) No child shall be required or permitted to work in any establishment in excess of such number of hours as may be prescribed for such establishment or class of establishments.

(2) The period of work on each day shall be so fixed that no period shall exceed three hours and that no child shall work for more than three hours before he has had an interval for rest for at least one hour.

(3) The period of work of a child shall be so arranged that inclusive of this interval for rest, under sub-section (2), it shall not be spread over more than six hours, including the time spent in waiting for work on any day.

(4) No child shall be permitted or required work between 7 p.m. and 8 a.m.

(5) No child shall be permitted or required to work overtime.

(6) No child shall be required or permitted to work in any establishment on any day on which he has already been working in another establishment.

Comment

This section prescribes working hours for a child labour.

Provision if mandatory or directory. The surest test for determination as to whether the provisions is mandatory or directory is to see as to whether the sanction is provided therein.

8. Weekly holidays— Every child employed in an establishment shall be allowed in each week, a holiday of one whole day, which day shall be specified by the occupier in a notice permanently exhibited in a conspicuous place in the establishment and the day so specified shall not be altered by the occupier more than once in three months.

Comment

This section lays down that a weekly holiday should be allowed to every child labour.

9. Notice to Inspector.

(1) Every occupier in relation to an establishment in which a child was employed or permitted to work immediately before the date of commencement of this Act in relation to such establishment shall, within a period of thirty days from such commencement, send to the Inspector within whose local limits the establishment is situated, a written notice containing the following particulars, namely:

(a) the name and situation of the establishment;

(b) the name of the person in actual management of the establishment;

(c) the address to which communications relating to establishment should be sent; and

(d) the nature of the occupation or process carried on it establishment.

(2) Every occupier, in relation to an establishment, who employs, or permits to work, any child after the date of commencement of this Act in relation to such establishment, shall, within a period of thirty days from the date of such employment, send to the Inspector within whose local limits the establishment is situated, a written notice containing the particulars as are mentioned in sub-section (1)

Explanation — For the purposes of sub-sections (1) and (2), "date of commencement of this Act, in relation to an establishment" means the date of bringing into force of this Act in relation to such establishment.

(3) Nothing in Secs. 7, 8 and 9 shall apply to any establishment wherein any process is carried on by the occupier with the aid of his family or to any school established by, or receiving assistance or recognition from, Government.

Comment

This section makes provision for furnishing of information regarding employment of a child labour to Inspector.

Explanation — It is now well settled that an explanation added to a statutory provision is not a substantive provision in any sense of the term but as the plain meaning of the world itself shows it is merely meant to explain or clarify certain ambiguities which may have crept in the statutory provision.

10. Disputes as to age — If any question arises between an Inspector and an occupier as to the age of any child who is employed or is permitted to work by him in an establishment, the question shall, in the absence of a certificate as to the age of such child granted by the prescribed medical authority, be referred by the Inspector for decision to the prescribed medical authority.

Comment

This section makes provision for settlement of disputes as to age of any child labour.

11.Maintenance of register — There shall be maintained by every occupier in respect of children employed or permitted to work in any establishment, a register to be available for inspection by an Inspector at all times during working hours or when work is being carried on in any such establishment showing —

(a) the name and date of birth of every child so employed or permitted to work;

(b) hours and periods of work of any such child and the intervals of rest to which he is entitled;

(c) the nature of work of any such child; and

(d) such other particulars as may be prescribed.

Comment

This section makes provision of maintenance of register in respect of child labour.

12. Display of notice containing abstract of Secs. 3 and 14. — Every railway administration, every port authority and every occupier shall cause to be displayed in a conspicuous and accessible place at every station on its railway or within the limits of a port or at the place of work, as the case may be, a notice in the local language and in the English language containing an abstract of Secs. 3 and 14.

Comment

This section makes provision for display of notice in a conspicuous place at every railway station or port of place of work regarding prohibition of employment of child labour, penalties, etc., in the local language and in the English language.

13. Health and safety —

(1) The appropriate Government may, by notification in the official Gazette, make rules for the health and safety of the children employed or permitted to work in any establishment or class of establishments.

(2) Without prejudice to the generality of the foregoing provisions, the said rules may provide for all or any of the following matters, namely;

(a) cleanliness in the place of work and its freedom from nuisance;
(b) disposal of wastes and effluents;
(c) ventilation and temperature;
(d) dust and fume;
(e) artificial humidification;
(f) lighting;
(g) drinking water;
(h) latrine and urinals;
(i) spittoons;
(j) fencing of machinery;
(k) work at or near machinery in motion;
(l) employment of children on dangerous machines;
(m) instructions, training and supervision in relation to employment of children on dangerous machines;
(n) device for cutting off power;
(o) self-acting machines;
(p) easing of new machinery;
(q) floor, stairs and means of access;
(r) pits, sumps, opening in floors, etc;
(s) excessive weights;
(t) protection of eyes;
(u) explosive or inflammable dust, gas etc.
(v) precautions in case of fire;
(w) maintenance of buildings; and
(x) safety of buildings and machinery.

Comment

This section lays down that the Government is required to make rules for the health and safety of the child labour.

14. Penalities—

Whoever employs any child or permits any child to work in contravention of the provisions of Sec.3 shall be punishable with imprisonment for a term which shall not be less than three months but which may extend to one year or with fine which shall not be less than ten thousand rupees but which may extend to twenty thousand rupees or with both.

(2) Whoever, having been convicted of an offence under Sec. 3, commits a like offence afterwards, he shall be punishable with imprisonment for a term which shall not be less than six months but which may extend to two years.

(3).Whoever—

(a) fails to give notice as required by Sec. 9; or

(b) fails to maintain a register as required by Sec. 11 or makes any false entry in any such register; or

(c) fails to display a notice containing an abstract of Sec. 3 and this section as required by Sec. 12; or

(d) fails to comply with or contravenes any other provisions of this Act or the rules made thereunder;

shall be punishable with simple imprisonment which may extend to one month or with fine which may extend to ten thousand rupees or with both.

Comments

This section makes provision for penalty for contravention of the provisions of the Act.

Penalty — Mens rea—Essential — Penalty proceedings are quasi criminal proceedings. Before penalty can be imposed it has to be ensured that *mens rea* has been established.

Penal provision - Object of — The law in its wisdom seeks to punish the guilty who commits the sin, and not his son, who is innocent.

15. Modified application of certain laws in relation to penalties.—

(1) Where any person is found guilty and convicted of contravention of any of the provisions mentioned in sub-section (2), he shall be liable to penalties as provided in sub-sections (1) and (2) of Sec. 14 of this Act and not under the Acts in which those provisions are contained.

(2) The provision referred to in sub-section (1) are the provisions mentioned below:

(a) section 67 of the Factories Act, 1948 (63 of 1948);
(b) section 40 of the Mines Act, 1952 (35 of 1952);
(c) section 109 of the Merchant Shipping Act, 1958 (44 of 1958); and
(d) section 21 of the Motor Transport Workers Act,1961 27, of 1961).

Comment

This section makes provision of penalties under the Act even when any person is found guilty and convicted of contravention of any of the provisions of Sec. 67 of the Factories Act, 1948, Sec. 40 of the Mines Act, 1952, Sec. 109 of the Merchant Shipping Act, 1958 and Sec. 21 of the Motor Transport Workers Act, 1961.

16. Procedures relating to offences—

1) Any person, police officer or Inspector may file a complaint of the commission of an offence under this Act in any Court of competent jurisdiction.
(2) Every certificate as to the age of a child which has been granted by a prescribed medical authority shall, for the purposes of this Act, be conclusive evidence as to the age of the child to whom it relates.
(3) No court inferior to that of a Metropolitan Magistrate or a Magistrate of the first class shall try any offence under this Act.

Comment

This section lays down that any person, police officer or inspector can make a complaint regarding commission of offences. It also lays down the procedure for disposal of such a complaint.

Court Duty of. — The Court should meticulously consider all facts and circumstances of the case. The Court is not bound to grant specific performance merely because it is lawful to do so. The motive behind the litigation should also enter into the judicial verdict. The Court should take care to see that it is used as an instrument of oppression to have an unfair advantage to the plaintiff.

17. Appointment of inspectors. — The appropriate Government may appoint inspectors for the purposes of securing compliance with the provisions of this Act and any inspector so appointed shall be deemed to be a public servant within the meaning of the Indian Penal Code (45 of 1860).

Comment

This section empowers the appropriate Government to appoint inspectors for securing compliance of the provisions of the Act. Such inspector is deemed to be a public servant within the meaning of the Indian Penal Code (45 of 1860).

Public servant. — Every public officer is a trustee and in respect of the office he holds and the salary and other benefits which he draws, he is obliged to render appropriate service to the State. If an officer does not behave as required of him under the law he is certainly liable to be punished in accordance with law.

18. Power to make rules. —

(1) The appropriate Government may, by notification in the official Gazette and subject to the condition of previous publication, make rules for carrying into effect the provisions of this Act.

(2) In particular and without prejudice to the generality of the foregoing power, such rules may provide for all or any of the following matters, namely:

(a) the term of office of, the manner of filling casual vacancies of, and the allowances payable to, the Chairman and members of the Child Labour Technical Advisory Committee and the conditions and restrictions subject to which a non-member may be appointed to a sub-committee under sub-section (5) of Sec. 5;

(b) number of hours for which a child may be required or permitted to work under sub-section (1) of Sec. 7;

(c) grant of certificates of age in respect of young persons in employment or seeking employment, the medical authorities which may issue such certificate, the form of such certificate, the charges which may be made thereunder and the manner in which such certificate may be issued:

Provided that no charge shall be made for the issue of any such certificate if the application is accompanied by evidence of age deemed satisfactory by the authority concerned;

(d) the other particulars which a register maintained under Sec. 11 should contain.

Comment

This section empowers the appropriate Government to make rule for carrying out the provisions of the Act.

Rules for effectuating the purpose of the Act. — The general power of framing rules for effectuating the purposes of the Act, would plainly authorize and sanctify the framing of such a rule.

19. Rules and notifications to be laid before Parliament or State Legislature —

(1) Every rule made under this Act by the Central Government and every notification issued under Sec. 4, shall be laid, as soon as may be after it is made or issued, before each House of Parliament, while it is in session for a total period of thirty days which may be comprised in one session or in two or more successive sessions, and if, before the expiry of the session immediately following the session or the successive sessions aforesaid, both Houses agree in making any modification in the rule or notification or both Houses agree that the rule or notification should not be made or issued, the rule or notification shall thereafter have effect only in such modified form or be of no effect, as the case may be; so, however, that any such modification or annulment shall be without prejudice to the validity of anything previously done under that rule or notification.

(2) Every rule made by a State Government under this Act shall be laid as soon as may be after it is made, before the Legislature of that State.

Comment

Under this section the rules and notifications are to be laid before Parliament or State Legislature for approval.

20. Certain other provisions of law not barred — Subject to the provisions contained in Sec. 15, the provisions of this Act and the rules made thereunder shall be in addition to, and not in derogation of, the provisions of the Factories Act, 1948 (63 of 1948), the Plantations Labour Act, 1951 (69 of 1951) and the Mines Act 1952 (35 of 1952).

Comment

This section lays down that the provisions of this Act shall be in addition to and not in derogation of, the provisions of the Factories Act, 1948, the Plantations Labour Act, 1951 and the Mines Act, 1952.

21. Power to remove difficulties—

(1) If any difficulty arises in giving effect of the provisional of this Act, the Central Government may, by order published in the official Gazette, make such provisions not inconsistent with the provisions of this Act as appear to it to be necessary or expedient for removal of the difficulty:

Provided that no such order shall be made after the expiry of a period of three years from the date on which this Act receives the assent of the President.

(2) Every order made under this section shall, as soon as may be after it is made, before the Houses of Parliament.

Comment

Under the provisions of this section the Central Government is empowered to remove difficulties which arise in giving effect to the provisions of this Act.

22. Repeal and savings. -

(1) The Employment of Children Act, 1938 (26 of 1938) is hereby repealed.

(2) Notwithstanding such repeal, anything done or any action taken or purported to have been done or taken under the Act so repealed shall, in so far as it is not inconsistent with the provisions of this Act, be deemed to have been done or taken under the corresponding provisions of this Act.

Comment

The Employment of Children Act, 1938 (26 of 1938) has been repealed by this section.

Implied repeal. —It is well settled that when a competent authority makes a new law which is totally inconsistent with the earlier law and that the two cannot stand together any longer it must be construed that the earlier law had been repealed by necessary implication by the latter law.

23. Amendment of Act 11 of 1948. — In Sec. 2 of the Minimum **Wages Act, 1948. —**

(i) For Cl. (a), the following clauses shall be substituted, namely;

"(a) 'adolescent' means a person who has completed his fourteenth year of age but has not completed his eighteenth year;

"(aa)'adult' means a person who has completed his eighteenth year of age;";

(ii) after Cl. (b), the following clause shall be inserted, namely:

(bb) 'child' means a person who has not completed his fourteenth year of age;".

Comment

Under this section Sec. 2 of the Minimum Wages Act, 1948 has been amended so as to define the terms "adolescent", "adult" and "child"

24. Amendment of Act 69 of 1951— In the Plantations Labour Act, 1951.—

(a) in Sec. 2, in Cls. (a) and (c), for the word "fifteenth", the world "fourteenth" shall be substituted;
(b) Sec. 24 shall be omitted;
(c) in Sec. 26, in the opening portion, the words "who has completed his twelth year" shall be committed.

Comment
Under this section Sec. 2 of the Plantations Labour Act, 1951, has been amended so far as it relates to the employment of child labour.

25. Amendment of Act 44 of 1958. — In the Merchant Shipping Act, 1958, in Sec. 109, for the word "fifteen", the word "fourteen" shall be substituted.

Comment
Under this section Sec. 109 of the Merchant Shipping Act. 1958, has been amended so far as it relates top the employment of child labour.

26. Amendment of Act 27 of 1961.— In the Motor Transport Workers Act, 1961, in Sec. 2, in Cls. (a) and (c), for the word "fifteenth", the word "fourteenth" shall be substituted.

Comment
Under this section, Sec. 2 of the Motor Transport Workers Act, 1961, has been amended so far as it relates to the employment of child labour.

The Schedule
(See Sec. 3)
Part A
Occupations

Any occupation connected with —
(1) Transport of passengers, goods or mails by railway;
(2) Cinder picking, clearing of an ash pit or building operation in the railway premises;
(3) Work in a catering establishment at a railway station, involving the movement of a vendor or any other employee of the establishment from one platform to another or into or out of a moving train;
(4) Work relating to the construction of a railway station or with any other work where such work is done in close proximity to or between the railway lines;
(5) A port authority within the limits of any port.

(6) Work relating to selling or crackers and fireworks in shops with temporary licences;
(7) Abattoirs/Slaughter House.

Part B
Processes

(1) *Beedi*-making.
(2) Carpet-weaving.
(3) Cement manufacture, including bagging of cement.
(4) Cloth printing, dyeing and weaving.
(5) Manufacturer of matches, explosives and fire-works.
(6) Mica-cutting and splitting.
(7) Shellac manufacture.
(8) Soap manufacture.
(9) Training.
(10) Wool-cleaning.
(11) Building and construction industry.
(12) Manufacture of slate pencils (including packing).
(13) Manufacture of products from agate.
(14) Manufacturing processes using toxic metals and substances such as lead, mercury, manganese, chromium, cadmium, benzene, pesticides and asbestos.
(15) "Hazardous processes" as defined in Section 3 (cb) and 'dangerous operations' as notified in rules made under Section 87 of the Factories Act, 1948 (63 of 1948).
(16) Printing as defined in Section 2 (k)(iv) of the Factories Act, 1948 (63 of 1948).
(17) Cashew and cashewnut descaling and processing.
(18) Soldering processes in electronic industries.

Supplement
Child Labour (Prohibition and Regulation) Act, 1986

In exercise of the powers conferred by section 4 of the Child Labour (Prohibition a nd Regulation) Act, 1986, the Central Government hereby adds the following occupation and processes in the Schedule to the said Act, namely:-

In the Schedule to the said Act, —

(1) In Part A, after item (5) and the entry relating thereto, the following item and entry shall be inserted, namely:-

(6) "Work relating to selling of crackers and fire works in shops with temporary licences.";

(2) In Part B, after item (11) and the entry relating thereto, the following items and entries shall be inserted, namely:-

(12) Manufacture of slate pencils (including packing).

(13) Manufacture of products from agate.

(14) Manufacturing processes using toxic metals and substances such as lead, mercury, managanese, chromium, cadmium, benzene, pesticides and asbestos.

The Child Labour (Prohibited and Regulation) Rules, 1988

G.S.R. 847(e), dated 10th August, 1988. — In exercise of the powers conferred by sub-section (1) of Sec. 18 of the said Act, the Central Government, hereby makes the following rules, namely:-

Comment

Rule-making power. — The general power of framing rules for effectuating the purposes of the Act, would plainly authorize and sanctify the framing of such a rule.

1. Short title and commencement.—

(1) These rules may be called the Child Labour (Prohibition and Regulation) Rules, 1988.

(2) They shall come into force on the date of their publication in the official Gazette.

Comment

These rules have been framed by the Central Government in the exercise of the powers conferred by Sec. 18 (1) of the Child Labour (Prohibition and Regulation) Act, 1986.

Rules - **Whether validity framed**. — The question whether rules are validly framed to carry out the purposes of the Act can be determined on the analysis of the provisions of the Act.

2. Definitions. — In these rules, unless the context otherwise requires, —

(a) "Act" means the Child Labour (Prohibition and Regulation) Act, 1986 (61 of 1986);

(b) "Committee" means the Child Labour Technical Advisory Committee constituted under sub-section (1) of Sec. 5 of the Act;

(c) "Chairman" means the Chairman of the Committee appointed under sub-section (2) of Sec. 5 of the Act;

(d) "Form" means a Form appended to these rules;

(e) "register" means the register required to be maintained under Sec. 11 of the Act;

(f) "Schedule" means the schedule appended to the Act;

(g) "Section" means a section of the Act.

Comments

This rule defines the various expression occurring in the Rules.

Interpretation by a court. — The Court can merely interpret the section; it cannot re-write, re-cast or re-design the section.

Otherwise - What amounts to. — The word "otherwise" is not to be construed *ejusdem generis* with the word "circulars, advertisements".

3. Term of office of the members of the Committee —

(1) The term of office of the members of the Committee shall be one year from the date on which their appointment is notified in the official Gazette:

Provided that the Central Government may extend the term of office of the member of the Committee for a maximum period of two years:

Provided further that the member shall, notwithstanding the expiration of his term, continue to hold office until his successor enters upon his office.

(2) The members appointed under sub-rule (1) shall be eligible for re-appointment.

Comment

"Shall" cannot be interpreted as "may"

Proviso. — In Abdul Jabar Butt v. State of Jammu and Kashmir, it was held that a proviso must be considered with relation to the principal matter to which it stands as a proviso.

4. Secretary to the Committee—The Central Government may appoint an officer not below the rank of an Under-Secretary to the Government of India as Secretary of the Committee.

Comment

This rule empowers the Central Government to appoint an officer not below the rank of an under-Secretary to the Government of India as the Secretary to the Child Labour Technical Advisory Committee.

5. Allowances to non-official members— The non-official members and Chairman of the Committee shall be paid such fees and allowances as may be admissible to the officers of the Central Government drawing a pay of rupees four thousand and five hundred or above.

6. Resignation —

(1) A member may resign his office by writing under his hand addressed to the Chairman.

(2) The Chairman may resign his office by writing under his hand addressed to the Central Government.

(3) The resignation referred to in sub-rule (1) and sub-rule (2) shall take effect from the date of its acceptance or on the expiry of thirty days from the date of receipt of such resignation, whichever is earlier, by the Chairman or the Central Government, as the case may be.

7. Removal of Chairman or member of the Committee— The Central Government may remove the Chairman or any member of the Committee at any time before the expiry of the term of office after giving him a reasonable opportunity of showing cause against the proposed removal.

Comment

This rule lays down procedure for removal of Chairman or member of the Committee by the Central Government.

8. Cessation of membership—If a member

(a) is absent without leave of the Chairman for three or more consecutive meetings of the Committee; or

(b) is declared to be of unsound mind by a competent court; or

(c) is or has been convicted of any offence which, in the opinion of the Central Government, involves moral turpitude; or

(d) is, or at any time, has been adjudicated insolvent or has suspended his debts or has compounded with his creditors, shall cease to be a member of the Committee.

Comment

This rule deals with the matter relating to cessation of membership.

9. Filling up of casual vacancies. — In case a member resigns his office under rule 6 or ceases to be a member under rule 8, the casual vacancy thus caused shall be filled up by the Central Government and the member so appointed shall hold office for the unexpired portion of the term of his predecessor.

Comment

This rule empowers the Central Government to fill up casual vacancies and it lays down that the member so appointed shall hold office for the unexpired portion of the term of his predecessor.

10. Time and place of meetings. — The Committee shall meet at such times and places as the Chairman may fix in this behalf.

11. Notice of meetings. — The Secretary to the Committee shall give at least seven days notice to every member of the Committee of the time and place fixed for each meeting along with the list of business to be transacted at the said meeting.

12. Presiding at meetings. — The Chairman shall preside at every meeting of the Committee at which he is present; if however, the Chairman is unable to attend a meeting, any member elected by the members present among themselves shall preside at the meeting.

Comment

"Shall". — It is well-known principle that in the interpretation of statutes that where the situation and the context warrants it, the word "shall" used in a section or rule of a statute has to be construed as "may".

13. Quorum. — No business shall be transacted at a meeting of the Committee unless atleast three members of the Committee other than the Chairman and the Secretary are present:

Provided that any meeting in which less than three of the total members are present, the Chairman may adjourn the meeting to a date as he deems fit and inform the members present and notify other members that the business of the scheduled meeting shall be disposed of at the adjourned meeting irrespective of the *quorum* and it shall be lawful to dispose of the business at such adjourned meeting irrespective of the member of members attending the meeting.

Comment

Scope of proviso — The scope of a proviso is well settled. In Ram Narain Sons Ltd. v. Asstt. Commissioner of Sales Tax, it was held: "It is a cardinal rule of interpretation that a proviso to a particular provision of statute only embraces the field which is covered by the main provision. It carves out an exception to the main a provision to which it has been enacted as a proviso and to no other."

14. Decision by majority — All questions considered at a meeting of the Committee shall be decided by a majority of votes of the members present and voting and in the event of equality of votes, the Chairman, or in the absence of Chairman, the member presiding at the meeting, as the case may be, shall have a second or casting vote.

Comment

This rule lays down that the matters considered by the Committee in its meeting should be decided by a majority votes of the members present. The rule further lays down that the Chairman or in his absence the member presiding at the meeting shall have a casting vote.

15. Sub-Committee — The Committee may constitute one or more Sub-Committees, whether consisting only of members of the Committee or partly of members of the Committee and partly of other persons as it thinks fit, for such purposes, as it may decide and any Sub-Committee so constituted shall discharge such functions as may be delegated to it by the Committee.

16. Register to be maintained under Sec. 11 of the Act. —

(1) Every occupier of an establishment shall maintain a register in respect of children employed or permitted to work, in Form A.

(2) The register shall be maintained on a yearly basis but shall be retained by the employer for a period of three years after the date of the last entry made therein.

Comment

Under this rule every occupier of an establishment is required to maintain an yearly register showing the children employed or permitted to work and to retain such registers for a period of three years.

17. Certificate of age —

1) All young persons in employment in any of the occupations set-forth in Part A of the Schedule or in any workshop wherein any of the processes set forth in Part B of the Schedule is carried on, shall produce a certificate of age from the appropriate medical authority, whenever required to do so by an Inspector.

(2) The certificate of age referred to in sub-rule (1) shall be issued in Form 'B'.

(3) The charges payable to the medical authority for the issue of such certificate shall be the same as prescribed by the State Government or the Central Government, as the case may be for their respective Medical Boards.

(4) The charges payable to the medical authority shall be borne by the employer of the young person whose age is under question.

Explanation - For the purposes of sub-rule (1), the appropriate "Medical authority" shall be Government medical doctor not below the rank of an Assistant Surgeon of a District or a regular doctor of equivalent rank employed in Employees' State Insurance Dispensaries of hospitals.

Comment

Explanation — It is not well settled that an explanation added to a statutory provision is not a substantive provision in any sense of the term but as the plain meaning of the word itself shows it is merely meant to explain and clarify certain ambiguities which may have crept in the statutory provision.

Supplement
The Child Labour (Prohibition and Regulation) Act, 1986

S.O. 333(E), dated 26th May, 1993. — In exercise of the powers conferred by sub-section (3) of Sec. 1 of the Child Labour (Prohibition and Regulation) Act, 1986 (61 of 1986), the Central Government hereby appoints the 26th day of May, 1993 as the date of which the provisions of Part III of the said Act shall come into force in respect of all classes of establishments, throughout the territory of India, in which none of the occupations and processes referred to in Sec. 3 of the said Act is carried on.

BIBLIOGRAPHY

PRIMARY SOURCES

Government Documents, United Nations Publications

Bouhdiba, Abdelwahab, *Exploitation of Child Labour: Final Report of the Special Rapporteur of the United Nations Sub-Commission on Prevention of Discrimination and Protection of Minorities* (Geneva: UNO, 1983).

Gupta, Meena, *The Jaggampet National Child Labour Project—A Status Paper* (New Delhi: International Labour Organisation, 1994).

Gupta, Meena, *The Markapur National Child Labour Project—A Status Paper* (New Delhi: International Labour Organisation, 1994).

Gupta, Meena, *The Sivakasi National Child Labour Project— A Status Paper* (New Delhi: International Labour Organisation, 1994).

International Labour Organisation, *A Programme of Action Against Child Bondage* (Geneva: International Labour Office, 1992).

ILO, *International Programme on the Elimination of Child Labour Document* (Geneva: ILO, 1992).

ILO, *Report of the Director-General to the International Labour Conference, 69th Session* (Geneva: ILO, 1983).

ILO, *Towards the Abolition of Child Labour: ILO Policy and Its Implications for ILO Technical Cooperative Services* (Geneva: ILO, 1993).

Ministry of Labour, *Child Labour in India* (Unpublished, 1994).

Ministry of Labour, *Child Labour in the Indian Carpet Industry* (New Delhi: Government of India, 1994).

Ministry of Labour, *Children and Work. Workshop of District Collectors/District Heads on Elimination of Child Labour in Hazardous Occupations* (New Delhi: Government of India, 1995).

Ministry of Labour, *Circular on Identification, Release and Rehabilitation of Child Labour. Workshop of District Collectors/District Heads of Elimination of Child Labour in Hazardous Occupations* (New Delhi: Government of India 1995).

Ministry of Labour, *Draft Recommendations of Working Groups. Workshop of District Collectors/District Heads on Elimination of Child Labour in Hazardous Occupations* (New Delhi : Government of India, 1995).

Ministry of Labour, *Enforcement of Child Labour (Prohibition and Regulation) Act 1986 - Background Paper for Sub-Committee Appointed by the Standing Labour Committee* (New Delhi: Government of India, 1994).

Ministry of Labour, *Enforcement of Child Labour (Prohibition and Regulation) Act, 1986 and Factories Act, 1948* (New Delhi: Government of India, 1995).

Ministry of Labour, *Grant-in-Aid Scheme for Financial Assistance to Organisations (Voluntary and Non-Governmental) for Taking up Action Programmes/Projects for the Benefit of Child Labour and Women Labour. Workshop of District Collectors/District Heads on Elimination of Child Labour in Hazardous Occupations* (New Delhi : Government of India, 1995).

Ministry of Labour, *Report on Child Labour Schools for Working Children in Carpet Industry in Varanasi-Bhadoi-Mirzapur Belt* (New Delhi: Government of India, 1990).

Ministry of Labour, *Report of the Committee on Child Labour* (Nasik: Government of India, 1979).

Ministry of Labour, *Report of the Task Force on the Implementation of the Child Labour (Prohibition and Regulation, Act, 1986 and the Legal Action Plan Contained in the National Child Labour Policy* (New Delhi: Government of India, 1989).

Ministry of Labour, *Scheme for National Child Labour Projects* (New Delhi: Government of India, 1987).

Ministry of Labour, *Working Group Papers for Elimination of Child Labour, Workshop of District Collectors/District Heads on Elimination of Child Labour in Hazardous Occupations* (New Delhi: Government of India, 1994).

Planning Commission, *Studies on Child Labour Commissioned by the Planning Commission: Salient Features of Nine Studies* (New Delhi: Government of India, 1992).

Statistics on Children (New Delhi: Government of India, 1995).

United Nations International Children's Emergency Fund. *The Right to be a Child* (New Delhi: UNICEF, 1994).

UNICEF, *The State of the World's Children*, 1984 (Oxford: UNICEF, 1984).

UNICEF, *The State of the World's Children*, 1994 (Oxford: UNICEF, 1994).

UNICEF, *The State of the World's Children*, 1997 (Oxford: UNICEF, 1996).

UNICEF, *UNICEF India Policy on Child Labour* (New Delhi: UNICEF, 1994).

SECONDARY SOURCES

Books and Reports

Arimpoor, Joe, *Street Children of Madras. A Situational Analysis* (Noida: National Labour Institute, 1992).

Bequele, Assefa and Boyden, J., (eds), *Combating Child Labour* (Geneva: International Labour Organisation, 1988).

Brownlie, Ian.(ed). *Basic Documents on Human Rights* (Oxford: Oxford University Press, 1981).

Calam, Richel and Franchis, Christina, *Child Abuse and Its Consequences* (Cambridge: Cambridge University Press, 1987).

Carlton, Frank Tracy, *The History and Problems of Organised Labour* (Boston: D.C. Heath and Company, 1920).

Challis, J. and Elliman, D., *Child Workers Today* (Sunbury: Quartermaine House Ltd., 1979).

Chand, Attar, *Politics of Human Rights and Civil Liberties* (New Delhi: UDH Publishers, 1985).

Child Labour in the Brassware Industry of Moradabad (Noida: Child

Labour Cell, 1992).

Child Labour in Gem Polishing Industry of Jaipur (Jaipur: Institute of Development Studies, 1991).

Child Labour in the Lock Industry of Aligarh (Noida : Child Labour Cell, 1992).

Child Labour in the Match Industry of Sivakasi (Noida: Child Labour Cell, 1993).

Child Labour in Tile Factories of Jaggampeta: An Evaluation (New Delhi: New Concept Consultancy Service, 1994).

Chowdhry D. Paul, *Child Welfare and Development* (New Delhi:Atma Ram and Sons, 1980).

Costin, Leela, B., *Child Welfare:Policies and Practice* (New York: McGraw Hill, 1972).

D'Lima, Hazel and Gosalia, Rima, *Street Children of Bombay: A Situational Analysis* (Noida: National Labour Institute, 1992).

D'Souza, Alfred, (ed.), *Children in India* (New Delhi: Manohar Publications, 1979).

Folk, Richard, *Human Rights and State Sovereignty* (New York: Holmes and Meir Publishers, 1981).

Fernandez, Walter, Burra, Neera and Anand, T.S. *Child Labour in India. A Summary of a Report Presented by the Indian Social Institute* (New Delhi: Indian Social Institute, 1986).

Freeman, Charles, *Human Rights* (London: B.T. Batsford Publishing Ltd., 1988).

Gangrade, K.D. and Gathia, A. Joseph, *Women and Child Workers in the Unorganised Sector* (New Delhi: Concept Publishing Company, 1983).

George, Ivy, *Child Labour and Child Work* (New Delhi: Ashish Publishing House, 1990).

Gokhale, Sharad D. and Sohani, Neera, K., *Child Labour in India* (Bombay: Somaiya Publications Pvt. Ltd., 1979).

Gupta, Manju and Voll, Klauss, (eds.), Child Labour in India. Young Hands at Work (New Delhi: Atma Ram and Sons, 1987).

International Labour Organisation, *Child Labour: A Briefing Manual* (Geneva ILO, 1986).

Jain, Mahavir, *Child Labour in India. A Select Bibliography* (Noida: National Labour Institute).

Joyce, James Avery. *The New Politics of Human Rights* (London: Mac Milan Press Ltd., 1978).

Juyal, B.N., *Child Labour and Exploitation in the Carpet Industry: A Mirzapur-Bhadoi Case Study* (New Delhi: Indian Social Institute, 1986).

Juyal, B.N., *Child Labour in the Carpet Industry of Mirzapur-Bhadoi - A Situational Analysis of the Government of India's National Child Labour Project* (New Delhi: ILO, 1983).

Kanbargi, Ramesh, (ed.), Child Labour in the Indian Sub Continent Dimensions and Implications (New Delhi : Sage Publications, 1991).

Kulshreshtha, Jinesh Chandra, *Child Labour in India* (New Delhi: Ashish Publishing House, 1988).

Luard, Evan, *The International Protection of Human Rights* (London: Camelot Press Ltd.,1967).

Macfarlane, M.J., *The Theory and Practice of Human Rights* (London: Maurice Temple Smith Ltd., 1985).

Mendelivich, Elias, *Children at Work* (Geneva: International Labour Office, 1979).

Mishra, G.P. and Pande, P.N. *A Study of Child Labour in Carpet Industry of Mirzapur* (Unpublished, 1992).

Mishra, G.P. and Pande, P.N., A Study on Child Labour in Glass Industry of Firozabad (Unpublished, 1992).

Mittal, Mukta, Child Labour in Unorganised Sector (New Delhi: Anmol Publications, 1994).

Mosely, Henry W. and Chen, Lincoin C., (eds.), *Child Survival: Strategies for Research* (Cambridge: Ca mbridge University Press, 1984).

Naidu, Usha and Kapadia, Kamini, (eds), *Child Labour and Health - Problems and Prospects* (Bombay: Tata Institute of Social Sciences, 1982).

Nangia, Praveen, *Child Labour: Cause Effect Syndrome* (New Delhi: Janak Publishers, 1987).

Newbery, Paula R. (ed.), *The Politics of Human Rights* (New York: New York University Press 1980).

Pandhe, M.K., (ed.), *Child Labour in India* (Calcutta : India Books Exchange, 1979).

Panicker, Rita and Nangia, Parveen, *Working and Street Children of Delhi* (Noida: National Labour Institute, 1992).

Phillips, W.S.K., *Street Children of Indore: A Situational Analysis* (Noida: National Labour Institute, 1992).

Rao, B.V.R. and Mallik B., *Street Children of Hyderabad: A Situtational Analysis* (Noida: National Labour Institute, 1992).

Reddy, N., *Street Children of Bangalore: A Situational Analysis* (Noida: National Labour Institute, 1992).

Rehman, M.M. *Society, Economy and Education of the Deprived* (Delhi: Anupama Publishers, 1992).

Rodgers, G. and Standing, G. (eds.), *Child Work, Poverty and Underdevelopment* (Geneva: International Labour Office, 1981).

Sekar, Helen, R. and Pinto, G.J., *The Situation of Working Children in Tamil Nadu:* A Workshop Report (Noida: National Labour Institute,. 1992).

Shah, P.M., (ed.), *Child Labour: A Threat to Health and Development* (Geneva: Defence for Children International, 1985).

Sharma, B. K. and Mittar, V. *Child Labour and Urban Informal Sector* (New Dellhi: Deep and Deep Publication, 1990).

Sieghart, Paul, *The Lawful Rights of Mankind* (Oxford: Oxford University Press, 1984).

Singh, A. N., *Child Labour in India. Socio-Economic Perspectives* (New Delhi: Shipra Publications, 1990).

Sinha, Swapan Kumar, *Child Labour in Calcutta—A Sociological Study* (Calcutta: Naya Prakash Publishers, 1991).

Vajapur, Abdulrahim, (ed.), *Essays on International Human Rights* (New Delhi: South Asian Publishers, 1991).

Varandani, G. *Child Labour and Women Workers* (New Delhi: Ashish Publishing House, 1994).

Weiner, Myron, *The Child and the State in India, Child Labour and Education Policy in Comparative Perspective* (Oxford: Oxford University Press, 1991).

Working Children of the Pottery Industry of Khurja (Noida Child Labour Cell, 1992).

Zimmern, Alfred, *The League of Nations and the Rule of Law* (London: Macmillan and Co., 1939).

Articles

"Action Plan Prepared to Abolish Child Labour in Andhra Pradesh", *The Times of India,* October 5, 1995.

Agnivesh, Swami, "Ratification of Convention Mere Window Dressing," *Mainstream,* October 2, 1993, pp. 23-28.

"Amendments Proposed to Child Labour Act," *The Economic Times,* October 16, 1994.

Anand, Umesh, "Carpet Industry in Slumber as European Ban on Exports Looms Large", *The Times of India,* February 16, 1994.

Arellano, Terry, "Child Labour in South Asia", *Asian Labour Update,* Issue 14, January-March, 1994, pp. 11-13

Banarji, Sumanta, "Child Labour in India", *Economic and Political Weekly,* Vol. XV, No. 25, 1980, pp. 1007-1009.

Baxi, Upendra,. "Unconstitutional Politics and Child Labour", *Mainstream,* October 2, 1993, pp. 17-20.

Bequele, Assefa and Boyden, Jo, "Working Children: Current Trends and Policy Responses", *International Labour Review,* Vol. 127, No. 2, September-October 1998, pp. 153-171.

"Bill to Better Child Labour's Lot", *Labour Gazette,* Vol. LXVI, No. 2, October, 1986, pp. 63-64

Bhaskaran, Nandini, "Child Labour in Carpet Industry. Coming to Grips with a Knotty Issues", *The Times of India,* August 19, 1994.

Bhattacharya, Santwana, "As Blind as Ever", *The Indian Express,* May 14, 1995.

Bonnet, Michel, "Child Labour in Africa", *International Labour Review,* Vol. 132, No. 3, September-October 1993, pp. 371-389.

Burra, Neera, "Exploitation of Child Workers in Aligarh Lock Industry", *Economic and Political Weekly,* Vol. 22, No. 28, July 1987, pp. 1117-1122.

Burra, Neera, "Exploitation of Children in Jaipur Gem Industry, I: Structure of Industry" *Economic and Political Weekly*, Vol. 23, No. 3, January 1988, pp. 75-79.

Burra Neera, "Exploitation of Children in Jaipur Gem Industry, II: Health Hazards of Gem Polishing", *Economic and Political Weekly,* Vol., 23, No. 3, January 1988, pp. 131-138.

Burra, Neera, "Child Labour and Education", *Child, Family, Community,* Digest 28, May 1989.

Burra,Neera, "Child Labour in India: Poverty, Exploitation and Vested Interest", *Social Action,* Vol. 26, No. 3, July-September 1986, pp. 241-263.

Burra, Neera, "Health Hazards", *Seminar,* No. 350, October 1988, pp. 24-28.

"Campaign Against Child Labour to be Stepped Up", *Labour Gazette,* Vol. LXXII, No. 1, September 1992, p. 3

"Carpet Industry Warned Against Child Labour," *Labour Gazette,* Vol. LXXIII, No. 1, September 1993, p. 6.

Chand Malini and Jain, Devaki, "Rural Children at Work: Preliminary Results of a Pilot Study", *The Indian Journal of Social Work,* Vol. 11, No. 3, October 1979, pp. 311-322.

Chatterjee,Meera, "Health for All: Wither the Child? *Social Action*, Vol. 35, No. 3, July-September 1985, pp. 224-250.

"Child Labour in Agarbatti Industry. The Smell of Exploitation", *The Times of India,* January 21, 1994.

"Child Labour in Coke Factory", *Blitz,* February 19, 1994.

"Child Labour Doubles to 250 Million", *Business Standard,* November 18, 1996.

"Child Labour High in Delhi: Study", *The Economic Times,* August 15, 1994.

"Children March Against Bonded Labour", *International Labour Review,* Vol. 32, No. 2, May-June 1993, pp. 133-134.

Chitnis, Suma, "The Education of Socially Disadvantaged Children—An Unfulfilled Promise and a Challenge", *The Indian Journal of Social Work,* Vol. 11, No. 3, October 1979, pp. 267-281.

"Combating Child Labour", *Hindustan Times,* May 22, 1994.

Debroy, Bibek, "A Labour of Hercules", *The Economic Times,* May 30, 1994.

Dey, Anindita, 'Sanctions Alone Will Not End Child Labour", *The Pioneer, May 19*, 1994.

Dixit, J. N., "Government Promoting Rights of the Child", *Mainstream*, October 2, 1993, pp. 20-22.

"Education Key to End Child Labour", *The Times of India,* February 19, 1995,.

"Explosion of Child Exploitation in South Asia", *SAARC Link*, Issue 2, January 1993, pp. 1-2.

Fernandes, Walter, "New Laws and Human Rights", *Social Action,* Vol. 37, No. 3, January-March 1987, pp. 73-81.

"Forty Three Kids Rescued from Bonded Labour", *The Pioneer,* April 25, 1994.

Geoghegan, Michel, "International Year of the Child 1979: UN Agencies and Children in Developing Countries," *Social Action* Vol. 29, No. 1, January-March 1979, pp. 1-11.

Gopalan, Muthuswami, "Child Labour", *Social Welfare,* Vol. 23, No. 8, November 1979, pp. 1-3.

"Government Not Serious About Child Labour: Panel", *The Pioneer,*April 27, 1994.

"Government Claims Convention on Child Labour Observed", *Labour Gazzette,* Vol. LXXII, No. 7, March 1993, pp. 464-465.

"Government Launches Project on Child Labour Laws," *Labour Gazette,* Vol. LXXII, No. 11, July 1993, p. 670.

Gupta, Meena, "Special Problems of Enforcement of Child Labour Laws and Regulations," *Awards Digest,* Vol. XVIII, No. 3-6, March-June 1992, pp. 40-44.

Gupta, Monobina, "Will the Rod Ever Be Used to Punish", *Telegraph,* March 13, 1994.

Gurha, Ritu, "When Industry Laboured on a Childish Cause," *The Economic Times,* May 21, 1995.

"ILO Opposes US Curbs Against India", *The Times of India,* April 16, 1994.

"ILO Asks Trade Unions to Solve Child Labour Problem", *Labour Gazette,* Vol. LIX, No. 8, April 1980, pp. 607-609.

"IPEC in the Dock", *Business Standard,* April, 4, 1994.

"India Has Latgest Child Labour Force in the World" *Labour Gazette,* Vol LIX No.5 January 1980, p.238,

"India Has 100 Million Child Labours", *The Times of India,* May 21,

1995

"In the Name of Labour", *The Times of India,* January 25, 1995.

"Jha Krishna, "The Tinkle and the Silence", *Hindustan Times,* January 9, 1994.

Joshi, Uma, "Working 9 to 5 When You're 9 or Even 5.", *Blitz*, February 19, 1994.

Kalra, Aparna, "Child Labour Law Gets on Edge", *Business Standard,* March 15, 1994.

Kathuria, Shalini, "Court Bar on Unions for Child Labourers", *The Pioneer,* February 22, 1994.

Katyal, Sugita, "Free the Children or Face the Music", *Business World,* 15-31 July, 1995, pp. 56-57.

Khandekar, Mandakini, "Policies for Children's Services in the 80s: Some Suggestions," *Indian Journal of Social Work*, Vol. 11, No. 3, October 1979, pp. 333-342.

Kothari, Smitu, "There's Blood on Those Matchsticks", *Economic and Political Weekly,* Vol. XVIII, No. 27, July 2, 1983, pp. 1191-1202.

Krishnan, G. V., "Kanyakumari Child Workers Make a Precarious Living: Study", *The Times of India,* August 11, 1993.

Kulkarni, Manu N., "Matchmaking Children in Sivakasi", *Economic and Political Weekly,* Vol. 18, No. 43, October 1983, pp. 1855-1856.

"Law Against Child Labour Ineffective," *Labour Gazette,* Vol. LXVII, No. 3, November 1987, p. 113.

"Laws Against Child Labour are Ineffective", *The Times of India,* September 11, 1995.

"Lost Childhood", *The Times of India,* September 15, 1995.

"Maximum Child Labour in India," *Labour Gazette,* Vol. LIX, No. 2, October 1979, pp. 93-94.

Mehta, Prayag, "Mortgaged Child Labour of Vellore, Women Beedi Workers' Tale of Woe", *Mainstream,* Vol. 22, No. 1, September 1983, pp. 15-17.

Mendelievich Elias, "Child Labour", *International Labour Review,* Vol. 118, No. 5, September-October 1979, pp. 557-567.

Mishra, Dipak, "Children Run Away from UP Carpet Slavery", *The Times of India,* August 1, 1995.

Mohammed, H. Shaukat, "*Bonded Babies",* Week, January 9, 1994.

"More Teeth for States Soon to Deal With Child Labour", *The Hindu,* March 2, 1994.

Morley, David, "International Year of the Child: A Time to Look at Child Health", *Social Action,* Vol. 29, No. 3, July-September 1979, pp. 213-220.

Mukherjee, R. N., "The Latest Bill on Child Labour", *Labour Gazette,* Vol. LXVI, No. 2, October 1986, pp. 82-83.

Mukherjee, Shikha, "Bengal Begins Survey to Assess Child Labour", *The Times of India,* October 6, 1995.

Mundle, Sudipto, "The Bonded of Palmau", *Economic and Political Weekly,* Vol. 11, No. 8, May 1976, pp. 653-656.

Murthy, P.V.V., "Bonded Child Labour in Beedi Industry," *The Hindu,* April 11, 1994.

Nandgaonkar, Satish, "Supreme Court Recognition a Boost for Child Labourers", *The Independent,* February 21, 1994.

"National Child Labour Authority Soon", *The Observer,* September 15, 1994.

"New Welfare Schemes for Child Labour", *Labour Gazette,* Vol. LXVII, No. 2, October 1988, p. 49.

"People Don't Count—Only Votes Do", *The Times of India,* March 31, 1996.

Poddar, Tanushree, "Realities of Child Labour", *Deccan Herald,* May 10, 1994.

"Portrait of a Family that Supports Child Labour", *The Metropolis,* October 8, 1994.

Prasad, T., "Preventing Exploitation of Children," *Economic and Political Weekly,* Vol. 29, No. 5, August 1982, pp. 15, 16-35.

Raman, Sunil, "Global Ban on Carpet Looms", *The Economic Times,* March 11, 1994.

Rodgers, Gerry and Standing, Guy, "Economic Roles of Children in Low-Income Countries", *International Labour Review,* Vol. 120, No. 1, January-February 1981, pp. 31-37.

Rao, Amiya, "Silicosis Death of Slate Workers", *Economic and Political Weekly,* Vol. 15, No. 44, November 1980, p. 1883.

"Rupees 850-cr. Scheme to Eradicate Child Labour", *The Economic Times,* May 23, 1995.

Saksena, K.P., "Human Rights in Asia: Assessing the Prospects for a

Regional Approach," *International Studies,* Vol. 21, No. 1, January-March 1982, pp. 1-15.

Sarma, A. M., "Child Labour in Indian Industries," *The Indian Journal of Social Work,* Vol. 11, No. 3, October 1979, pp. 345-352.

Sawhney, Inder, "Ending the Era of Child Servitude", *The Times of India,* November 29, 1994.

Sawhney, Inder, "UNICEF Abhors Social Clause Linkage"; *The Times of India,* January 24, 1995.

Sehgal, Rashme, "The Wrongs Multiply", *The Telegraph,* April 3, 1994.

Sekar, Helen, R., "Child Labour (Prohibition and Regulation) Act, 1986: Critique", *Awards Digest,* Vol. XVIII, No. 3-6, March-June 1992, p. 35-39.

Singh, Sheotag, "For a World Free of Child Labour", *The Economic Times,* November 4, 1994.

Srivastava, R. C., "Moradabad Children an Exploited Lot", *The Times of India,* November 23, 1994.

Standing, G., "State Policy and Child Labour", *Development and Change,* Vol. 13, No. 4, October 1983, pp. 611-631.

"Steps to Curb Child Labour" *Financial Express,* September 19, 1994.

Sunderan, P. K., "They Drop Out of School to Supplement Family Income", *The Times of India,* February 6, 1995.

"Supreme Court Order Corpus Fund in Bid to Check Child Labour", *The Times of India,* December 11, 1996.

Suri, Sanjay, "Holland Endorses India's Kaleen Label", *The Economic Times,* April 1, 1996.

Swaminathan, Mina, "Children of the Urban Poor: Problems and Opportunities", *Social Action* Vol. 29, No.3, July-September 1979, pp221-234

Swepston, Lee, "Child Labour: Its Regulation by ILO Standards and National Legislation," *International Labour Review,* Vol. 121, No. 5, September-October 1982, pp. 577-592.

"War Against Child Labour", *The Hindu,* March 9, 1994

"Wage for Child Labour Soon", *The Economic Times,* February 20, 1994.

"Weaving Off the Debts", *The Hindustan Times,* January 1, 1994.

Weiner, Myron, "Child Labour in Developing Countries: The Indian Case", *New Wave,* March 27, 1994, pp. 8-10.

Weiner, Myron, "India's Case Against Compulsory Education", *Seminar,* No. 413, January 1994, pp. 83-87.

Weiner, Myron, "India's Case Against Compulsory Education", *Seminar*, No. 413, January 1994, p. 83-87

Index